T0389545

Re/centring Lives and Lived Experience in Education

Bold Visions in Educational Research

Series Editors

Kenneth Tobin (*The Graduate Center, City University of New York, USA*)
Carolyne Ali-Khan (*College of Education & Human Services, University of North Florida, USA*)

Co-founding Editor

Joe Kincheloe (with Kenneth Tobin)

Editorial Board

Daniel L. Dinsmore (*University of North Florida, USA*)
Gene Fellner (*College of Staten Island, City University of New York, USA*)
Alejandro J. Gallard (*Georgia Southern University, USA*)
S. Lizette Ramos de Robles (*University of Guadalajara, Mexico*)
Kashi Raj Pandey (*Kathmandu University, Nepal*)
L. Earle Reybold (*College of Education and Human Development, George Mason University, USA*)

VOLUME 76

The titles published in this series are listed at *brill.com/bver*

Re/centring Lives and Lived Experience in Education

Edited by

Ellyn Lyle

BRILL

LEIDEN | BOSTON

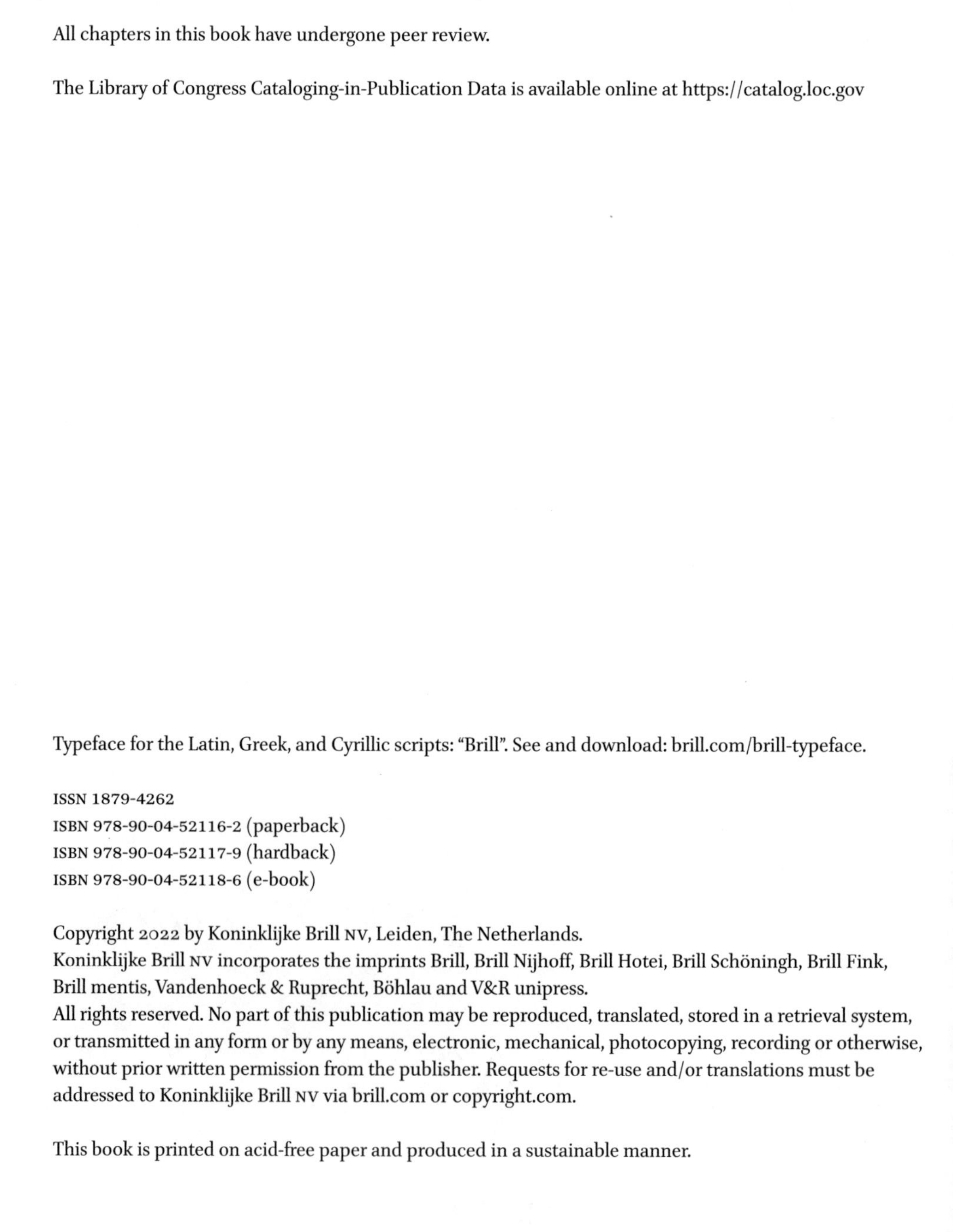

Cover illustration: Artwork by Mavourneen Trainor Bruzzese

All chapters in this book have undergone peer review.

The Library of Congress Cataloging-in-Publication Data is available online at https://catalog.loc.gov

Typeface for the Latin, Greek, and Cyrillic scripts: "Brill". See and download: brill.com/brill-typeface.

ISSN 1879-4262
ISBN 978-90-04-52116-2 (paperback)
ISBN 978-90-04-52117-9 (hardback)
ISBN 978-90-04-52118-6 (e-book)

Copyright 2022 by Koninklijke Brill NV, Leiden, The Netherlands.
Koninklijke Brill NV incorporates the imprints Brill, Brill Nijhoff, Brill Hotei, Brill Schöningh, Brill Fink, Brill mentis, Vandenhoeck & Ruprecht, Böhlau and V&R unipress.
All rights reserved. No part of this publication may be reproduced, translated, stored in a retrieval system, or transmitted in any form or by any means, electronic, mechanical, photocopying, recording or otherwise, without prior written permission from the publisher. Requests for re-use and/or translations must be addressed to Koninklijke Brill NV via brill.com or copyright.com.

This book is printed on acid-free paper and produced in a sustainable manner.

Contents

Foreword

There are books that are living entities formed from blood and bone, soil and song. Every once in a while, I come across one knowing it holds words I will return to again and again. The pages of this book breathe from the inside out and give life. I return to the land daily to walk its terrain, listen for its pulse, and be wooed to how I am as an earthling, connected to and in place. I will return to *Re/centring Lives and Lived Experience in Education* as a place to roam in its wisdom and teachings. This amazing collection of scholars is marinated in the soil of hybridity, transdisciplinarity, lived experiences, and teaching practices. As I traverse the breadth and depth of their vibrant scholarship, I move in the terrain of what it means to be broken open to relationship with myself, others, and the more-than-human world. I reevaluate my own pedagogy and praxis as I find resonance and remember—I am not alone. Here are writers who crave and model a whole scholarship, a brave scholarship—one where aesthetic articulation and criticality are not separated. These writers are storying worlds that cultivate what it means to be human in provocative, poetic, and profound ways.

I invite you to walk into this collection as terroir that breaks open possibility—the possibility of navigating issues that matter, but with a kind of vulnerability that exudes authenticity. The root word of vulnerability comes from *vulnere*—to break open. Here, in *Re/Centring Lives,* I am guided to a way of being that is central to *currere*, and I attune to the inner life connected to the outer life. More than ever in this time, clariant voices are needed to say *yes* to all the textures of humanness—in our classrooms and creations, messes and mysteries.

Beauty is palpable in this diverse and inclusive text, where writers open up pathways to resilience. A resilience borne of the earth and story, body and boldness, creativity and courage. I walk the path and discover the glorious impossible—the attention to small things that hold worlds. I am rebodied to find my own centre and encouraged to keep walking the road where scholarship and artistry go hand to hand, foot to foot. May you pick this book up and rediscover what deeply animates you and uncover wonder.

Celeste Nazeli Snowber, PhD
Professor | Poet | Performer
Simon Fraser University

Acknowledgment

A note of gratitude to Dr. Wendy Kraglund-Gauthier for her discerning eye as copyeditor. Wendy, your support and skill have been invaluable in this collection. Thank you.

Notes on Contributors

Jennifer Blue
has spent 22 years working in healthcare where she consistently advocates for uncompromised safety and excellent patient experiences. She began working in Infection Prevention and Control in Toronto shortly after SARS changed the face of healthcare safety. She is currently the Director of Infection Prevention and Control for a multisite hospital organization in southern Ontario.

Chantelle Caissie
has a rich and diverse background in health and community services, with a Bachelor of Arts Degree in Psychology, a Graduate Certificate in Addictions and Mental Health Counselling, and a Master of Education degree in Adult Education. As a health professional transitioning into the education sector, Chantelle has challenged dominant academic discourse, hoping to encourage a shift away from objectivity toward exploring the tender and vulnerable spaces of our interior lives imperative to our growth as both working professionals and human beings.

Philip Davis
(Haudenosaunee) has resided in St. Catharines, Ontario, Canada most of his life. Phil has been an active member of his community for many decades. His cultural knowledge and congenial disposition have offered him numerous opportunities to share his knowledge, to educate, and to learn more about himself and others. He enjoys life, particularly when sharing enlightening experiences with others whenever possible. Phil is currently the cultural coordinator at the Niagara Regional Friendship Centre and the Indigenous liaison and consultant with Dreamwalker Dance Company.

Danielle Denichaud
has professional roots grounded in an eight-year career as a Contemporary Dance Artist, followed by 10 years as a Holistic Health Consultant and Movement Educator in Montréal. She obtained a B.A. (Honours) in Child Studies from Concordia University and a M.A. in Social Justice Education at the Ontario Institute for Studies in Education where she is currently pursuing a Ph.D. in Curriculum & Pedagogy. Her doctoral research and work as knowledge mobilizer with Dreamwalker Dance Company explore symbiotic bridges between the performing arts and community well-being, social justice education and embodied learning, environmental education, and holistic health promotion.

Alysha J. Farrell
lives and works in Brandon, Manitoba, which is located on the traditional homelands of the Dakota, Anishanabek, Cree, Oji-Cree, Dene, and Métis peoples. She is an Associate Professor in the Faculty of Education at Brandon University and is passionate about nurturing ecosophical orientations in the study of curriculum, pedagogy and educational leadership. Her forthcoming book is called *Ecosophy and Educational Research for the Anthropocene: Rethinking Research through Relational Psychoanalytic Approaches.*

alexandra fidyk
is a philosopher, poet, professor (University of Alberta, Faculty of Education), and Jungian somatic psychotherapist who engages with youth and teachers on issues of wellbeing, mental health, body-centred and creative processes, and trauma-sensitive pedagogy. She has won university and national awards for teaching, transdisciplinary research, and scholarship, the latter of which unfolds through hermeneutics, poetic inquiry, and life writing to explore questions central to living well.

Crystal Gail Fraser
(she/her) is Gwichyà Gwich'in and originally from Inuvik and Dachan Choo Gę̀hnjik in the Northwest Territories. She is an Assistant Professor in the Department of History, Classics, & Religion and the Faculty of Native Studies at the University of Alberta. Crystal's dissertation "T'aih k'ìighe' tth'aih zhit dìidìch'ùh (By Strength, We Are Still Here): Indigenous Northerners Confronting Hierarchies of Power at Day and Residential Schools in Nanhkak Thak (the Inuvik Region, Northwest Territories), 1959–1982" won the Canadian Historical Association's prestigious John Bullen Prize in 2020.

Lucrécia Raquel Fuhrmann
is a PhD candidate at University of Regina. She was born and raised in Brasil, where she lived in three different states that have borders with Spanish-speaking countries. She has a master's degree in education and a bachelor's degree in language – português brasileiro. She is a teacher and has worked in which is the equivalent of K–12 in Brasil, but she is on leave from her activities for studying. Her research interests are language, identity, immigration, literature, and reading. She is also interested in working with scientific methodology with students in elementary school.

Barbara Gilbert Mulcahy
completed a PhD in Education in 2018. She has been teaching in the Faculty of Education at Memorial University since 2013. She taught as a high school

English teacher in the public education system for five years and as an English as a Second Language (ESL) instructor at the Association for New Canadians (ANC) for 11 years. Her area of interest and expertise is literacy and language education. Her research interests also include issues of language, culture, identity, and curriculum and pedagogy.

Shawnee Hardware
is a Professor of Early Childhood Education at George Brown College. She is also a research associate with the Toronto District School Board and a visiting scholar at Memorial University of Newfoundland's Faculty of Education. She draws on years of work and community leadership experiences from Jamaica, Japan, Newfoundland and Labrador, Peru, and Toronto. Shawnee completed her doctoral studies at York University, and her Master of Education in Curriculum, Teaching, and Learning Studies at Memorial University of Newfoundland.

Benjamin Hertwig
is a veteran of the war in Afghanistan, a writer, and a PhD student. He is the recipient of a Gold National Magazine Award for his work on the war, and his first book was a finalist for the 2017 Governor General's Award.

Anita Lafferty
is a PhD candidate at the University of Alberta in the Faculty of Secondary Education. She is of Dene and Cree descent and a member of the Łíídlı̨ı̨ Kų́ę́ First Nation in Northwest Territories, Canada. Her doctoral research examines approaches of Indigenous curriculum perspectives that are grounded in Dene k'ęę (philosophy) on the Land. Her research interests include learning from/with the Land, experiences of Indigenous youth, identity, healing, and matriarchal knowledge. She takes a multidisciplinary approach in her research, drawing on the disciplines of multimedia, art, poetry, and storytelling.

Eric Lai
is a regular force Canadian Armed Forces veteran with two deployments in Afghanistan. He is an avid community volunteer, husband, and UBC student as well as recipient of the General Campaign Star and Sacrifice medal.

Tim Laidler
is a veteran and community advocate and committed to the cause of assisting war veterans and service to his community. Laidler's community service was recognized with a Queen Elizabeth II Diamond Jubilee Medal, and he was selected as UBC's Young Alumnus of the Year in 2014. Founder and executive

director of the non-profit Veterans Transition Network, he is also the Executive Director of the Institute for Veterans Education and Transition at UBC.

Clement Lambert
is the Chair and Associate Professor in the Department of Teaching and Learning, College of Education Northern Arizona University (NAU). His education leadership experiences with an emphasis on literacy education span three decades in a variety of contexts including five years at the K-12 level, and 27 years at the tertiary education level. For more than 20 years, he has been an education leader within Caribbean and North American contexts. He has also served on various committees and acted as the principal investigator for a major research grant proposal.

Natalie LeBlanc
is Assistant Professor in Art Education at the University of Victoria in British Columbia where she teaches studio and digital art courses to undergraduate and graduate students. Her art practice, research, and teaching are highly intersecting. Her award-winning doctoral research explored the generative and pedagogical possibilities of closed and abandoned schools in Canada through digital photography and site-specific installation. Her current research examines how conceptual art practices inform artistic and arts-based research methodologies, evocative modes of learning and researching in and through art.

Hilary Leighton
is Associate Professor at Royal Roads University and psychotherapist and Registered Clinical Counsellor in private practice. A lifelong apprentice to nature and psyche, she draws wisdom from eco- and depth psychology, systems theory, and embodied, nature-based, and arts-informed practices to extend the notion of the individual psyche to a world ensouled. Through teaching and learning, she inspires a whole-human, ecologically intelligent epistemology, and she cultivates reconnection with the sentient Earth. Her examination and reflection of the ethical dilemma, suffering, and loss of human relationships with wildness initiates learning as a regenerative journey toward maturation and a more soul-furthering way of belonging.

Ellyn Lyle
is interested in creating spaces for learners to engage meaningfully with their studies and is drawn to inquiries that seek to re/humanize education. Having joined the academic community full time in 2011, she is currently Dean in Yorkville University's Faculty of Education. The use of critical and reflexive

methodologies shape explorations within the following areas: intersections of self and subject and their implications for teacher and learner identity; praxis and practitioner development; lived and living curriculum; and undivided ways of knowing and being.

Esther Maeers
is a PhD student in the Faculty of Education at the University of Regina where she also teaches in the early childhood department as a sessional instructor. Esther is a research assistant at both the University of Regina and the University of Saskatchewan. Her interests are focused on early childhood education, objects, teenage mothers and parent engagement. Prior to beginning her doctoral studies, she was a pre-kindergarten teacher for 12 years. Aside from being a student and teacher, Esther is a mother to three amazing children and a Nana to three wonderful grand babies.

Lorrie Miller
comes to the Institute for Veterans Education and Transition after seven years working in teacher education at UBC as a program coordinator in the B.Ed. program and post-degree diplomas. Part of her work involved a multi-country and multi-institutional education project in Dadaab, Kenya, under the umbrella of Borderless Higher Education for Refugees (BHER).

Andrea Nann
is an award-winning artist who choreographs, performs, produces, and presents dance to reach across distance, to experience herself and others in celebration of possibility, diversity, connection, and belonging. She believes that dance can shift attitudes and ways of being, tuning us into what makes each of us distinct, to what we share and, ultimately, how we can live together in wonderment and peace. As artistic director of Dreamwalker Dance Company, Andrea creates works for stage, film, and outdoor sites. She channels her community building passion into various participatory, collaborative, multi-arts experiences.

Mahtab Nazemi
is Assistant Professor at Thompson Rivers University, with previous experiences at University of Washington, Antioch University, and McGill University. Additionally, Dr. Nazemi is a member of Michigan State University's Diversity Scholar Network. Prior to working in higher education, Dr. Nazemi taught French Immersion and Mathematics in the K–12 system. Dr. Nazemi's research employs critical race, decolonial, and anti-racist feminist theories to uncover and address neoliberalism and institutional racism in educational settings.

Through centring counter-narratives and lived-experiences, Dr. Nazemi's research aims to expose and respond to oppression and marginalization occurring at the intersections of race, gender, and sexuality.

Steven Noble
is an adjunct instructor in adult education and educational leadership who engages in researching social identity margins within community settings through the use of popular theatre, social ritual, and performative language in order to find liberatory pathways. Much of his work has been understanding the performed dynamics of oppression and social justice work with the active participation of those people directly involved: *nothing about us, without us.* Steven received his Master's (Counselling Psychology and Educational Studies) and Doctorate (Adult Education and Community Development) from University of British Columbia.

Debbie Pushor
is a mother of three adult sons and a former public-school teacher, consultant, principal, and central services administrator. She currently works as Professor in the Department of Curriculum Studies at the University of Saskatchewan in Canada. In her program of research, Debbie has engaged in narrative inquiries into parent engagement and leadership, a curriculum of parents, and parent knowledge. She is currently engaged in research on systematic parent engagement. In her undergraduate and graduate teaching, Debbie makes central an often absent or underrepresented conversation about the positioning of parents in relation to school landscapes.

McKenzie Robinson
is Project Coordinator at the Institute for Veterans Education and Transition. He was deployed to Afghanistan in 2009–2010 and was part of a force protection platoon as dismounted infantry and driver. McKenzie currently serves in the primary reserves and is enrolled at UBC taking on IVET projects and duties.

Jee Yeon Ryu
completed her PhD in Curriculum Studies at The University of British Columbia, specializing in music education and arts-based research methodologies. As a pianist/teacher/researcher, she integrates a variety of artistic genres into her teaching and research practices, including music, poetry, video, stories, and creative writing. Currently, Jee Yeon teaches and supports aspiring education graduate students at Yorkville University.

Muna Saleh
is Assistant Professor in the Faculty of Education at Concordia University of Edmonton (CUE), a former elementary and secondary school teacher, the mother to three awesome humans, and the author of *Stories We Live and Grow By: (Re)Telling Our Experiences as Muslim Mothers and Daughters*.

Carmen Schlamb
is Professor of Environmental and Sustainability Studies at Seneca College in Toronto, Ontario. She holds a PhD in education (educational sustainability) and has research interests in ecological identity, narrative inquiry, and self-study. She is particularly interested in how storytelling can support greater understanding of environmental relationships and promote action for a sustainable future. When not teaching, Carmen likes to be out on the water in cottage country paddling her hybrid canoe.

Michelle Silagy
is a Contemporary Dance Artist and Inclusion Pedagogue whose dance making and teaching practice span 32 years. Silagy received her B.A. (Honours) in drama from San Diego State University (CA), is a School of Toronto Dance Theatre (STDT) graduate, and she completed an MFA Dance degree at York University. Silagy is a Master DanceAbility International Facilitator with certifications in Vienna, Montevideo, Uruguay, and Mexico. As Artistic Director of the Young Dancers' Program at STDT, Silagy folds sensorial influences into creative spaces with multigenerational learners.

Celeste Nazeli Snowber
is a dancer, writer, and award-winning educator who is a professor in the Faculty of Education at Simon Fraser University. She has published widely in the area of arts-based research and her books include *Embodied Inquiry: Writing, Living and Being through the Body*, as well as two collections of poetry. Her latest book of poetry, *The Marrow of Longing*, explores her connection to her Armenian identity. Celeste continues to create site-specific performances in the natural world between land and sea.

darlene st. georges
is a visual artist, poet, and creation-centred scholar. She is assistant professor of art education at the University of Lethbridge, Alberta, Canada. Her theoretical and practice-based research recognizes the creative, critical, spiritual, and performative ways of knowing in the world. Generating and sharing counter-narratives and creation stories invites innovation in learning and embraces an

unfolding metamorphosis of scholarship in provocative, creative and intellectual ways. See www.darlenestgeorges.com

Poh Tan
is completing her second PhD from the Educational Theory and Practice program at Simon Fraser University. Her research focuses on understanding the development of scientific literacy through different lenses, including Indigenous Hawaiian epistemology. Dr. Tan is a two times TEDx speaker and the inaugural recipient of the Kris Magnusson Emerging Leaders Award for leadership and advocacy for positive change. With a PhD in Experimental Medicine, she is also a scientist, author, entrepreneur, educator, mother, and volunteer. She has published many peer-reviewed research articles both in fields of stem cell biology and science education, and she has authored and co-authored book chapters and co-published children's books.

Patrick Tomczyk
completed his PhD at the University of Alberta in the Faculty of Education. While there, he held a Doctoral Fellowship from the Social Sciences and Humanities Research Council of Canada. His research focuses on the intersections of queer theory, pedagogy and arts-based research, as they relate to lived experiences of sexual and gender minority youth. The aim of his research is to create social change that fosters equity, diversity, and inclusion to create safer learning environments. Dr. Tomczyk is a school administrator, as well as a certified counselor with the Canadian Counseling and Psychotherapy Association.

CHAPTER 1

Living and Being with/in Education

Ellyn Lyle and Chantelle Caissie

Instructions for living a life:
Pay attention.
Be astonished.
Tell about it.
OLIVER (2009, p. 37)

∴

We are sentient beings: emotional, perceptive, intuitive, sensitive, responsive, and attentive. Complex composites of all our experiences, we cannot help but engage a messy process as we undertake learning with and through each other. Our pursuit of knowledge is driven by and mediated through our ontological perspectives, our epistemological assumptions, even our metaphysical entanglements. As such, teaching and learning are deeply personal endeavours even as they are profoundly relational. As we engage in this complex process of meaning-making, we must do so from a place of consciousness—an *awakeness* that deliberately accounts for who we are as we come to know. Drawing from the enduring wisdom of Parker Palmer (2017), we are reminded that this awakeness begins with our inwardness but extends to include the subjects with whom and which we engage. Such an acknowledgement requires a conscious commitment to accounting for lives and lived experience with/in teaching and learning spaces.

We recognize that cultivating spaces for the co-curricular inclusion of lived experience is both personal and political as it chafes against those well-established systems that continue to prioritize dehumanized approaches to education. Resisting the tendency to abstract self from subject, we reject claims that research rigor is improved by the pursuit of objectivity. We maintain that such objectivity is made impossible by our very *humanness*—the thoughts, feelings, assumptions, and biases born of our experiences and motivating us toward inquiry. While we value *the empirical* as a necessary constituent of research integrity, we extend empiricism to include insights garnered from

© KONINKLIJKE BRILL NV, LEIDEN, 2022 | DOI:10.1163/9789004521186_001

experience (etymology online) and, in so doing, recognize people as valuable data sites. Said another way, we value people as rich sources of experiential knowledge and actively seek to elevate experience as equal to theory.

Resisting brackets of conventional research led us to Elizabeth St. Pierre's work advancing post-qualitative inquiry (PQI). This approach to inquiry defies methodological containment in favour of at/tending to the deeply intimate tenets of living in real time (St. Pierre, 2017, 2018, 2019). Shifting away from traditional methods where insights are too often lost within parenthetic references, PQI encourages us to engage in an organic spirit of writing so that we are able to look "not on things already made, but on things in the making" (St. Pierre, 2018, p. 604). We began to wonder about the capacity of organic writing to cultivate more hospitable spaces for lives and lived experience within the field of education. Finding resonance in post-qualitative inquiry, we are drawn to photopoetics as a creative vehicle for exploring the terroir of living and being with/in education (Kay, 2013). Having no particular destination in mind, we begin from the only place we can—where we are.

The Self as an Entry Point

Ellyn

I am the second daughter of three born to a teacher and a farmer. Raised on an acreage nestled along the banks of Malpeque Bay, I was an amphibious creature from the start. I moved seamlessly between the land and the bay, nurturing and being nurtured, as I was attentive to what each had to teach me. While the lessons were many and varied, their seeming practicality were rich with metaphorical possibility. I learned that, in tending the land, I was at/tending to myself even as I honoured those who came before me and worked to preserve resources for those who would come after me. In this way, the land taught me about stewardship and sustainability—about respect. As I planted, watered, weeded, and harvested, I developed an enduring awe of the honesty and wonder of life spent in cultivation.

My relationship with water is more complicated. I am drawn to the Atlantic like ancient mariners to the call of the Siren. But, unlike them, the call cannot lure me from the proximity of the shore. Even as I delight in being enveloped by the salty buoyancy, my inner equilibrium diminishes the farther I get from the land. I've thought about this a lot, how my enchantment transforms to anxiety, and I have come to recognize my need to feel grounded. I long for the sea because I am in awe of its ability to wash clean and leave behind a fresh canvas. That is the enduring wisdom that life along the water's edge has offered me—the possibilities born in letting go. It took me years to understand intellectually what I knew viscerally—that finding grace in letting go creates the breaking open that Elizabeth St. Pierre (2018) references. I began to think about the *washing away* as a *vanishing point* for its ability to conjure both a sense of possibility and a sense of loss (Lyle, 2021a). Because of this duality, I often associate water with *equanimity*—the ability to maintain grace and calm even in difficult times. While I am now several thousand miles from the place that cultivated these understandings within me, I carry them with me acknowledging that such insights were made possible in the leaving. Expansiveness, it seems, requires relinquishing the well-trod familiarity of such deep intimacy.

wandering the liminal space
each ebb and flow
teaches me impermanence—
consciousness an artful scribble
on life's Buddha Board
wiped clean with the passing of time
i learn the possibilities born of letting go
—expansiveness

Lingering (Photograph by Ellyn Lyle, used with permission)

Chantelle

Restless,
anxiously sinking
in an oversized chair, stained,
by a timeless encounter with
a courageous heart—

I am reminded that a lesson in learning
begins only if we are prepared to
listen—

Moving beyond what can be measured
or quantified, I challenge the field of
education
to find the person, in the personal.

Breaking free from the bars of creative captivity,
I move towards a vulnerable praxis—
creating space to bathe in the magic of living,
even if the magic hurts

Grace (Photograph by Ellyn Lyle, used with permission)

I was born into a middle-class household and raised in a subdivision where laughter was boundless and the sun's setting dictated when it was time to go home. Of these early days, when I still lived courageously guided by my curiosity, my memories are joyful. Very quickly after entering the school system, though, shame and fear transformed joy into anxiety and self-doubt.

I struggled to learn
in the same way
a flower struggles to bloom in the absence of the sun.

Reading was slow,
an aggravating undertaking,
as if the words on the page strategically planned their assault.
Numbers and equations mocked my efforts—
The symbols breaking out into a chorus of laughter—
A reminder of my lacking

As I packed my books,
prepared to leave the classroom for yet another one-to-one session
their words hit me like a ton of bricks—
—she's an idiot, that's why she gets to leave.

According to the Canadian grading system, where my academic worth and capacity to contribute were reduced to a numerical value, I was below average. Having my worth and human potential questioned as a child left a scar that time still struggles to heal. As I progressed through formal schooling, learning spaces became blighted by a system warped by division. I became an expert at hiding my humanity. In tucking my softness under my shell, I forgot that teaching and learning must engage the heart and that expansiveness is only possible through the grace found in vulnerability.

In my forgetting, and upon dragging myself through the painful completion of 12 years in this context, I made the conscious decision to pursue a career in health and social services. I became an advocate for marginalized populations, hopeful that creating space for others to address the complexities of life would somehow mitigate my disappointment with the dehumanization I experienced in formal learning. After almost 10 years as a health professional, I realized that the fragments of myself could not be re-assembled through the work engaged with other human beings. I needed to reconnect (with) my own fragments. Celeste Snowber and Sean Wiebe (2009) tell me that connection lives at the site of the *in-between*—the space within ourselves that invites us to break open and acknowledge the comedic, joyful, and harrowing experiences of living and learning. As I learn to respect myself as a rich and valuable data source, it becomes easier to recognize how reflexive consciousness propels forward momentum.

As I entered graduate studies, I began the process of untangling the fragmented threads of my disconnection. Encountering the work and wisdom of Parker Palmer (2017), I came to understand that, for better or worse, teaching and learning are human endeavours and that acknowledging the centrality of self is neither selfish nor narcissistic. I drew courage from Joanne Yoo (2019) and began to experiment with *dangerous writing*. At first, my writing was reckless, triggered by raw emotion, and my words were unable to find a soft place to land. Over time, I realized that giving myself permission to explore the strange and confusing complexities of living cultivates space to find beauty in my blemishes. Writing dangerously became an avenue where I could wander through magnificent and painful experiences of being human—where I would come to understand that worth was not something to be measured but esteemed. Like Elizabeth St. Pierre (2018), I understand now that writing is *always becoming*. As I untangle the threads of my interior landscape, I invite others to pause—to sit with their humanity and to speak back to what fractures. Only in the reconstitution of ourselves can we create spaces for living and being with/in education.

Reconstituting Selves

Expressive writing is intimately entwined with life, and it moves beyond expression toward self-construction (Leggo, 2004). Yet, as human beings governed by constructs not of our own making, too often we find ourselves compromising our creative voices to author-vacant texts that perpetuate a narrative of privilege and exclusion (Badley, 2017, 2020a). Exhausted by systems that draw power from division, we turn to writing dangerously as an expressive act of self-preservation and freedom. This poetic and emancipatory practice allows us to create a space that playfully re/negotiates teaching and learning, writing and being. Through emerging conversations with text, we have come to understand that living and teaching in ways that re/centre human being require us to resist decontextualized and dehumanized practices.

Transcendence (Photograph Ellyn Lyle, used with permission)

Own your story—
take all the broken shards
and assemble them
with your trembling hands,
piece by piece,
gaining confidence
in the reconstitution
of you.
Whole once more,
polish yourself to a shine
that illuminates
all those around you
so they cannot help
but to see.
—*transcendence*

There are openings in writing—invitations to explore our interiority in ways that disrupt normative styles of learning. When we allow our humanity to be present on the page, we affirm that our lives matter (Badley, 2020; Yoo, 2019). Through experimenting with creative and metaphorical writing, we have discovered that the fragile and textured details of human experience hold restorative possibilities for living and learning—possibilities we may have never encountered without writing. Although neither of us identify as poets, we have found a sense of calm and mutual understanding made accessible through vulnerable and poetic writing, and we are committed to creating brave spaces for students to explore the same.

Creating Brave Spaces

Recentring lives and lived experience is reliant on creating brave spaces for both individual and collective humanness. While these spaces are made brave by many defining characteristics, we hold that, at the very least, they must evidence deep commitments to relationality, vulnerability, advocacy, and wonder and hope.

Relationality

We are always in relation—with the world around us, with previous iterations of ourselves, and with all the lives that have intersected with our own. Because each encounter writes itself on our lives, we must stop abstracting self from subject. Parker Palmer (2017) makes this same argument when he writes about the pathology of disconnectedness that is deliberately cultivated in education contexts. This disconnectedness, he says, leverages human vulnerability to create a culture that explicitly devalues deep personal and relational knowledge. In re/positioning vulnerability as a strength and seeking to include it in teaching and learning spaces, we are more prepared to engage with empathy and understanding when we encounter experiences that are different from our own. This is the heart of *relational knowing*—the process of connecting with realities not our own (Palmer, 2017).

Cultivating brave spaces that value the lushness within relationality can help us make sense of teaching and learning, not just from our minds, but from our hearts. In so doing, it renders more honest our teaching and learning engagements, and it has the capacity to advance pedagogical spaces where our vulnerabilities are safe in the presence of others (Lyle & Caissie, 2021; MacKenzie, 2019).

that which is unprotected
erodes
but is not lost—
earth washed to sea
it returns with the tide
to remind.
—soulscape

Soulscape (Photograph by Ellyn Lyle, used with permission)

Vulnerability

Creating contexts safe for the vulnerability that is born of human being has the capacity to breathe life back into education (Lyle & Caissie, 2021; Snowber & Wiebe, 2009). Vulnerability allows us to grapple with what matters while at/tending to the ever-unfolding emergence of who we are. Such openness supports both our individual and collective humanness in helping us to really see each other. This *witnessing* is perhaps among the greatest needs of the human spirit. As Parker Palmer (2017) reminds us, the human soul does not seek to be fixed; it longs to be seen, heard, and accompanied exactly as it is.

This witnessing, though, feels counter-intuitive in an educational culture that associates competence with confident speech, rather than attentive silence—that values producing answers more than generating questions. Silence, like the absence of certainty, is often mis/understood as a failure of sorts. We suspect this is because education has cobbled together a dangerous denial of vulnerability. By framing vulnerability as *weakness*, dominant discourse successfully leverages shame to perpetuate continued dehumanization (Groen, 2018; Palmer, 2017; Thomas, 2018; Yoo, 2020). Teaching and learning, though, *are* acts of vulnerability. Writing vulnerably, cultivating intentional space to delicately undress the inherent worth of the human soul, transforms learning from a conservatory of privilege into a space of restorative possibility and recognition (Badley, 2019; Colyar, 2009). Valuing ourselves and each other as rich sources of data allows us to broaden and deepen our teaching and learning experiences. Engaging poetically and aesthetically allows us just enough abstraction to make us more comfortable with exposure—a *modesty cover* of sorts. This un/veiling has the capacity to foster connection amidst vulnerability and re/instill hope in teachers and learners.

I am naked, vulnerable—
hold your gaze,
allow yourself to ease into my imperfection

Feel me,
trail your fingers along
the cracks in my foundation—
grant yourself permission to feel
the rough and jagged patterns of my exterior

Linger,
if only for a second longer,
to hear my truth.

Bury your hands and your heart
in the raw and fragile pieces of my humanity.

There is beauty in our missteps,
and forgiveness in our fractures—

So, allow them to see you,
naked and vulnerable.

Fractures (Photograph by Ellyn Lyle, used with permission)

Vulnerability cultivates a terroir of self-discovery. Within this space of the still-emerging, we are able to answer the call of others who are *willing* to be vulnerable and work together to advocate for education that explicitly seeks to advance humanness.

Advocacy

Cultivating spaces that permit vulnerable exchanges creates an ethical imperative to respect the myriad ways of being that congregate in teaching and learning spaces. Such regard lays the foundation for the creation of more culturally responsive pedagogies and socially equitable practices. As we explicitly seek to include a broader representation of human experiences, we must deepen our commitment to non-discriminatory pedagogies. This shift necessarily opens up education contexts to historically marginalized and underrepresented groups not only in the diversification of curriculum, but also in the inevitable ontological expansiveness. As we move toward un/privileging educational cultures that tend to value competition over collaboration, individuality over collectivity, fragmentation over holism, and insularity over globality, the landscape of education will inevitably shift to reflect this new richness.

join me in a soft revolution

let us use words
until words
are no longer heard

then

let us become water
and river our way
to new ground

where we can
know each other differently
—re/storying war

Revolution (Photograph by Ellyn Lyle, used with permission)

Employing poetic text in partnership with photographs acknowledges that both textual and visual literacy are interpretive acts mediated by the lens of lived experience. Photopoetic inquiry thus creates a space where we can weave together the intellectual, affective, and spiritual aspects of our lives as we seek understanding with and through each other (Lyle, 2021). In so doing, we deepen our regard for each other and the societies we create.

Wonder and Hope

Wonder is born of curiosity, but it takes willful courage to hope. Hope sheds light on those things we aspire to, and the anxiety related to our hopes reveals what we fear will be lost in the pursuit. Reminding us of the inevitability of erasure learned while wandering the *vanishing point*, we are propelled by hope even as the evidence of our journey is wiped away. Like the slow and relentless reclaiming of stone by water, we have confidence that the form, while changing, is still present as a part of the greater momentum.

As we continue to navigate the shifting landscapes of education, we are often reminded of the temporality of all things, and we have learned to find comfort in it. Such realization encourages us to seek a more expansive perspective. Lately, and increasingly, we shift our gazes toward the sky. Rather than contemplating the inevitable wiping clean of the canvas we tread between earth and water, we are finding assurance in the knowledge that we are all united under one canopy. In this acknowledgement, we are able to embrace the wonder of our shared existence and hope it inspires a reverence for the mutuality that has brought us together in this wonderful and wild grace of living with/in education.

I hope you know land—
that you pause to feel the warmth of mother earth,
allowing her to stain your skin coffee brown—
a gentle reminder that our body is our canvas—
if only we have the courage to paint.

I hope you know the sea—
selflessly offering her shoreline kisses,
prompting us to give love unconditionally—
but never losing sight of the strength and power,
beneath her depths.

I hope you know the sky—
that you bathe in her magic, her joy,
as she playfully colours a moment in time.

I hope you live with/in the stars—
my dearest cosmic being,
as your shine is limitless.

Guardian (Photograph by Kara Katmouz, used with permission)

In/Conclusion

Living and being with/in education is brave work. We necessarily bring the miraculous messiness of our lived experiences into our teaching and learning interactions. Photopoetic inquiry helps us navigate these spaces by drawing us into images where we might wander landscapes contemplating the complementary text while writing ourselves into being. This intertextuality is both evocative and provocative in its capacity to reveal what is hidden and encourage discoveries about ourselves and each other. Joanne Yoo (2020) reminds us that there is infinite wisdom and mystery that can be found through writing creatively. Letting go of rigid structures allows us to write the unknown into being. In conversation with the text, and with each other, we maintain that our greatest wisdom is garnered through a deep and brave examination of lives lived fully. While our search for meaning begins from our earliest consciousness, the busyness of *living* too often distracts us from the sanctity of *being.*

Photopoetic inquiry offers us a place to pause—to consider who we are and how our experiences have formed the tapestries of our lives. This way of inquiry is subtle and, in so being, lends itself to a range of explorations from the historically charged to the deeply human. In this way, photopoetic inquiry is not an indulgence; it is vital to our existence and to our pursuit of rehumanizing praxis (Lorde, 2007; Thomas, 2018).

References

Badley, G. F. (2019). Post-academic writing: Human writing for human readers. *Qualitative Inquiry, 25*(2), 180–191. https://doi.org/10.1177/1077800417736334

Badley, G. F. (2020). We must write dangerously. *Qualitative Inquiry, 27*(6), 716–722. https://doi.org/10.1177/1077800420933306

Colyar, J. (2009). Becoming writing, becoming writers. *Qualitative Inquiry, 15*(2), 421–436. https://doi.org/10.1177/1077800408318280

Etymology online. https://www.etymonline.com/

Groen, J. (2018). Inner and outer congruence: An academic's quest to find spiritual wellness and health. *Journal for the Study of Spirituality, 8*(2), 120–129. https://doi.org/10.1080/20440243.2018.1523049

Kay, C. (2013). Photopoetic moments of wonder: Photography as an artistic reflective practice in secondary dance education. *Physical & Health Education Journal, 79*(1), 22–26.

Leggo, C. (2004). Living poetry: Five ruminations. *Language & Literacy: A Canadian Educational E-Journal, 6*(2), 1–14.

Lorde, A. (2007). *Sister outsider: Essays & speeches by Audre Lorde.* Crossing Press.

Lyle, E. (2021a). Vanishing point. Walking: Attuning to an earthly curriculum (Special Issue). *Journal of the Canadian Association for Curriculum Studies, 18*(2), 6–20. https://jcacs.journals.yorku.ca/index.php/jcacs/issue/view/2293

Lyle, E. (2021b). Sisterhood and solidarity: Fostering equitable spaces for women in academia. In E. Lyle & S. Mahani (Eds.), *Sister scholars: Untangling issues of identity as women in academe* (pp. 1–10). DIOPress.

Lyle, E., & Caissie, C. (2021). Re/humanising education: Teaching and learning as co-constructed reflexive praxis. *LEARNing Landscapes, 14*, 219–230.

MacKenzie, S. (2019). (Re)acquaintance with praxis: A poetic inquiry into shame, sobriety, and the case for a curriculum of authenticity. *Journal of Curriculum Theorizing, 34*, 72–89.

Oliver, M. (2009). Sometimes. In *Red Bird.* Beacon Press.

Palmer, P. (2017). *The courage to teach.* Jossey-Bass.

Snowber, C., & Wiebe, S. (2009). In praise of the vulnerable: A poetic and autobiographical response to Salvio's abundant Sexton. *Journal of the American Association for the Advancement of Curriculum Studies, 5*(1), 1–18.

St. Pierre, E. (2017). Haecceity: Laying out a plane for post qualitative inquiry. *Qualitative Inquiry, 23*(9), 686–698. https://doi.org/10.1177/1077800417727764

St. Pierre, E. A. (2018). Writing post qualitative inquiry. *Qualitative Inquiry, 24*(9), 603–608. https://doi.org/10.1177/1077800417734567

St. Pierre, E. A. (2019). Post qualitative inquiry in an ontology of immanence. *Qualitative Inquiry, 25*(1), 3–16. https://doi.org/10.1177/1077800418772634

Thomas, M. (2018). The girl who lived: Exploring the liminal spaces of self-study research with textual critical partners. In D. Garbett & A. Ovens (Eds.), *Pushing boundaries and crossing borders: Self-study as a means for knowing pedagogy* (pp. 327–333). Self-Study of Teacher Education Practices (S-STEP).

Yoo, J. (2019). A year of writing 'dangerously': A narrative of hope. *New Writing, 16*(3), 353–362. https://doi.org.10.1080/14790726.2018.1520893

Yoo, J. (2020). Writing creatively to catch flickers of 'truth' and beauty, *New Writing, 18*(1), 1–11. http://doi.org/10.1080/14790726.2020.1726966

CHAPTER 2

The Gifting of Feather

A Kaleidoscopic Visioning to Reanimate Learning

alexandra fidyk and darlene st. georges

© KONINKLIJKE BRILL NV, LEIDEN, 2022 | DOI:10.1163/9789004521186_002

An Egyptian Creation Story and the Teachings of Maat

Bird and Feather are Teacher[1] ...

> As in many creation stories, land begins through the action of a bird or animal. For ancient Egyptians, *Khepri*—the Egyptian god embodied as sacred Scarab—is associated with the beginning. Scarab rolls up a piece of primordial earth and pushes the element into being in the presence of the morning sun. Khepri, depicted as a black dung beetle, sometimes with wings spread, sometimes with scarab head and human body, comes from *kheper* which means "to take shape" or "to come into being". (Martin, 2010, p. 236)
>
> Scarab, like Crane, Hummingbird, and Raven, evokes the qualities of immortality, sublimation, and transcendence. Revering its wisdom, its dwelling, "a subterranean, vertical shaft leading to a horizontal passage," appears to have inspired the architecture of Egyptian tombs (Andrews, as cited in Martin, 2010, p. 236). Scarab amulets, crafted out of stone, metal, and glass, were used to draw power to the living. In hope of return to earthly dwelling, the amulets were placed with the dead as prayers for new life.
>
> At the time of death, the heart—the centre of life: feeling, action, and memory—is weighed against a feather of Maat, Goddess of truth, harmony, and cosmic order. The result of this weighing determines the next realm.
>
> Known for the beauty and ethic of her teachings, Maat symbolizes the way to live. Her widespread wings and headdress composed of one feather, a symbol of truth, adorns her. Her teaching upholds the values of truth, balance, order, harmony, right way, morality, and justice, instructing people in their daily lives with family, community, and place. Over time, Maat's way becomes a living curriculum,

---

1 Here, we capitalize "Bird", "Feather", and "Teacher" when we enter into the archetypal realm. In this realm, primordial energy that rises to consciousness can become enfleshed through culturally meaningful symbols and images. When we use lower case, bird, feather, teacher, the entity is not archetypal; even though, it is alive and endowed with spirit. It is *not* an inanimate thing.

> embracing all aspects of existence. It is believed that cosmic harmony stems from living a right and ritual life.
>
> The death ritual, one of the most important rituals of ancient times, centres around the weighing of the extracted heart. Its weight determines the passage of the soul, "Ba" or "Ba-Bird"—symbolized by a bird with a human head. If the "right way" is respected—maintaining harmonious relations with other—the heart's weight is equal to the weight of Maat's feather. Entry to the land of the blessed is granted. Such access promotes living in balance with the stars, scarabs, and stones. Living lightly upon the earth lends itself to be, at the end, "light as a feather."

According to symbologist J. E. Cirlot (1971/2014), "Bird" generally symbolizes human souls with early examples found in the art of ancient Egypt. Many of the traits that we associate with birds—spirit, inner vision, transcendence—distill into the image of Feather. Hope, joy, imagination, intuition, breath, psyche, and flight are a few of these.

Everywhere in the world, feathers are endowed with magical powers, which accrue to the individual who wears them (Martin, 2010). Like magical transformation, feathers, unique to birds, are thought to have evolved from the scales of primordial reptiles, attesting to the unity of water and air. Earth traces reveal feathered dinosaurs that likely originated flight. These creatures appear the mythical ancestors of the winged serpent, the root of the twinned nature of the bird and snake.

Attending through Kaleidoscopic Visioning

Inspired by Maat's teaching, We ask Bird to participate in our creation storying by gifting its Feather to us—to initiate our wondering.[2] We ask how Feather and agential landscape might recentre our learning through lived experience,

2 As authors, we are intentional about not identifying who wrote which story or from whose life a memory emerged. As described, we attuned to Feather and honoured what appeared for storying. At times, we worked together as "we" where our particularities are written into the text; at times, we wrote separately as "I"; and again, at other times, we fell into the archetypal field where our particularities dissolved into "We", writing as One with Feather. We continue to seek fluidity across the usage of I, we, and We. We do, however, differentiate with capitalization to be consistent across the text.

in particular, through the places we inhabit: the coulees of southern Alberta, the great plain of northern Alberta, interior British Columbia, and the Sahara Desert of Egypt. With on-going Bird presence, we are gifted Feathers from diverse species and enriched with symphonic accompaniment.

We honour Bird by inquiring with Feather—knowledge keeper. We begin with a creation story and a death ritual watched over by Maat. With her teachings in heart, we wonder of our ethical responsibility to right action, that is, living in balance and harmony with other, community, and place through respect and relational accountability.[3] As We turn Feather over and over, memories, images, and stories rise, creating a kaleidoscopic movement. In attentive turning and pausing and wondering and imagining, We meet Feather in new configurations—not conceptual and verbal, but somatic and imaginal. We are led by the not-yet known and engage what emerges through the process of amplification. This fresh way, kaleidoscopic visioning,[4] opens "seeing" to encounter Feather's aesthetic complexity. We are discovering some of its dynamic dimensions, and in this turning, reciprocally, We are uncovering more of ourselves.

We find, as Jan Zwicky (2008) describes, the disciplined act of attending to things is "ontologically robust" (p. 86). Attending respects the deeply interwoven web in which all things dwell. It permits the underlying movement of energy in the unity of psyche and matter, of acausal and synchronistic happenings, to draw us into new experience and meaning through the constellation of the subtle body—a reality where psyche and matter are no longer clearly distinguishable. As We surrender ourselves to imaginal processes (unconscious and ancestral), with their roots in the reservoir of primordial images, these embodied experiences[5] give rise to fresh perceptions and not-previously-known meanings, renewing Our visioning. We experience these moments as constellating an ethos—a spirit or atmosphere characteristic of the image domain of the preverbal, preconceptual mind-body-being—which paradoxically enfolds and unfolds inside and outside of place, space, and time.

3 By ethical responsibility and relational accountability, we refer to the cosmic network of life that includes earth, water, tree, star, scarab, and stone. This relationship spirals through time, understood in lay terms as backward and forward.

4 In response to reviewer comments, we are not able to speak to how stories were selected or applied to the dynamics outlined as we served as conduits for archetypal energy seeking expression. When images, memories, and stories came to consciousness, we respected their manifestation in various forms as demonstrated in this chapter. Our processes seek to emphasize the integrity of an animated paradigm.

5 We understand experience as spherical, in that it includes components of beingness: mind, body, emotion, and spirit, as well as connections with otherworldliness: upperworlds, middle grounds, and underworlds. As a whole, all elements are held by creative life energy.

Close attention reveals a complexity of dimensions that opens up a unified whole, a meaningful symbolic form, moving beyond Feather's physicality of height, width, and length, as well as depth felt and perceived through the interplay of shadow and light. Through Our curiosity and respect, unique in-sight tumbles forth—even though Feather always already exists multi-dimensionally. Our intimate, tactile relations with Feather concretize the abstract and theoretical whereby our seeing transforms That is, We experience Feather as a reflection of the pulsating polyverse: Feather dwells in relationship with Other: animal, place, minerals, and tools. Through these relationships, Feather has weight; it varies in association with light and shadow and its own casting of shadow; Feather exists in time and is affected by time, bound to space and place; Feather possesses family, kin, and ancestors; it offers an aesthetic—beauty and ethic; it has function, and it arrives laden with presence. In what follows, we amplify these dimensions with life writing and storying—personal vignettes, memories, and images.

ecstatic flight between realms
shamanic drums keep time
signaling what passes, what's lost—can you feel
round, round the taut skins

bone, lucky charm, feather amulets divine
your pain and ours
four generations maybe more
fates tied

the dance of dimensions

Function

Feathers mature over time into branch like structures to support flight, affect temperature, and shed water. They are protected from winds, moisture, and sun. Feather's biological anatomy holds the knowledge of its function for flight.

elemental compositions of light and darkness—
Avian knowledge keepers
map an evolution of powered flight
across centuries of flying
with interlocking friendships
and ancestral memories
sketching constellations
with kaleidoscopic vision

I remember sitting on the bus in Montreal on a hot and humid July summer day. I recently moved back from living up North for five years, in a remote Cree community, situated along the James Bay coast. I was thinking of Archie, a good friend of mine, who I met while living there. He led the sweat lodges that I attended and always called me Sister. Archie and I often got together to tell and share stories, and we envisioned writing a play one day—something each of us had wanted to do for a long time.

In our initial visit, Archie invited me to his house to have some moose and dumpling soup—his specialty. He introduced me to his Mom, with whom he was living and caring. Together we spent hours poring over photographs. Remembering and telling stories with his photos was Archie's way of introducing me to his friends and family, his life, and inviting and enfolding me into his relational kinships.

Archie was a Healer. He taught me how to be with spirit, even when it was painful. In ceremony, he often began with smudging sage using Hawk Feather. Archie said: Hawk can glide on winds, and see both near and far, not only for hunting but also for relational connecting with land, and sky, and spirit world. Hawk is the carrier and communicator of knowledges between Earth World, Sky World, and Spirit World. Hawk weathers storms through breath, said Archie.

I left Moosonee to return to Montréal and said my farewell to Archie. Before I left, I invited him to my house and we spent hours poring over pictures and sharing our stories—mapping out our play of life. While on the bus that day, as I stared out the cracked open window, a white feather whisked its way through the opening and landed on my lap. What an unexpected gift! And, it was unusual for a feather to make its way through a crack in the window on a city bus. I immediately thought of Archie and felt I needed to share this with him. I called Archie when I got home. His mom picked up the phone. She told me that Archie had passed away—sudden heart attack. I lost my breath.

Today, I carry Hawk Feather to remind me how to look close and far, to soar, to weather storms with the power of flight and insight, returning me to breath, long deep rhythmic breaths—

Relationship

Elemental songs, webs of relations, intersecting lines of flight, grounding, place—

Amongst peacock, eagle, hawk, guinea fowl, and dove feathers, my writing space on this hot June evening on the northern plain of Alberta hosts shells, pussy willows, plants, round sea rocks, fertility dolls, desert glass, clay figures, ash, and a raven's wing—elements of earth rhythms that tether me to where I have lived, dwelt, and learned. Elemental songs that account for what was, is, and might have been sing through both hollowed and weighted bone. The things we carry, keep, wear—like mourning lockets—reveal our loves and losses. These living testaments of my many lives, aid as tactile embodiments of relations with wind, bird, and beetle that have and do inhabit the steppes of Saqqara; the sacred site of San Agustin, Colombia; coastal Iguana, Nicaragua; and the rocky shore of South Africa's cape peninsula. Each flows like the fertile Nile, Egypt's lifeblood, concealing lost treasures, turning the stories imprinted within sand and silt, redirecting

seeds
pods and
death.

Black and white and faded-colour images of four generations of parentage buoy me, bloodlines in a web of relations, wafting across realms of existence. A visible reminder that I am always enacting others' lives. My father died June 2019; his mother, my baba, died November 2002—they stand as guardians and pull me into tomorrow.

amber-hued morning air
sweet fragrance rides the wind
low over drifting sands

haunted songs carried, lost
loves, dreams, hope

death

seeds

Weight

215 Sentinels

while held captive in sleep
as long and deep as death
we stand in hues of sweat
that ignite our breath
as we unearth
constellations

On the heels of the COVID-19 global pandemic, and under an extreme heat dome, Avian guardians gathered outside the downtown Vancouver public art gallery. Wearing light summer dresses, hats, and sandals, they congregated under a pop-up tent and sat around white folding tables that supported a spread of scissors, fishing line, ribbon, and glue guns. At the center of this crafting cluster sat a large, white, plastic bag containing a communal collection of over twenty eagle feathers.

The tent, along with bottles of water, offered minuscule reprieve from the choking heat, while these Avian Protectresses laboured over their creations of assembled Eagle Feather amulets. In conversation, they poured out their vision and intention of installing these sacred objects at the memorial site they were shielding. Eagle Feather amulets were to bear witness and protect the children's spirits—remains of young bodies recently discovered in unmarked, shallow graves at residential schools across the country: Kamloops Indian Residential School, British Columbia, Canada: 215; St Eugene's Mission School for Indigenous Children, Cranbrook, British Columbia, Canada: 182; Marieval Indian Residential School, Saskatchewan, Canada: 751.

Eagle Feather carries the weight of these lives denied; holds the heaviness of this catastrophic loss; stands with the darkness of genocide, upon which the country of Canada has been built and now quivers. Children as young as three years old, stolen from their families, separated, humiliated, violated, and killed.

Eagle Feather gifts us with sentinel strength: to bear witness; to honour the children; to endure the darkness; and to conjure the wisdom to change. Bones of memory cannot be denied.

Pulsating Sands of Time

Warmed by life movement and slowed to stillness, blood memory carries story, image, knowledge of eons through the cellular structure of bird's feather. Offspring are born not only with the territorial knowledge of its parents and immediate kin, but also with what knowledge has been uncovered since existence—through the dark ages, over migration patterns, and into the coloured, textural specificities of space-place-time. A kind of epigenetics lying dormant until required now-here when it spontaneously appears.

Woven into the barbs and barbules of its intricate web, keratin carries forth the life-stories of the ancestors. Coded into turacin (red) and turacoverdin (green with some structural blue) pigments or simple black and white, throbs Feather's evolutionary origin and lineage—dating back some 250 million years ago—long before the origin of birds to their dinosaur kin.

In the delicate iridescent-turquoise Pigeon Feather, plucked from the hot sand of Saqqara, lives the daily activities of Kemetic (ancient Egypt) people, beating within the interlocking branching. This ancient way of life runs alongside the gallibaya-clad farmers tending vegetables under June's butter-sun. Fused into this scene, rushes the crack of a gun along with scattered horns and barking dogs. Braided deeper into such branching lies the distinct sounds of earthly predators, memories of intimate hide-a-ways, and the location of lush gardens flush with majestic wisteria and fresh water.

Time spirals within the plumage, a continuing reiteration of desert life and every-other-place from whence Pigeon arrived. Woven into the dynamism of its be-coming, eons spiral, braiding not-yet, already here, might have been, and have-been-here-before. Kairos enfolds here, there, now, then, and to-be—within the feather.

Presence

Feather calls for a return to life world ...

circling us with other eyes and throated whistles
air tribes pour out quilled songs
sounding the land
animating knowledge
recruiting myth

A dull ache emerges as I wade the surface of Old Man River, breathing sky. Tongues have been talking all morning: foxtail, sage, meadowlark, grasshoppers, telling stories, down in low rises and folds of the Coulees on Bull Trail. Circling, circling, circling, a Pelican pod soars, riding spiraling, thermal, air currents. They sketch lands, lakes, and rivers—places that form their blood-branched, winged architecture—with their rippling feathers. Their bodies of fine bones and air pockets have developed through Earth's epochs, over 30 million years. Their bodies heal fragmentation in my own body.

In deep lock, we move westward with mild throated winds, gathering momentum on this celestial journey. The land fades.

Stretched, winged shadows cast out consciousness, emancipating our bodies from colonial fixedness and igniting our remembering, with an intimate pull of memories in cells and marrow. Our bodies connect us in this place. Mouth empty, still in breath, we return slowly to the river's sediments and deep caverns beneath spruce, where we are oxidized.

Here, from the corner of my mouth, I can finally recognize the animal inside me. It is like the first time I actually know myself—a lodge of bones, darkening veins, an inspirited wing-span, and a tongue thick enough to hold constellations, yet thin enough to curl and sound a whistle.

As I stare out the window, into the yard, while the wind persists, I think that it takes courage to bring home your transfigured body—the relational self you discovered—and to weave ribbons of time to form a new horizon.

Familial Lines and Lineages

Running my fingers through the downy afterfeather softens my body. I drop into another space-time. Simple joy experienced through touch. I run the white and grey feather along my cheek. When or how have we forgotten the pleasure, the necessity of somatic presence? Is it cultural?

Cultural cosmologies endure because of their inhabitation of place; they survive for millennia through their stories, songs, myths, rituals, and symbols. The people, creatures, elements, and vegetation of a particular space-place-time create a genealogical record of birth, mating, death, and kinship. Its pages bound with the threads of bodily wisdom not only distill through the marrow of familial inheritance but also through the active engagement of intuition, memory, and imagination.

Just as a Columbidae feather—that of pigeon and dove—is coded by the brilliant sun, drifting Sahara sand, and the survival instinct of its family, it also stores its lineage, siblings, and parentage in its shaft and barbs, evolving from a single filament to vaned feathers with asymmetrical rachis.

Pigeon, descendent of Rock Dove, the oldest domesticated bird, was immortalized through etched likeness in pyramid walls some 5000 years ago. Just as this symbol preserved its place of reverence, visual, acoustic, and somatic experience becomes imprinted upon the feather. Memories and meanings transport the lived past alongside innumerable family trees—a telepathic tapestry among pigeons, mules, scarabs, and cats, and of collective memories of each species—into our here-now. Each chick inherits a collective memory of its clan and contributes to the ancestral code, affecting future offspring.

Cooing stirs my heart as I sip Turkish coffee from this 100-year-old balcony, breathing in golden hues of the Saqqara pyramids. At once, this sonogram cords me to the intimate cooing of doves perched on the powerline wiring my writing space to back-street Albertan neighbours. Sound creates a complete relativity of space-place-time. Each collapses into the other as sonorous lines of flight.

Light and Shadow

Light is a stream of small packets of energy; energy cannot create shadows. Three-dimensional objects block light and create shadows. The interplay of light and shadows with objects creates a fourth dimension.

sparing breath
sleek and shimmering
dancers of dreams
glisten with territorial hues
and blooming shades
riding the thermals
between worlds—
casting shadows on trails
they offer us slender vanes
before disappearing in hedges

Memories seemingly fade over time, or at least they take on their own life—just out of reach emerging and submerging on their own terms. I have learned to install hooks for my keys at home, in my office, and in my bag to maintain some sense of control from my lucid and nomadic recollections.

Often surfacing in dreams, my memories come through in symbols and images, and at times, as intense and riveting stories—inner movies with ontological breadth that bleed into day break, provoking my sense of being, sometimes for days.

The sheath enveloping and separating my memories, dreams, sensations, and experiences can be quite fluid and translucent at times. I feel my blood charging through my veins and hear my teeth hum to the pulsing echo of my erratic heartbeat. Awkwardly, I clench my jaw.

I am a survivor of multiple traumas—a riveting stone, burnished and glazed by the sun over time. My shadows exist in stilled silver air and can be seen in my body's gestures, in my skin's melding folds and crevices. The slow drifts of sacred soil from Earth's movements soothe my disrupted rhythms, dislodging the violence from my entrenched terrain, accounting for my happiness.

Mourning Dove teaches me how to move with this interference of light, to exist between shadows, and along edges under soothing sonic vibrations among gentle breezes. Thrice charmed, Dove's feather is finely layered with iridescent hues and shades that hold the nourishing moisture of morning's dew, enabling it to survive successfully through periods of drought. Dove returns me to my core, that narrow space that remains open under the weight of forgiveness, provoking intermittent sensual invocations that lace my dreams and memories with hope and joy.

Aesthetic of a Thousand Eyes

In ancient thought, beauty "referred to the right placing of the multiple things of the world" (Hillman, 1992, p. 43). There is a right order to things that when experienced, a body-mind resonance unfolds. Such order reflects an ethic, an attitude of acceptance for the way things are—relational. It is an affirmation, an appreciation of life—as it exists in rhythm, pattern, and form. In its ancient, pagan coupling, "ethic" was inherent to "aesthetic." The two were one (Fidyk, 2017, p. 125).

I had just placed the porcelain bird figurine with iridescent green feathers into the sand tray. It had called to me so it was the right figure. I was perplexed, however, by the pattern on its back and the plumage on its head. I called it a wattled crane, a large species found south of the Sahara Desert, yet the plumage, length of tail, crown, and patterning, suggested otherwise.

The following day, when returning to sand tray process, a large peahen stopped me on the road. Here was the living form of what my mind could not identify—peafowl! The dissonance held in my body quickly dissolved. Her metallic blue crown with fan-shaped feathers stood distinct. Her green-blue and bronze body feathers—things of and for perception by the senses—radiated and made her vulnerable. Her presence confirmed the right ordering of things in the tray. I placed her likeness again that day—under a banyan tree and adjacent to a clay house. With two long peacock feathers cupping the base of the tree as grounding for the male whose screaming I heard that morning.

Oh Solar Bird, Bird of immortality with your thousand eyes—guide us to respect our relations and to trust resonance.

burnt marrow
defies life spirit, heart
ache misread

living testaments splinter
pierce
bone dry, hungry

eyes misread
brown like Mother Earth
bleed red

Recentring Education through Kaleidoscopic Visioning

Attending deeply to Feather—a particular being of place—revealed a microcosm of the animated pluriverse in which We dwell. In "setting things side by side" (Zwicky, 2003, p. L7)—Feather in place—We uncovered patterns of what-is, what has "come into being"—interwoven and interstoried. When We set this thing alongside other things, We rediscovered the beauty, complexity, and holographic nature of things in relation—*beings in relation*. As such, Our kaleidoscopic visioning aids to reanimate learning, not unlike the Scarab rolling up a piece of primordial earth and pushing it into being.

Animated learning invites us "to come into being"—through body, story, memory, and image—and to fold self into storying. It resists flattening and deadening things, and welcomes poly-dimensionality. These relations enliven Us, recentring *beings in learning and education*. Our animated learning through kaleidoscopic visioning unfolds spontaneously: respecting life worlds; honouring other-and-Other; wondering; trusting of and for the unity of embodied experience and the unbidden; being open to discovery—unfamiliar dimensions imprinted by what has lived, is living and, in turn, imprints upon all beings unfolding.

Such engagement teaches us ways to imagine curriculum and pedagogy as embedded in the things we encounter in place; it teaches us how new patterns arise from slow, attentive turning—an ancient ritual often remembered only in dance. It teaches us how to recentre living and learning through witnessing, relations, and reciprocity. Radically, by offering Our breath to Feather, a kind of resuscitation occurs—of ourselves—transmuting Feather from a thing to a *being* that breathes life back. Afterall, it is the ritual of weighing one's heart, one's life—action taken and not taken *in this moment*—in relation to the weight of Maat's feather that determines what next unfolds.

The heart's weight is equal to the weight of Maat's feather.

Authors' Note

We note the apparent contradiction of identifying photographer and digital rendering artist and not the stories constituting the main text. We discussed this dilemma at length. However, it is not a contradiction. Simply, we include this identification for self-preservation within the audit culture of academe. The photographs were taken by a. fidyk and d. st. georges; the digital rendering is by d. st. georges.

References

Cirlot, J. E. (2014). *A dictionary of symbols* (J. Sage, Trans.). Welcome Rain. (Originally published in 1971)

Fidyk, A. (2017). An aesthetic of the underworld. In P. Sameshima, A. Fidyk, K. James, & C. Leggo (Eds.), *Poetic inquiry: Enchantment of place* (pp. 211–219). Vernon Press.

Hillman, J. (1992). *The thought of the heart and the soul of the world.* Spring Publications.

Martin, K. (Ed.). (2010). *Book of symbols.* Taschen.

Zwicky, J. (2003). *Wisdom & metaphor.* Gaspereau.

Zwicky, J. (2008). Lyric realism: Nature poetry, silence and ontology. *The Malahat Review, 165*(Winter), 85–91.

CHAPTER 3

The Monarch Lecture

Alysha J. Farrell

Wildlife biologist, Kasey Fowler-Finn, and her project partner, sound artist Stephen Vitiello, staged an exhibit for the St. Louis Museum of Art called *Too Hot to Sing* to illustrate the impact of climate change on the calls of tiny sap feeding insects called treehoppers. As viewers explored the exhibit, the treehopper's call became increasingly distant and infrequent as the temperature increased. Kika Tuff, who created the displays to illustrate the context for the sound installation, remarked:

> You can read the data on how much the frequency of a treehopper song has changed. It's so different when you go into a room and listen to how a soundscape changes with temperature. What you'll find in the exhibit, as it gets warmer, things just start to drop off. It's a "Silent Spring" kind of idea. It gets too hot, and [the treehoppers] just retreat to the shade and they just don't call anymore. (Chen, 2020, para. 11)

After hearing an excerpt from the exhibit, I was inspired to visit Fowler-Finn's digital sound library. Immediately, I was sensory-struck by the treehopper duet (Fowler-Finn Lab, 2018). Sitting alone in an empty university classroom, goosebumps rippled across my body as I thought about the millions of tiny creatures across the planet who are falling silent amid the climate crisis.

This was not my first evocative experience with eco-grief. Many moons ago, as a way to grieve the disappearance of the monarch butterfly from my own backyard, I got a tattoo. The tattoo not only inscribed a text of mourning on my body but, as a teacher educator, it has also become a visceral reminder of the disenfranchisement of eco-grief across the field of education. Disenfranchised grief refers to encounters in which a mourner is denied the comfort or catharsis shared grief brings (Doka, 1989). As it relates to teacher education, disenfranchised eco-grief is perpetuated in the absence of climate change curricula across programs, the minimization of the emotional dimensions of learning amid the climate crisis, and in the widespread refusal to acknowledge that we are educating young people for a world that is prepared to go on without them. The 10-minute play that comprises the bulk of this chapter explores the intersections

© KONINKLIJKE BRILL NV, LEIDEN, 2022 | DOI:10.1163/9789004521186_003

among mourning, embodied curriculum, and what it means to emotionally dwell with teacher candidates amid the Earth's decreasing habitability.

The Classroom as Holding Environment

Time is of the essence and young people have swallowed the ticking clock. A survey carried out by *ComRes,* asked 2000 children from the United Kingdom between the ages of eight and 16 if they thought adults were doing enough about climate change. 53% of the respondents believe the adults in their lives are not doing enough, and 61% of the 14–16-year old cohort said adults need to do more (Newsround, 2019). When educators minimize the threats to the survival of the human species by rigidly adhering to the curriculum-as-plan, it exerts a dehumanizing force in the emotional landscapes of young people by making adults emotionally illegible. As an example, after watching a documentary about deforestation, one of the participants in an arts-based study I am leading on the emotional impacts of the climate crisis told me she could not understand how adults could know about habitat loss, climate change, and animal extinctions and do nothing about it. At one point during the interview she fumed, "Adults are insane!" Later in our conversation, she referenced the silence of her high school teachers. She wondered aloud if they knew about clearcutting or if they just didn't care. Her anger, fear, and disappointment about the emotional illegibility of her former teachers in relation to global warming was palpable.

Within an intersubjective psychoanalytic frame (Mitchell, 2000; Stern, 2003, 2015) the environment (home, classroom, forest, beach) is part of the relational field. Young people come to know themselves by making meaning of their own reflections in the eyes of significant Others. Affective fusions and dislocations make imprints on a student's mental topography in ways that facilitate or inhibit their attachment, sense of security, and their ability to tolerate the disillusion of what Winnicott (1965) refers to as the *holding environment. Holding* refers to a protected caregiving space in which children trust their environment and feel a sense of safety. Analysts and teachers provide emotional holding by attuning to a child's feelings without judgement. When significant adults accept the whole child and demonstrate knowledge of the child's uniqueness, the adult's acceptance and recognition metamorphosizes into the child's positive self-image and an increased capacity for self-regulation. For these reasons, students' complicated feelings about oceans of plastic or uncontrolled wildfires should be openly discussed in classrooms. An integral aspect of this difficult pedagogical praxis is to give language to loss before students engage in preservative repression.

Grief is the term used to describe the web of unwieldly emotions experienced after a significant loss. The Climate Psychology Alliance (2021) adapted Worden's (1983) work on grieving to describe what it looks like to embrace or reject the tasks of mourning in the context of climate change. To embrace the work of grief involves accepting a loss, working through excruciating emotions, adjusting to a new interpersonal field, developing a new sense of one's identity, and finding a place to contain the loss. Rejecting the task of grief manifests as denying the facts and irreversibility of the loss, idealizing what was lost, bargaining, numbing, becoming bitter, feeling helpless, or turning away from loved ones and the vitality of life. Climate grief can emerge when we experience physical ecological losses, the loss of environmental knowledge, and when we anticipate loss (Cunsolo et al., 2020).

Inspired by conversations with graduate and undergraduate students about eco-justice, and informed by the young people who have courageously shared stories with me about their own climate grief, I wrote a 10-minute play called *The Monarch Lecture*. In my experience, drama-pedagogies can enhance emotional awareness within and between individuals and groups by allowing people to be participants and observers at the same time (Kershaw & Nicholson, 2011; Mackay et al., 2016; Vettraino et al., 2017). As an audience interprets the actions of the characters on stage through their own lived experiences, they become more perceptive of their own emotional registers and those of Others (Farrell, 2020). With this in mind, I hope the encounter between Larissa and Dr. Kelly evokes spirited performances and dialogue in teacher education classrooms about what it means to emotionally dwell with one's students.

The Monarch Lecture

AT RISE: A dated university classroom in a Faculty of Education building somewhere in Western Canada. There is a large wooden table with a desktop lectern center stage. ***Dr. Kelly****, a 56-year-old associate professor is hurriedly packing her laptop, tablet, and water bottle into a weathered computer bag. From stage right,* ***Larissa****, an education student in her final year, enters and moves toward Dr. Kelly.*

Dr. Kelly (*Looks up, a little annoyed to find Larissa just staring at her. Forces a smile.*) What can I do for you?

Larissa (*Looks like she's just about to say something but then takes her backpack off her shoulder and begins to root around in it, pulling a few things out. She mumbles to herself and is becoming increasingly frustrated.*) Just a sec.

Dr. Kelly (*Concerned. She moves to the front of the table closer to Larissa.*) Everything okay?

Larissa (*Finds a balled-up piece of paper in her bag and then thrusts it toward Dr. Kelly.*) This.

Dr. Kelly (*Takes the ball of paper from Larissa's hand and begins to unfurl it and scan it.*) Ouch.

Larissa (*Sits on the ground in a tight ball.*) She's ruined me.

Dr. Kelly (*Reading from the letter.*) "Takes too many liberties with the curriculum. "Inability to take—"

Larissa (*Loud voice, with finger pointed in the air.*) "Constructive criticism." (*Lower voice, with anger.*) So says the old battle-axe.

Dr. Kelly (*Perplexed.*) "During the last two weeks of practicum, missed three days…late twice…unreliable—"

Larissa The students hate her, you know. She's boring them to death. That's the real crime.

Dr. Kelly You need to make an appointment with the field experience office today and arrange to make up those days.

Larissa Why should I—

Dr. Kelly Today, Larissa.

Larissa Seriously, how am I supposed to learn to be a good teacher from someone who is so awful?

Dr. Kelly (*Sits down beside Larissa.*) I'm sure she's objectively terrible. Her Grade 1 students are probably plotting her demise as we speak. But how did we get here? I told you to come and see me if you had any trouble during your practicum. (*Pause.*) We could go together and see about another placement for next term? (*Pause.*) What? You've got better things to do with your time than to stuff whiny six-year-olds into their smelly snow pants?

Larissa Were you ever a real teacher, you know, a teacher of tiny humans?

Dr. Kelly I was a high school drama teacher for a spell. Does that count?

Larissa Barely.

Dr. Kelly (*With concern.*) Last term, you mentioned you were struggling a bit with anxiety. It must have been tough to be placed in a classroom where you felt judged.

Larissa You wanna be my counsellor now?

Dr. Kelly (*Gestures to the whole room.*) Nope. In a culture of hyper individualism such as this, listening to you is an act of subversion. I'm feeling rebellious today.

Larissa (*Pause.*) You'll think I'm crazy.

Dr. Kelly Try me.

Larissa (*Pause.*) I read an article about the heat dome. A heat dome happens when the warm air goes up really high in the atmosphere and it makes a thick layer. A marine biologist said the extreme temperatures fried one billion sea creatures on the west coast in July. (*Starts to fidget.*) She said the ecosystem is totally screwed now too because the mussels and clams filter the ocean to keep it clear enough for the sunlight to reach the eelgrass beds. And because of climate change, we could get these types of heat waves every five to 10 years, which is a big problem because it won't give the ocean a chance to recover between the die-offs. (*Gets still and then looks anxiously at* DR. KELLY.) Then I read about web-bulb temperatures—what happens when it's too hot and humid for human sweat to evaporate, which made me think a lot about human die-offs, and my die-off. (*Gets up and moves downstage.*) And why the hell are we talking about preparing students for 21st century learning in Professor Litman's Ed Tech class without talking about the climate emergency? It's insane.

Dr. Kelly If it makes you feel any better, he's a real nightmare during faculty council meetings, too.

Larissa (*Walks over to front table. Picks up and shakes half-empty coffee in a disposable cup.*) This isn't funny. We're in deep shit if your generation doesn't stop drinking drive-thru coffees and manicuring your stupid lawns. (*Spills coffee on the front of her shirt.*) Perfect.

Dr. Kelly (*Gets up and hands Larissa some paper towels.*) I don't understand what this has to do with missing practicum days.

Larissa (*Tries to dry her shirt with the paper towel.*) We should become activists, you know. Tie ourselves to machines so they can't build anymore pipelines. Something useful.

Dr. Kelly I think my days of chaining myself to a front-end loader are behind me. (*Pause.*) Was there a specific moment when the whole teaching thing started to feel absurd to you?

Larissa You mean, pointless?

Dr. Kelly Okay, pointless.

Larissa After lunch one day, the old battle axe—

Dr. Kelly Really?

Larissa Fine. My cooperating teacher asked me to read a story to the kids. Everything was going fine until I noticed Rayleen, driving the little blue car I gave her up and down her pant leg as I read the line, "The world's your oyster, kid!" I started to think about what kind of future there is for kids like her, when things really go for shit. In a world of food shortages, what chance does Ray have? And don't give me some sentimental BS like, "That's why we need you in the classroom, to make sure kids like Rayleen are not shoved to the margins."

Dr. Kelly (*Hand up as if to swear an oath.*) I wouldn't dare.

Larissa The same night, I woke up shaking, and I freaked out because I couldn't calm myself down. My mom took me to the hospital because she thought I was having a heart attack. Seven hours in emergency waiting for the psych doc, and ta-da! Absence number one. Happy?

Dr. Kelly No, actually. That sounds pretty awful.

Larissa What's awful is what a clueless person I am. In other parts of the world, so many people have been suffering because of global warming. It's only because I saw some pictures of a bunch of fried starfish in the same place I used to walk with my Grannie that I actually cared enough to start educating myself. What kind of person does that make me?

Dr. Kelly A person who had their ethical bones rattled. The suffering Other invaded your self-satisfied life and that's uncomfortable because it's demanding a response from you. (*Pause.*) You want to tell me about absence number two?

Larissa Slept through my alarm after the fire drill dream. In case you're curious…

Dr. Kelly You can tell me.

Larissa In the dream, the fire bell goes off and I rush the Grade 1s down the hall, get them outside, and lined up. I count heads and realize one student is missing. As I watch the smoke get more intense, I just keep counting their heads even though every cell in my body is screaming, "Go find Rayleen!" But I don't. I just keep counting heads, over and over again.

Dr. Kelly What do you think it means?

Larissa (*Jumps up and lies on the table.*) I don't know, Dr. Freud. What do you think it means?

Dr. Kelly What could counting heads over and over represent in the field of teaching?

Larissa Seriously?

Dr. Kelly Humor me.

Larissa (*Sits up. Reluctantly at first.*) Maybe we avoid what we know because it's too terrifying. In the dream, I know at some level I'm missing a kid but instead of running into the school to find her before the whole school catches fire, I keep counting because I'm too scared to move. What we obsess over to avoid facing our fear can distract us to death.

Dr. Kelly That's pretty insightful. What would be an example of something distracting us to death in education?

Larissa Rigidly sticking to the curriculum guide…God forbid we take too many liberties with it.

Dr. Kelly What should we be focusing on?

Larissa (*A little more animated.*) How about we teach kids that all living things have value. That a cow is not your hamburger. Human beings have a responsibility to love and care for animals. That we're part of nature, not outside of it. If the bees die, we all die.

Dr. Kelly A little harsh for Grade 1, but go on.

Larissa (*A little more animated.*) Or how about we teach kids that the lowest emitting countries are experiencing the worst impacts of climate change. We don't need any more assholes taking cruises because they believe happiness is measured in the number of Instagram posts they make on vacation.

Dr. Kelly And what about absence number three?

Larissa Before bed, I read a bunch of posts on the insect apocalypse and then I just kept going.

Dr. Kelly (*Gives Larissa an "are you kidding me look."*) Seriously?

Larissa I know, but listen. The monarch butterfly population has fallen by 90% over the last 20 years. Scientists don't know exactly why, but they think it could be due to a combination of land use changes, pollution, and insecticides. Do you want to live in a world without butterflies?

Dr. Kelly No, the world is definitely better with butterflies.

Larissa (*Starts slower and then picks up speed.*) The current rate of global species extinction is hundreds of times higher compared to the last 10 million years, and the rate is picking up speed. How is this not what we're talking about in every class, every post, and—

Dr. Kelly (*Gestures to have Larissa sit beside her.*) Camus's novel, *The Plague*, speaks to that very question.

Larissa *The Plague*?

Dr. Kelly The story takes place in a modern town somewhere on the Algerian coast. Camus tells us the people of Oran live, "money-centred and de-natured lives. They barely notice they are alive." One day, Dr. Rieux, the narrator of the story, comes across a dead rat, and then another, and then another. Soon, Oran is covered in thousands of dead rats. The mysterious disease spreads uncontrollably to humans. A real zoonotic horror show. But even after the disease kills a quarter of the people in town, most citizens disavow the deadliness of the plague.

Larissa Like those people who think the warnings of climate scientists are part of some government conspiracy?

Dr. Kelly Most humans work hard to avoid difficult knowledge. The people in Oran deny the deadliness of the disease. They've convinced themselves it can't happen to them. They're too modern, too smart, too tech savvy. Camus points out, it's actually the denial of our human fragility and the precarity of our species that drives us to become the narcissistic, consuming assholes we are. Walking around in denial in the middle of a plague, that's delusional. Your fear, the fire drill nightmare, it means you are awake to the danger climate change poses. Anxiety is a healthy response to the legitimate danger we face.

Larissa So, you're saying we should just deal with our fear, show up and teach, even though the future isn't a given anymore?

Dr. Kelly Actually, Camus wants more from you. Like Dr. Rieux, you have to honour and care for the lives of others in spite of the danger you face and do your part. Where there is suffering, bring relief. Join the healers.

Larissa Teaching as healing?

Dr. Kelly Remember the promise I made during your first class with me? If you take Philosophy of Ed, you'll become slightly more enlightened to feel modestly less miserable.

Larissa (*Looks up and smiles a little.*) What do you have to be miserable about anyway?

Dr. Kelly (*Pause.*) Three years ago, my wife Ella died.

Larissa Oh God, I'm so sorry, I—

Dr. Kelly It's okay, thank you…About a year after she died, I ran into a good friend at a research conference. We went for a drink and he told me I was, by far, "the most pathetic-looking person at the conference." It was the first time I cracked a smile since she passed. (*Pause.*) Sitting in that noisy bar, I confessed that each time I exhaled, it was like letting her go all over again. (*Pause.*) Instead of responding with some cheap platitude, he said, tell me more about that. He didn't try to blow sunshine; he just sat with me, and we wallowed in it for a while.

Larissa That doesn't sound very helpful.

Dr. Kelly Actually, it was a relief. By not retreating, he somehow opened a space for me to say the unsayable while drinking very expensive Irish whiskey. Emotional dwelling with others is where it's at when your world goes to hell, my friend.

Larissa Maybe that's how teaching can be healing. You make room for messy feelings and then use them to create spaces of compassion for the other, including the monarchs and the starfish.

Dr. Kelly That's what you could do for your future students in the place where the wheat fields meet the smoky skies. (*Pause.*) Are you going to make up the days you missed?

Larissa (*Starts packing up her backpack.*) I don't know. But I have to say the thought of building a small army of tiny eco-justice warriors in smelly snow pants, is starting to have some appeal.

Dr. Kelly (*Wryly.*) Goodbye. I feel sorry for your future principal.

Larissa (*Said as she exits stage left.*) You know you love me.

Dr. Kelly (*Gathers belongings.*) What have I unleashed on the world?

(*Fade to black.*)

The Next Act

In performative education systems that are myopically focused on closing achievement gaps, the moral purpose of education is subsumed by an elaborate fantasy that masks incongruencies and problematic intersections among social mobility and the curriculum-as-plan. Mechanisms like standardized tests construct learning as a competitive system in which external accountability measures are instruments of the social good. As a proxy for inclusion, neoliberal interventions are a wolf in sheep's clothing, compelling teachers to internalize feelings of shame when bad test scores are strategically severed from the wider context. In the play, Larissa is disoriented by the pressure to adhere to prescriptive curriculum and the severance of the wider ecological crisis from her Ed Tech class. "If the bees die, we all die." Separating humans from the natural world, passive learning, competition, repetition, and separate disciplines must be relinquished (von Bülow & Simpson, 2021) if students are to enact more ecosophical ways of being in the world.

Exploring the affective dimensions of the climate crisis could propel us to enact more eco-compassionate curricula. It might begin with teachers understanding the classroom space as a holding environment (Winnicott, 1971/2005), one that is open to the world. Pedagogy, then, would become the art of being more attentive to students as they grow increasingly aware of what emotions escape their consciousness but still manage to influence their actions. These are the moments in the play when Dr. Kelly invites Larissa to consider her absences as manifestations of anxiety and grief.

Through Dr. Kelly's actions, we see education as a process of enhancing students' capacity to introject loss. After experiencing the traumatic loss of her wife, Dr. Kelly is acutely aware that when unprocessed grief is swallowed whole, ghostly reverberations of melancholy can fester and interfere with one's capacity to engage fully in the world. That said, it becomes a moral imperative to understand oneself as a compassionate witness in the classroom. As an illustration, Dr. Kelly encourages Larissa to understand teaching as taking responsibility for the Other, even when the Other cannot or will not return the gesture.

Many of our students are experiencing fear, helplessness, and grief related to environmental degradation (Hickman, 2019, 2020; Lertzman, 2015), yet the affective dimensions of teaching and learning in the midst of the climate crisis are muted, if not disavowed in teacher education programs. Eco-grief and anxiety will continue to "broaden and deepen in the years to come, [and] meeting the mental health needs of humanity will be a critical and central challenge" (Davenport, 2017, p. 13). In response, we need to lean into our students' and our own emotional discomfort so we can collectively face our finitude head-on. To do this difficult work, we will need classrooms in which teachers are prepared to weave stories that acknowledge what we have lost and to foster an intergenerational commitment to build eco-attuned communities grounded in reciprocity and love. "It's what you do for your future students in the place where the wheat fields meet the smoky skies."

References

Camus, A. (1947). *The plague.* Kindle Edition.

Chen, E. (2020, February 6). *Songs from a tiny bug tell a story about climate change at SLU Museum of Art.* NPR. https://news.stlpublicradio.org/health-science-environment/2020-02-06/songs-from-a-tiny-bug-tell-a-story-about-climate-change-at-slu-museum-of-art

Climate Psychology Alliance. (2021, April 23). *Handbook: Grief.* https://climatepsychologyalliance.org/handbook/321-grief

Cunsolo, A., Harper, S. L., Minor, K., Hayes, K., Williams, K. G., & Howard, C. (2020). Ecological grief and anxiety: The start of a healthy response to climate change? *Planetary Health, 4*(7), e261–e263. https://doi.org/10.1016/S2542-5196(20)30144-3

Davenport, L. (2017). *Emotional resiliency in the era of climate change: A clinician's guide.* Jessica Kingsley.

Doka, K. J. (1989). *Disenfranchised grief: Recognizing hidden sorrow*. Jossey-Bass.

Farrell, A. J. (2020). *Exploring the affective dimensions of educational leadership: Psychoanalytic and arts-based methods*. Routledge.

Fowler-Finn Lab. (2018). *Sound library*. https://www.fowlerfinnlab.com/sound-library

Hickman, C. (2019). Children and climate change: Exploring children's feelings about climate change using free association narrative interview methodology. In P. Hoggett (Ed.), *Climate psychology: On indifference and disaster* (pp. 41–59). Palgrave Macmillan.

Hickman, C. (2020). We need to (find a way to) talk about…eco-anxiety. *Journal of Social Work Practice, 34*(4), 411–424. https://doi.org/10.1080/02650533.2020.1844166

Kershaw, B., & Nicholson, H. (2011). *Research methods in theatre and performance.* Edinburgh University Press.

Lertzman, R. (2015). *Environmental melancholia: Psychoanalytic dimensions of engagement.* Routledge.

MacKay, M., Parlee, B., & Karsgaard, C. (2020). Youth engagement in climate change action: Case study on Indigenous youth at COP24. *Sustainability, 12*(16), 6299. https://doi.org/10.3390/su12166299

Mitchell, S. A. (2000). *Relationality: From attachment to intersubjectivity.* The Analytic Press.

Newsround. (2019, July 17). *Climate change: 'Adults need to do more!'* BBC. https://www.bbc.co.uk/newsround/48965605

Stern, D. B. (2003). *Unformulated experience: From dissociation to imagination in psychoanalysis.* Routledge.

Stern, D. B. (2015). *Relational freedom: Emergent properties of the interpersonal field.* Routledge.

Vettraino, E., Linds, W., & Jindal-Snape, D. (2017). Embodied voices: Using applied theatre for co-creation with marginalized youth. *Emotional and Behavioral Difficulties,* 22(1), 79–95. doi:10.1080/13632752.2017.1287348

von Bulow, C., & Simpson, C. (2021). What matters most? Deep education conversations in a climate of change and complexity. In J. Bendell & R. Read (Eds.), *Deep adaptation: Navigating the realities of climate chaos* (pp. 224–239). Polity Press.

Winnicott, D. W. (1965). *The maturational process and the facilitating environment.* International Universities Press.

Winnicott, D. W. (2005). *Playing and reality.* Routledge. (Original work published 1979)

Worden, J. W. (1983). *Grief counselling and grief therapy*. Tavistock.

CHAPTER 4

"We Are Not Seen as Human"

Re/telling Stories of Dis/citizenship

Muna Saleh

"Ma feehum yakhdouha mineena…sah?"
Fatima's[1] question continues to weigh heavily on my heart and mind.
"They can't take her away from us…right?"

I remember when Fatima asked me a variation of this question during our first research conversation in the early fall of 2019. Fatima was eight months pregnant and had been up most of the night to use the washroom and to make sure that her eldest daughter, Eman, was comfortable.

I had planned for our first conversation to be relatively short so we could get to know one another slowly. However, every time I tried to ease into ending the conversation, Fatima would ask more questions. I recall getting a strong sense that Fatima may not have many opportunities to ask questions in Arabic about citizenship, schools, policies, and other social codes/structures. I also remember feeling admiration for her strength and forthrightness in the midst of challenges I could only imagine navigating. I remember feeling enveloped by the warmth that radiated from her and throughout the home she made alongside her husband, Mahmoud, and their children Ali, Eman, and Mariam.

During that first conversation, Fatima shared how, in the midst of bombings and gunfire, she and her family escaped her small village in Syria in December 2011. She said they were originally grateful to be in a refugee camp in neighbouring Jordan…until they realized that they didn't have access to schooling for their children or medical/therapeutic supports for Eman (who has cerebral palsy) and Mariam (who is hard of hearing).

Fatima shared her elation when, in December 2016, she and Mahmoud were contacted by re/settlement officials and informed that they were selected for re/settlement in Canada. She expressed her anxiety and excitement as she boarded an airplane for the first time, and laughingly recounted her surprise at how warm it was when they arrived in the summer of 2017, because she assumed that Canada was always chilly. Fatima stressed that, while they're grateful for escaping what she characterized as the despair of the refugee camp, they've been confronted

© KONINKLIJKE BRILL NV, LEIDEN, 2022 | DOI:10.1163/9789004521186_004

with many different challenges since their arrival in Canada. She mused, "We were happy before the war...but the good thing is we have each other, Alhamdulillah."

Over the multiple conversations that Fatima and I engaged in, Mahmoud, Ali, Eman, Mariam, and (later) baby Hannah often joined us for brief periods. In February 2020, during our last in-person conversation before COVID-19 lockdowns in March, Mahmoud entered the living room and asked if I could translate a letter that Mariam's school had sent in English. Both Fatima and Mahmoud had previously expressed their desire to be able to communicate with their children's teachers and school administrators without the need for translators (who are not always reliable/available) or their eldest, Ali (who translates as best he can).

After I translated the letter, Fatima and Mahmoud shared a troubling experience with Mariam's school. They discussed how, during a meeting the month before with Mariam's teacher, school administrators, and occupational therapist, they were told (according to the translator) that they were in violation of Mariam's human rights by not ensuring she wears her hearing aids at all times. Fatima said that she tried telling Mariam's teacher multiple times that Mariam complains of severe discomfort and pain from her hearing aids, so she cannot force her to wear them, but "they don't listen to me."

After she and Mahmoud shared their outrage at being judged as bad parents, Fatima asked why, rather than making them feel threatened, Mariam wasn't supported with better hearing aids or even surgery to help her. She asked, "Why are they talking about human rights? We did the impossible for our children." Fatima paused before asking, "But...they can't take her away from us...right?"

Because of the stories she had previously shared with me, I recognized that this question was shaped by Fatima's knowing of governments that can (and do) commit violence against their own citizens. Over time, I also began to understand that Fatima was hearing stories from other Syrian mothers who arrived in Canada of the need to be careful during interactions with school officials and service providers, because they could recommend that "the government take your children away if they think you are not raising them right."

Narrative Re/tellings

Re-reading my storied account of part of my narrative inquiry[2] (Clandinin, 2013; Clandinin & Connelly, 2000) alongside Fatima, I think of Sara Ahmed's (2017) words: "A story always starts before it can be told" (p. 4). I think about how a story must also be told before it can be retold,[3] and how it is through the (often tension-filled) process of telling and retelling stories of lived experiences that we might begin to live out other stories (Clandinin, 2013)—perhaps even stories that sustain who we are and are always in the process of becoming (Cardinal et al., submitted). I think about the stories I have re/told and re/lived as a Muslim woman, educator, and scholar of colour, intergenerational survivor of violent Palestinian displacement (Saleh, 2020), and mother to three (including a dis/abled daughter), who has intimate knowledge of, and experiences with, dehumanizing systems, practices, and narratives (Saleh, 2021b)—including within school systems.

However, although I have relationally re/told my (autobiographical) stories alongside those of former participants/co-inquirers in previous narrative inquiries alongside Muslim girls and women (Saleh, 2019, 2020), I have never lived the (re)trauma(tization) of displacement and (un/re)settlement (Tweedie et al., 2017) as a newcomer to *amiskwaciywâskahikan* in Treaty 6 lands, in what is now known as Canada. As someone born and raised within these lands, I have never experienced the profound uncertainties and anxieties of mothering/caregiving across different, often violent, geographical contexts (Dossa, 2008). I have never navigated unfamiliarity with not only different dialects and languages, but also (the lack of) social and educational systems, supports, and norms in new lands (Awuah-Mensah, 2016). Here, I am reminded of Sara Ahmed's (2017) words: "When you are a stranger—maybe you are a tourist, or just newly arrived, and you don't know these unwritten rules…you can become quite an imposition, a burden, a thing" (p. 45).

I have recently written about the (intergenerational) narrative reverberations (Young, 2005), trauma (Menakem, 2017), un/knowings, resonances, tensions, and wonders that echoed within me during my first conversation alongside Fatima (Saleh et al., forthcoming). I wrote about thinking with my own non/ethical ways of being in relation alongside Fatima, because I had (inadvertently) imposed stories upon her—stories of what I assumed her experiences would be—before I had even met her. I wrote about leaving Fatima's home following that initial conversation, vowing to try to "walk in a good way" (Young, 2005, p. 179) alongside Fatima, her family, and other co-inquirers. For, not only does a story need to be told before it can be retold, *how* it is retold matters. As Barry Lopez (1990) reminds me,

> The stories people tell have a way of taking care of them. If stories come to you, care for them. And learn to give them away where they are needed. Sometimes a person needs a story more than food to stay alive. That is why we put these stories in each other's memories. This is how people care for themselves. (p. 60)

Throughout this chapter, as I re/center Fatima's re/tellings of lived experiences and my understandings of them, I try to take good care of Fatima and the stories she lived and re/told alongside me. *Insha'Allah khair.*

(Storied) Process of Living and Inquiring alongside Fatima

In my (sometimes contentious) advocacy as a caregiver to a dis/abled child across curriculum-making worlds[4] (Huber et al., 2011), I have often wondered about the lived experiences of other Muslim women who live and mother at the intersections (Crenshaw, 1989) of (marginalizing and violent) systems. In August 2019, Fatima was one of two women who responded to my research call for participants/co-inquirers who are Muslim mothers with refugee experiences and caregivers to dis/abled children. Fatima arrived in Canada in 2017, through the government-assisted refugee program following long periods of displacement from Syria, and is mothering two dis/abled daughters. Between September 2019 and July 2020, I engaged in multiple research conversations in the Arabic language alongside Fatima within her home or via telephone conversations.

As we were still in the midst of conversations, guided by the three narrative inquiry dimensions of temporality (past, present, and future), sociality (personal and social), and place(s) (Clandinin & Connelly, 2000), I began the process of looking across field texts[5] to discern narrative threads (Clandinin, 2013) by identifying patterns of continuities, discontinuities, silences, resonances, tensions, and wonders within and across field texts. Throughout this process, I made notes of what I understood to be threads resonating within and across our re/tellings and discussed these notes with Fatima, asking variations of the following questions: Is this how you understand the stories we inquired into? Is anything missing? Fatima approved of the threads I identified and helped to elucidate and/or identify narrative threads.

Narrative Threads That Resonated across Fatima's Stories

Fatima's stories illuminated two interconnected narrative threads: (a) the many ways that Fatima draws upon her embodied knowledge, faith, and loved ones to sustain herself and her family; and (b) even as she contends with (ongoing) discrimination and (re)trauma(tization). In the following sections, I center Fatima's lived experiences of dis/citizenship, including feeling/being unheard and silenced in school curriculum-making worlds.

Dis/citizenship

> You know how it is for a refugee…we are not seen as human.

As I continue to think with Fatima's stories, I wonder about who is *included* in our classrooms, schools, and communities? Who is not? Who is deemed a citizen? Who is not? Why? As Frederick and Shifrer (2019) note:

> Ideals of good citizenship, including independence, rugged individualism, and moral and intellectual competence, were delineated through the othering of bad citizens, those who were defined as dependent, incompetent, and morally depraved.…Thus, notions of deviance, disability, and normalcy were imbued into citizenship laws, practices, and cultural values. (p. 206)

Rather than dominant (individualistic, neo/liberal, and ableist) narrativizations of citizenship, Goodley and Runswick-Cole (2016) argue for relational, transformative understandings of dis/citizenship and dis/abilities that engage with the "theoretical, practical and political work that takes place either side of the binary, a binary denoted by the presence of '/'…[and] consider[s] how we value the human and what kinds of society are worth fighting for" (p. 3).

Fatima's oft-repeated question of "they can't take her away from us…right?" gives a sense of her uncertainty about who and what to trust as a Syrian newcomer with refugee experiences, as a mother/caregiver to dis/abled daughters, and as a Muslim woman in hijab during a time of ongoing xenophobia, ableism, sexism, (gendered) Islamophobia, and anti-Muslim hate (Saleh, 2021a). Alongside experiences of discrimination, similar to the findings of Cranston et al.'s (2021) research alongside Arabic-speaking and recently arrived refugee parents, Fatima's stories highlighted how language barriers continue to profoundly shape her experiences in relation to educators and service providers within and across formal schooling, medical/rehabilitational, and re/settlement organizations. Indeed, after sharing her experiences with being made to feel like an inadequate parent by Mariam's school team, Fatima shared another story of being made to feel like "an insect" by a settlement agency worker after advocating for a better wheelchair for her eldest daughter, Eman. After sharing these stories of discrimination and dis/citizenship, Fatima said in a heartbreakingly matter-of-fact manner, "You know how it is for a refugee…we are not seen as human."

Sadly, school systems have been complicit in, and sometimes explicitly contribute to, Islamophobia (Amjad, 2018). Numerous studies have illuminated how Muslim students (and their families) with refugee experiences contend with Islamophobia and other forms of discrimination and racism in formal schooling contexts—including from their teachers and other educators from within schooling contexts (Guo et al., 2019; Kovinthan Levi, 2019; Shamim, 2019). While not all of Fatima's post-migration stories centered around experiences of dis/citizenship, many of her tellings underscore Erevelles and Minear's (2010) assertion that those who are "located perilously at the intersections of race, class, gender, and disability are constituted as non-citizens and (no)bodies by the very social institutions (legal, educational, and rehabilitational) that are designed to protect, nurture, and empower them" (p. 127).

Feeling/Being Unheard and Silenced

> They don't listen to me.

Although much has been written and discussed within education research and literature in relation to any combination of the terms *diversity*, *equity*, and/or *inclusion*, my research alongside Fatima highlights the many ongoing barriers to accessibility, opportunity, and agency that continue to characterize formal schooling and education systems for dis/abled children and their families/caregivers (Moore, 2017; Yoon, 2019). In many school systems, inclusion seems to be understood as physically "including" the bodies of dis/abled children and youth in classroom and/or school spaces, while simultaneously excluding them from full citizenship in different ways, including through curriculum, pedagogy, and government funding models whereby "inclusion" is approached as "the continuation of traditional practices of the segregation and integration of students into an unchanged school system" (Gilham & Williamson, 2014, p. 559). These pervasive approaches to *inclusion* underscore how "a fantasy of inclusion is a technique of exclusion" (Ahmed, 2017, p. 112).

What does *full citizenship* entail? Particularly for those who live at the intersections of ableism and other oppressive systems (Crenshaw, 1989; Crenshaw et al., 2019), including racism, sexism, misogyny, poverty, homophobia, transphobia, xenophobia, and Islamophobia? Because, although Fatima understandably expressed that her anxieties would be significantly eased with attaining Canadian citizenship,[6] "citizenship is not just an issue of individual status; it is also a practice that locates individuals in the larger community" (Devlin & Pothier, 2006, pp. 1–2). While many educators and scholars have emphasized the concept of *belonging* in discussions of citizenship, I resonate with Bettina Love's (2019) conceptualization of *mattering*. She explained that:

> We who are dark want to matter and live, not just to survive but to thrive.... It would mean we matter enough that our citizenship, and the rights that come with it, are never questioned, reduced, or taken away regardless of

> our birthplace or the amount of melanin in our skin. Mattering, citizenship, community sovereignty, and humanity go hand in hand with the ideas of democracy, liberty, and justice for all, which are the unalienable rights needed to thrive. (Love, 2019, pp. 1–2)

Inherent in the concept and practice of mattering is being recognized, heard, and valued. When Fatima lamented that "they don't listen to me" after sharing her experiences with Mariam's school team, she was inherently signifying that not only her words, but her lived experiences and embodied knowing were not acknowledged and respected. She was signifying that she was made to feel like she did not matter. Fatima's stories of being/feeling unheard and silenced resonated with the stories of Syrian students with refugee experiences who participated in Guo et al.'s (2019) research and their assertion that "teachers and administrators need to listen more carefully to refugee children's needs" (p. 98). As Fatima's stories elucidated, this includes listening more carefully to not only (dis/abled) children (with/out refugee experiences), but their families/caregivers as well. Because, for Fatima, Mahmoud, Ali, Eman, Mariam, and Hannah, mattering in formal schooling contexts necessarily involves recognizing and respecting their embodied knowing by de-centering school-centric epistemologies and ontologies that can often be shaped by (and/or fully rooted in) ableism, (gendered) Islamophobia, classism, sexism, racism, and xenophobia.

Drawing upon Embodied Knowledge, Faith, and Loved Ones

> We were happy before the war…but the good thing is we have each other, Alhamdulillah.

As I continue to try to "walk in a good way" (Young, 2005, p. 179) and take care of Fatima's stories (Lopez, 1990), I am trying to balance re/presenting the difficult stories that we re/told alongside each other without reducing Fatima's stories to being only of challenges, or even somehow romanticizing her stories and the curriculum she co-composes. As I have stressed throughout this chapter, Fatima's stories do not solely revolve around navigating dis/citizenship, discrimination, and (re)trauma(tization). Alongside her family, she also lives a familial curriculum of faith, love, gratitude, acceptance, hope, and humour. I will never forget the love and joy I witnessed when I visited with Fatima, Mahmoud, Ali, Eman, and Mariam a few weeks after Fatima gave birth to Hannah. Memories of our laughter (and good-natured arguments about who will hold Hannah next) continue to make me smile. I will never forget the warmth I felt radiating throughout their home. However, as Sara Ahmed (2017) emphasizes,

> We all have different biographies of violence, entangled as they are with so many aspects of ourselves: things that happen because of how we are seen; and how we are not seen. You find a way of giving an account of what happens, of living with what happens. (p. 23)

I am reminded of how, after sharing some of her experiences with violent dis/placement from Syria and ongoing hardships in the process of re/settlement, Fatima mused, "We were happy before the war…but the good thing is we have each other, Alhamdulillah." As Fatima finds/creates "a way of giving an account of what happen[s/ed], of living with what happen[s/ed]" (Ahmed, 2017, p. 23), she draws on her faith, loved ones, and embodied knowing (including of better times) to sustain her.

Imagining Forward: Thinking with Fatima's Stories

Every time I present this research, someone inevitably asks me a variation of the question, "So what are the lessons from your research alongside Fatima?" This is a question that gives me great discomfort, because I am fearful of reducing Fatima's stories to a list of *best practices* that can be approached as a checklist to *prove* that an institution or organization is "inclusive," "accepting," and/or "diverse" (Ahmed, 2017). So, rather than attempting to do this, I invite you to reflect and imagine forward alongside me by thinking with Fatima's stories and our re/tellings: How might Fatima's stories have been re/told had Mariam's school team carefully listened to her rather than judged her for refusing to force Mariam to wear an assistive device she finds painful? How might her stories have been re/told if more care had been taken to make her feel like her embodied knowing—and by extension that *she*—matters? How might we re/center lived experiences and begin to live out different stories within school landscapes? How might we ensure that caregivers like Fatima never say the words, "You know how it is for a refugee…we are not seen as human," or "they don't listen to me," or "they can't take her away from us…right?"

Notes

1 All names used throughout this chapter are pseudonyms.

2 As both phenomena and methodology, narrative inquiry is a relational inquiry process whereby researchers understand that we are part of the storied research landscape (Clandinin & Connelly, 2000).

3 In narrative inquiry, the term *retelling* signifies the inquiry into stories that are lived and told (Clandinin, 2013).

4 Drawing upon Maria Lugones' (1987) conceptualization of various "worlds" we each inhabit, Huber et al. (2011) re/conceptualizes curriculum as (co-)composed within and across two worlds: school and familial curriculum-making worlds. They argue that while school landscapes are recognized as places of curriculum-making, the curriculum composed within familial contexts (including community places) is not often recognized as equally important to the co/composition of lives.
5 Field texts (Clandinin & Connelly, 2000) of this research include audio files and transcripts of research conversations, voice notes sent through text, a co-composed annal of Fatima's experiences, and my research journal.
6 Fatima is still considered a 'Permanent Resident' in Canada. To qualify for Canadian citizenship, a Canadian Language Benchmarks (CLB) Level 4 or higher in speaking and listening in English or French is required.

References

Ahmed, S. (2017). *Living a feminist life*. Duke University Press.

Amjad, A. (2018). Muslim students' experiences and perspectives on current teaching practices in Canadian schools. *Power and Education, 10*(3), 315–332.

Awuah-Mensah, L. (2016). Examining the experiences of government assisted refugee women with settlement services in Kitchener-Waterloo. *Social Justice and Community Engagement, 15*.

Cardinal, T., Saleh, M., Quiles-Fernández, E., Murphy, M. S., & Huber, J. (submitted). *Stories as good medicine: Narrative inquiry as a way of understanding experience.*

Clandinin, D. J. (2013). *Engaging in narrative inquiry*. Left Coast Press.

Clandinin, D. J., & Connelly, F. M. (2000). *Narrative inquiry: Experience and story in qualitative research*. Jossey-Bass.

Cranston, J., Labman, S., & Crook, S. (2021). Reframing parental involvement as social engagement: A study of recently arrived Arabic-speaking refugee parents' understandings of involvement in their children's education. *Canadian Journal of Education, 44*(2), 371–404.

Crenshaw, K. W. (1989). Demarginalizing the intersection of race and sex: A Black feminist critique of antidiscrimination doctrine, feminist theory and antiracist politics. *University of Chicago Legal Forum*, 139–167.

Crenshaw, K. W., Harris, L. C., HoSang, D. M., & Lipsitz, G. (2019). *Seeing race again: Countering colorblindness across the disciplines*. University of California Press.

Devlin, R., & Pothier, D. (2006). Introduction: Toward a critical theory of dis-citizenship. In R. Devlin & D. Pothier (Eds.), *Critical disability theory: Essays in philosophy, politics, policy, and law* (pp. 1–22). UBC Press.

Dossa, P. (2008). Creating alternative and demedicalized spaces: Testimonial narrative on disability, culture, and racialization. *Journal of International Women's Studies, 9*(3), 79–98.

Erevelles, N., & Minear, A. (2010). Unspeakable offenses: Untangling race and disability in discourses of intersectionality. *Journal of Literary & Cultural Disability Studies, 4*(2), 127–145.

Frederick, A., & Shifrer, D. (2019). Race and disability: From analogy to intersectionality. *Sociology of Race and Ethnicity, 5*(2), 200–214.

Goodley, D., & Runswick-Cole, K. (2016) Becoming dishuman: Thinking about the human through dis/ability. *Discourse: Studies in the Cultural Politics of Education, 37*(1), 1–15.

Gilham, C., & Williamson, W. J. (2014). Inclusion's confusion in Alberta. *International Journal of Inclusive Education, 18*(6), 553–566.

Guo, Y., Maitra, S., & Guo, S. (2019). "I belong to nowhere": Syrian refugee children's perspectives on school integration. *Journal of Contemporary Issues in Education, 14*(1), 89–105.

Huber, J., Murphy, M. S., & Clandinin, D. J. (2011). *Places of curriculum making: Narrative inquiries into children's lives in motion*. Emerald.

Kovinthan Levi, T. (2019). Preparing pre-service teachers to support children with refugee experiences. *Alberta Journal of Educational Research, 65*(4), 285–304.

Lopez, B. (1990). *Crow and weasel*. North Point Press.

Love, B. L. (2019). *We want to do more than survive: Abolitionist teaching and the pursuit of educational freedom*. Beacon Press.

Lugones, M. (1987). Playfulness, "world"-travelling, and loving perception. *Hypatia, 2*(2), 3–19.

Menakem, R. (2017). *My grandmother's hands: Racialized trauma and the pathway to mending our hearts and bodies*. Central Recovery Press.

Moore, S. (2017). *One without the other: Stories of unity through diversity and inclusion*. Portage & Main Press.

Shamim, A. (2019). *The successes and challenges of Syrian refugee families in Canada: A follow-up study* [Master's thesis]. University of Toronto.

Saleh, M. (2019). *Stories we live and grow by: (Re)telling our experiences as Muslim mothers and daughters*. Demeter Press.

Saleh, M. (2020). Honouring our grandmothers: Towards a curriculum of rahma. *Cultural and Pedagogical Inquiry (CPI), 12*(1), 8–21.

Saleh, M. (2021a). The urgency of (explicitly) teaching against Islamophobia. *Annals of Social Studies Education Research for Teachers, 2*(1), 1–7.

Saleh, M. (2021b). "We need a new story to guide us": Towards a curriculum of rahma. *Curriculum Inquiry, 51*(2), 210–228.

Saleh, M., Quiles-Fernandez, E., Cardinal, T., Murphy, S. M., & Huber, J. (forthcoming). *Wakefulness to the multiplicity of stories we live by, with, and in: Resonant threads, tensions, and wonders around relational ethics and narrative inquiry.*

Tweedie, M. G., Belanger, C., Rezazadeh, K., & Vogel, K. (2017). Trauma-informed teaching practice and refugee children: A hopeful reflection on welcoming our new neighbours to Canadian schools. *BC TEAL Journal, 2*(1), 36–45.

Yoon, I. H. (2019). Haunted trauma narratives of inclusion, race, and disability in a school community. *Educational Studies, 55*(4), 420–435.

Young, M. (2005). *Pimatisiwin: Walking in a good way – a narrative inquiry into language as identity*. Pemmican Publications.

CHAPTER 5

A Pedagogy of Relatedness

Braiding Re(story)ative Co-inquiry through Métissage

Hilary Leighton

How can we help our students find their way in the dazzling darkness of these complex and difficult times that we struggle to understand ourselves? Cartesian-Newtonian perspective-based assumptions persist in dominating, separating, and colonizing curriculum to inform a modern worldview that fosters "the myopia of our independently trained minds" (Meyer, 2013, p. 98) while festering a mistrust in the importance of lived experience. This particular approach is insufficient for preparing students for the trouble we're in. Bolstered by (an often tacit) commitment to standardized uniformity and assimilation, mainstream systems of education still privilege rational linearity and empirical verifiability. This drives an unhealthy reliance on techno-scientific solutions to solve what may in fact need (dis)solving.

Speaking back to the systemic marginalisation of humanness in education, *pedagogies of relatedness* refuse to segregate or diminish the ways of knowing that the inside-subjective-cerebral, the outside-objective-physical, *and* the transpatial-ethereal-spiritual convey. In other words, we must design more inclusive, experiential learning that intersects *body, mind, and spirit* (Meyer, 2013). This aligns with many Indigenous worldviews with their primacy of "relationality, dynamic coherence, interdependence and mutual casuality" (Meyer, 2013, p. 98) and best informs the design of a more symbiotic syllabus responsive to the web of life.

Disrupting classical knowledge systems that divide us from each other, from our own bodies, and from the living world is to actively engage in a more "holographic epistemology" that values "knowledge that comes from direct experience, a knowing that has been encountered, registered and remembered in bone and muscle" (Meyer, 2013, p. 96). A curriculum that recognizes the indissoluble unity between humans and nature has its roots in general systems theory, quantum mechanics, and "native common sense" (Meyer, 2013). Further, it recognizes all parts of the living world as co-constitutive and contingent on each other for inseparable wholeness and health (Capra, 1996).

New epistemes of interdependency, collaboration, and attunement that serve the enlargement of *both-and-all* rather than *either-or* thinking (Neumann,

© KONINKLIJKE BRILL NV, LEIDEN, 2022 | DOI:10.1163/9789004521186_005

1969) provide a third way stance that is "neither this or that, but this *and* that" (Pinar, 2004, p. 9). Practices that embrace tensionality allow complex interactions and rich interplay of thought and feeling and create the energetic conditions for a new, integrative ethic toward broader, conscious awareness (Neumann, 1969). In this way, métissage can teach us that when we authentically share, listen, relate, and open to new *and* old tensions, let our words and worlds collide, mix, and blend together, we are profoundly (re)membering ourselves as part of something larger and inseparable.

The following chapter provides powerful, yet elegantly simple examples of what happened when environmental students wove threads of their individual identities, relationships, memories, and beliefs into new combinatorial storylines to disclose more complete but complex views of life, chaos, birth, death, grief, and intense beauty using métissage. Regenerative learning spaces that simultaneously invite and hold the contrariness of solitary experiences and our relatedness to the collective, "wake us up from too long a dormancy" (Leighton, 2014, p. 313) in education. They can serve to remind us that no matter our ancestries, roots, responsibilities or affiliations, we belong together, and we need each other if we are to adequately meet the world and find our way. Each exemplar is provided with full and informed consent.

The Art of the Braid

Métissage, an Indigenous-inspired approach from the French Métis meaning "to mix" (Lowan-Trudeau, 2015), can act as an emancipatory form of counter-narrative. Adapted from literary and cultural studies (Lionnet, 1989), it is used as a method for research and life-writing that invites meaning-making through the powerful blending of polyphonic perspectives to reveal a new, concomitant, living story. Breaking with conventional storytelling, a poesis such as this that joins together seemingly disparate stories to create a dynamic story-mix (Hasebe-Ludt, Chambers, & Leggo, 2009), can weave new and significant patterns of thought and provide leeway for imagining what could not have been possible through just the telling of one story alone.

The following raw, honest, and vulnerable interactions were gathered at an Environmental Education and Communication Network (EECOM) conference in 2018 held at a former residential-school-turned-hotel-casino-campground-golf course called the St. Eugene Resort located within the traditional territory of the Ktunaxa Nation by the St Mary's River in the East Kootenays. Shared ownership of the commercial enterprise consists of four Ktunaxa communities all dedicated to making something beautiful and regenerative out of the shadows of a horrific and difficult past to ensure a positive future for their people. The setting could not have been more evocative.

To enact métissage is to make it pedagogical and performative. Workshop participants were invited to collaborate through an organic praxis of braiding one discrete line at a time of their individual stories until all lines and all stories were blended and then spoken aloud. A collective inquiry that provides such a spontaneous, generative arts-informed space asks that we "suspend currently held thought-patterns particularly around knowledge, science and reality" (Meyer, 2013, p. 98). It can illuminate systemic issues of identity and relatedness, and division and loss, where peoples and places, humans and more-than-humans, darkness and light, the known and the strange, find deep confluence and surprising semiotic connections within the weave.

In (what one hopes is) the aftermath of Western colonialism, these extraordinary times beg for (re)connection through relationship toward increased consciousness of self and world. Mobilizing radical collaboration through intertwining autobiographical stories can be an effective way to disrupt and evict tired, habitual narratives, ventilate and shift our thinking, and dissolve dualisms to help us find footing on more common ground. However, to have a substantive experience of métissage within the short limitations of a conference workshop, the students were encouraged to embrace an ethos of cooperation and trust in one another as this heuristic process of making something they would not understand until they did it, held no promise of turning out well. The added pressure of performance adrenalized groups into action.

Following a writing prompt I provided, the students each wrote a 5-minute piece. Next, in small groups, they listened carefully to each other's words to identify natural breaks and resonant, bright threads to pull and weave together into something far greater and more complex than any one particular story could ever have been. Groups soon found their own techniques to arrangement, crafting crude scripts to help organize themselves. With barely enough time to rehearse, each group performed. It never failed. Participants appeared deeply moved and changed by each other's words when mixed with their own—right up to and including the moment they spoke their new story into the world.

Where I Am From

Already sensitized by the stories they had been hearing about lived residential school experiences from the Ktunaxa Knowledge Keepers at the conference, I asked participants to write from the prompt, *Where I am from*. I was purposeful in my instruction to avoid asking about *the lands* they were from or the *places* they were from, which allowed a wider array of imaginative thought. Each voice is represented here by a different colour.

Stardust made us all.
Chaos
We're so different, yet the same
A rhizomatic mapping,
a weaving of my dreams with yours

Every atom, every drop of water,
every multi-cellular animal
Unknown
There is more that binds us together than separates us
If we are under the same sky, sun and moon,
is it okay that our stories be different?

The mitochondria that cleave energy,
the chloroplast that eats sunlight
are small aberrations in genetic codes
that made our life, *this* life possible
Scary
We all feel the same,
breathe the same,
dream the same.
Afterall, that is already the grand narrative…
your story makes mine

Beautiful

As evidenced in the piece below, each participant's writing could have just as easily stood alone in every case:

Stardust made us all.
Every atom, every drop of water,
every multi-cellular animal
The mitochondria that cleave energy,
the chloroplast that eats sunlight
are small aberrations in genetic codes
that made our life, *this* life possible.
Beautiful

Chaos
Unknown
Scary

We're so different, yet the same
There is more that binds us together than separates us
We all feel the same,
breathe the same,
dream the same.

A rhizomatic mapping,
a weaving of my dreams with yours
If we are under the same sky, sun and moon,
is it okay that our stories be different?
Afterall, that is already the grand narrative…
your story makes mine.

However, when combined, a far more powerful *grand narrative* emerged that held dynamic tensions spanning the infinite cosmos to the smallest mitochondria, telling a larger, more vibrant, universal story of where *we* are *all* from. In this transcendent space, students leave one world and enter another, more possible world where "knowing, doing and making merge" (Pinar, 2004, p. 9) through braiding text. There is no need to compete with each other or for one *better* story to prevail; rather, a panoramic experience stretches words across worlds and speaks to a more vast, all-encompassing view.

In the next piece, student found links between family trees and forest trees through visible and invisible root systems above and below ground.

I like to acknowledge that I am from the trees
and trees have an underworld
My roots go back to an ancient time
England, Scotland and an island called Skye

This is paradise
A place of simplicity, of beauty raw and real
Waterfall streams, ocean dreams
My roots stretch far and wide and ground me

Trees are so tall
their roots allow for this
The land is my home

Family is everything
where wildness still thrives
A dark, cool supportive place
we rarely get to see

Re(story)ation

Laurel Richardson and Elizabeth St. Pierre (2005) argue that personal stories are always "situational," "partial," and "local" (p. 962), a fraction of reality. However, if we are willing to consider most basic human truths are accessible through subjectivity (van Manen, 1990) and that knowledge is both relational *and* contextual (Kimmerer 2013; Meyer, 2013; Yunkaporta, 2020), then as stories deeply intertwine and each artful line weaves in and through the other, all contributors equally enlarge its emergent meaning-making possibilities. The act itself binds us, lifts our spirits, and brings happy surprise at the discoveries made at the nexus of co-inquiry, co-creation, and co-expression.

But writing or talking about why we need new stories is not going to deeply change the world. We can admit that just knowing the story that natural science is telling us right now about the urgency of the ecological crisis, for instance, has not been motivation enough for us to make wholesale change (Noble et al., 2021).

After his decision to migrate to the country, author and self-proclaimed recovering environmentalist, Paul Kingsnorth (2017) offers, "Deep change is going to come…[only] through a radical alteration in people's lived experiences" (p. 39). If our teaching practices can foster a willing embrace of nature as a natural *relative* rather than natural *resource*, we can begin to live into that reciprocity between ourselves and all living beings tied to our very survival. With this knowledge, cracks appear in the siloes of current existence, creating openings for a new story to emerge out of the rubble of our old lives for the sake of the whole.

To "tug on one leaf is connected to everything in the world" (Kingsnorth, 2017, p. 43) is not news and is even an older story than what Francis Thompson (2012) cautioned over one hundred years earlier in 1917:

> All things by immortal power,
> Near or far,
> Hiddenly
> To each other linked are,
> Thou canst not stir a flower
> Without the troubling of a star
> (p. 384)

Today's systems science (Holling & Gunderson, 2002; Lazlo, 1996) is the same ancient poetry of the cosmos that land-based peoples have always known (Meyer, 2013; Yunkaporta, 2020). In environmental education, we tell the web of life story (Capra, 1996) to try to make the invisible network of connections more visible for students, connecting how we live to where our destiny lies. These teaching stories turn out to be really old ones, just in new form (Kingsnorth, 2017; Meyer, 2013; Shaw, 2011; Yunkaporta, 2020). Indigenous educator Veronica Arbon acknowledges, "There is a critical need for a *new old way* [emphasis added] now" (in Meyer, 2013, p. 98). To bring the wisdom of ancient ontologies with their treatment of knowledge as a living presence to new experimental spaces of spontaneous and simultaneous learning, "facilitates the flow of living knowledge" (Yunkaporta, 2020, p. 86). The new-old-now.

Mythologist Martin Shaw (2011) believes the stories we need now turned up right on time thousands of years ago and may not even come *from* us but *through* us like an echolocation from a sentient, dreaming Earth. Through expressions of poetry, music, dance and art, Andalusian poet and playwright, Frederico Garcia Lorca understood these moments to be sacred transmissions filled with mythic substance, known as *duende* (Buhner, 2010). Primal material of life and death rising up from the dark earth through the soles of our feet, pulling us toward what is most wild and alive, provide a kind of elation found in a deep but fleeting sense of connectivity, a rootedness with everything at once (Weller, 2011).

Forest child, daughter of a gardener and welder
The place I am from is Canada
I am from the Prairies

The place I am from has five giant willow trees in the yard
I was like a leaf blowing on the wind to where the breeze took me
I am from the moss and needled soil from behind my fenced yard

Taking mental notes on the new events in the pond
A river that carves its way through the landscape
creating a valley which is rich in land and love
Feeling thankful for this movement

I am from the shores of the silent thinking
of the blue and greens of the West coast timber
This is the spot
The place I am from has maple trees that turn red
in September and October

and light up the world to remember
It's okay to fall
...I am falling toward

The smell of fall leaves and spring pansies
Daughter of seasons
The sweetness in the spring will come

Borders and boundaries no longer separate this world from that, as these wild students are leaf, wind, soil, silence, turning, falling, and becoming. Unique yet in unison, they let the world sing through them, rising up as tree intelligence, moss embrace, and flowering sweetness carried through memory, skin, and bone. Line-by-line, each group set to work braiding up their stories, embroidering tattered threads of thought through resonance and repetition to tell of how they had always belonged to the living earth. And an intimacy was born between strangers through intertextual relations and wild affiliations in just mere minutes. As we witness each other in our full humanness, we begin to see ourselves in the *I-thou* of each other (Buber, 1970), and we can no longer stay distant (even from those whose motivations may run counter to our own). In this way, relatedness runs through both the warp and the weft of métissage, (in)forming implications for peace- and capacity-building too.

Are we always (re)telling a more eternal, never-ending story when we share what it is to experience this human life? One might say there is a sacredness, a feeling of the holy and the eternal, something older and greater than the dark night we find ourselves in that arises in such "a regenerative upwelling" (Shaw, 2011, p. XIV) once our stories are let loose in the world. It is noteworthy that word *holy* shares its etymological roots with whole, health, and heal.

Somehow, a combinatorial approach always feels slightly hopeful, more truthful to me in terms of knowing the world than individual stories can convey. Life writing allows the writer "to know 'something' without claiming to know everything" (Richardson & St. Pierre, 2005, p. 961) so then when an imaginative blending of storylines occurs, each crystallizes into a more complex, multi-faceted aggregate of the phenomenon without diluting the unique strands each person brings.

Dynamic Coherence

In performance, students spontaneously stepped up or leaned in as they spoke their lines, bringing past-tense lived experience into (a)live experience. In a (dis)play that broke the spell of individualistic tendencies (or the worst kind of performing), the students riffed off each other's intonations and body-cues, presenting a fluid, nuanced, grace-filled *movement*—a dance between words and worlds.

Where am I from? Where are any of us from?
In a dark room, we are all the same, same colour, mostly sharing the same parts
The place I am from is not where my parents are from
and it's not where my children will say they are from
Aren't we all from the same place? The uterus?
I am at the confluence of the Bow and Elbow rivers,
a place known by the Blackfoot as Moh-kíns-tsis
a place where the people meet

A discovery of space which I transformed into my place
using names of my own curiosity
We all originated in the centre of our mothers, made of blood and breath and bone
and journeyed...
To the confluence of the Svislač and the Niamiha Rivers:
a place known since the 1300s as Minsk
via the feet of our carriers

I am from a place of mysteries, half told stories and forgotten dreams
I hold that everywhere I go
Where our mothers feet land in the moment that we surface for air,
is that where we are from?

In what could only be called a *hermetic* moment, human mothers and Earth Mothers meet at the shape-leaping confluence of bone and blood, uteruses and rivers, darkness and dreams in a wildly coherent new narrative. Redolent of the mythic maxim, *as above, so below* with its nod to the messenger god Hermes and his tricky work in the in-between of this world and the underworld (Hauck, 1999), something had definitely been delivered "up" and everyone "got it." Perhaps the ground may have even slightly shifted underfoot as we sat in a moment of silence to take it all in. Of course, we come from human parents as well as the humus of earth! I wondered, *does the power of stories work by osmosis? How are we changed by what we weave and hear? What if what is revealed is what needs to be born? Can this method help us more bravely face some of our dark difficulty together?*

Molecular research in neuroscience has shown that narrative structures can have a profound impact on the human brain and body (Levinson, 2018).

Recent studies have further demonstrated a causal effect of change on prosocial behaviours too (Zak, 2015). The release of the brain chemical oxytocin—a small peptide synthesized in the hypothalamus of the brain (the same chemical associated with milk letdown in new mothers and the high associated with experiencing the chanting of monks) reproduces a correlation of increased empathy to "suggest that emotionally engaging narratives inspire post-narrative actions" (Zak, 2015, n.p.). It would follow then, that stories have some (al)chemical potential to change *and* recharge us. When spoken aloud, these litanies felt shimmering and alive, transformative in an earthy and prayerful way. Duende.

(Re)pairing

However, if we persist in educating to separate the ideas inside of us from the ideas outside of us, then we will continue experiencing the world as "distinctly dysfunction and determinedly disenchanted" (Blackie, 2018, p. 111). Pedagogies designed to welcome and acknowledge a full gamut of thought and feeling help release trapped and held emotional and psychic energy and, in turn, sustain our vitality and imaginative capacity necessary to address future work (Macy & Brown, 1998). It is also a sign of profound care to keep ourselves clean in this way; to perform a kind of *soul hygiene* (Weller, 2011).

Next, the students completed one of three open sentences adapted from the ecologically conscious practices found within The Work That Reconnects (TWTR):

> What I find most difficult about being alive at this time is…What I find most beautiful about being alive at this time is…and, the ways I might contribute to the healing of the world are… (Macy & Brown, 2014, pp. 99–100)

I divided them into groups of three, each having written from a different open sentence in order to experiment with the arrangement of beauty, fear, and possibility within one weave.

Disconnection caused by misunderstanding
I am astonished by how often I am close to tears
Sometimes tears of sadness
But most often, tears of a powerful nature
feelings of transformation
I will teach the ones that come after me

to be themselves because that is enough
Alienation stemming from selfish goals
I see beauty in the hope and simplicity and love
in my children's faces
I will be a listening ear

Misled, misinformed, good intentions
I am astonished by how stagnant society
is in a time of possibility
I will celebrate the minor victories
and not just the destinations
I am astonished by the connections that exist,
evolve and commune

I will put myself in other peoples' shoes
I see beauty everywhere around me
I will smile, smile at everyone

A generally-held societal view is that which is difficult is not worth much attention, but can we instead imagine our troubles as simply having different, generative and even transformative potential? Often in story-mixing lived experiences, what is difficult breaks open against hope or love as lines juxtapose in a (re)pairing, a (re)formed adjunct newness.

Feelings…
I find most difficult
I find most beautiful

I talk about…
Societal norms
Diversity and beautiful people

I have a lot of…
waste abiotics
powerful narratives

I must…
Change, can we change?
Look, listen, say yes

Feel my way back
to living Earth

Writing about the Japanese art of repairing broken pottery with gold, Tiffany Ayuda (2018) suggests that kintsukuroi or kintsugi is:

> built on the idea that in embracing flaws and imperfections, you can create an even stronger, more beautiful piece of art. Every break is unique and instead of repairing an item like new, the 400-year-old technique actually highlights the "scars" as a part of the design. (n.p.)

In much of Western culture, we just are not taught that wholeness and brokenness "are contingent on each other, and co-constitutive" (Akomolafe, 2017, p. 17), more like intimates than opposites in anything other than a linear reality because, in fact, the one rises out of the other. Think of the mosaic. It begins with what is fractured to make something of beauty as it upholds intentional breaks to find "perfection in imperfection" (Tempest Williams, 2009, 5:38) and celebrates a new narrative.

Appreciating what is imperfect as exquisite, is captured in the both-and-all spirit of the 15th century traditional Japanese aesthetic of Wabi-Sabi where an object's beauty and brokenness are worthy of celebration. Just as our difficult feelings, anxieties, angst, pain, and despair are as much part of our humanness as our love, joy, exuberance, and levity, to press them together through stories initiates us toward "a wider heart for the village" (Shaw, 2011, p. 57); it holds implications for healthy psychological shifts where positive integration brings greater potential for maturation and wholeness (Jung, 1953/1968). "Using [kintsugi] as a metaphor for healing ourselves teaches us an important lesson: …in the process of repairing things that have broken, we actually create something more unique, beautiful and resilient" (Ayuda, 2018, n.p.).

Interstices

Métissage does not rely on just *what* is written. The interstices between perspectives allows stories the chance to openly converse *with each other* where new patterns (e)merge, meaning bends and reshapes itself into a kind of evolving communal intelligence, made stronger by all who participate. In this regard, it is method, practice, process, and system all at once!

Psychologist-educator, Bayo Akomolafe (2017) offers that something more complex happens when we allow ourselves to break open as this entrusts us with a "richer world where cynicism, despair, and failure are not orphaned apparitions of an immaculate world…but part of how the world substantiates itself" (pp. 16–17). In this way, we might consider those more dissonant and jagged-edged lines not as an ugliness in the story-mix, but as a vital interruption of the conversant asking us to turn toward what is a hidden, truth-in-waiting.

Akomolafe (2017) reminds us that what happens in the spaces in-between things on their way to becoming, "is the world on its ongoing practices of worlding itself" (p. 12). Educational theorist, Ted Aoki (1993) knew that, if we let it, the unpredictable, in-betweennesses of things can do its quiet third-way work of transformation and meaning-making within our curriculum. Back-loops of not knowing can be darkly generative, "just as embodied, resilient, voluptuous as proud light" (Akolomafe, 2017, p. 12) if we are willing to stay open, experiment, and have faith in how natural and human systems work (Holling & Gunderson, 2002). Before coming to any semblance of wholeness, breaking down is necessary if each story fragment is to be (re)assembled like puzzle pieces to fit into a larger picture of world (Tempest Williams, 2009), and métissage *is* the golden joinery.

Mutual Causality

I talk about feelings a lot
living experiences and reflecting
approaching all situations with love and care

I will support and encourage the awakening of others
I become bombarded with the issues of the world
I will hold your hand through it
with love and compassion

I have a lot of feelings
share knowledge, have conversations and reflect
I may not be the changing force
but we are
Is anyone else feeling this?

Indigenous scholar Tyson Yunkaporta (2020) offers that connectedness can create a much-needed healthy balance for individualism through diversity and such interactions promote change with their power to energize knowledge, rekindle its living presence. The interchange at the crisscross of lived experiences evokes a form of adaptation where generative, emergent properties occur naturally. If we allow ourselves to be transformed by these interactions and the knowledge we gain, then we begin to act more like a planet—the self-organizing, symbiotic system we are a part of.

In a most cooperative move from I/me to We/us, these students saw the world anew through their enchanted kaleidoscopic lens of pluralism. Shifts in *thinking-with* rather merely *thinking-about* our shared ecological context invites the ancient evocation of *participating consciousness* (Berman, 1984), where one's personal sense of agency *and* a collective responsibility are tethered in an ethical (even evolutionary?) obligation to act more wisely in service of a greater good.

When we see the world as kin (Kimmerer, 2013), "what appeared to be 'other' can be equally construed as a concomitant of 'self,' like a fellow-cell in the neural patterns of a larger body" (Macy & Brown, 2014, p. 41). When old adages of otherness finally rupture and a space is opened for healing, stories we can tell, teach, enact, embody, and energize hold profound implications for justice, equality, diversity, inclusion, and love; they are powerful and timely medicines. Through this relational process, I understand that big, beautiful stories will always get their paws on us, carry us out beyond the confines of our comfortable lives to (dis)orient, put their untamed claims upon us, cover us in dark feathers, make us fall in love with them, restor(e) our faith in the world, and *move us* to change.

With galaxies in their eyes, students were luminous as stars, supercharged by their shared experience, lit from within. Each group seemed to transcend the knowledge they arrived with as expanded understandings became re(story)ative narratives. In this holographic space, meant to "bring both the feasting hall of life's abundance and the desolate tundra of challenge and despair" (Shaw, 2011, p. xv) into relationship, these students were free to blossom while dropping their petals at the same time—living into the wild-possible, folding and unfolding, métissage-collage of the new-old, both-and-all.

Witnessing the state of disconnection between humans
With loving compassion
Sharing experiences and creating connections with people
no matter where they are

The disconnection between humans and the world
How can I live?
Approaching all situations with loving care
I feel the death of the world in my bones

Being alive! (unison)

Loving the world,
sharing love,
spreading love

Being alive! (unison)

Acknowledgement

Kind thanks to Métis Elder, Bill Bresser, of the Heron People's Circle, Royal Roads University who guided the use of métissage for this research.

References

Akomolafe, B. (2017). *These wilds beyond our fences. Letters to my daughter on humanity's search for home*. North Atlantic Books.

Aoki, T. (2005). Legitimating lived curriculum: Toward a curricular landscape of multiplicity. In W. Pinar & R. Irwin (Eds.), *Curriculum in a new key: The collected works of Ted T. Aoki* (pp. 199–215). Lawrence Erlbaum.

Ayuda, T. (2018). *How the Japanese art of Kintsugi can help you deal with stressful situations*. NBC News. https://www.nbcnews.com/better/health/how-japanese-art-technique-kintsugi-can-help-you-be-more-ncna866471

Berman, M. (1981). *The reenchantment of the world*. Cornell University Press.

Blackie, S. (2018). *The enchanted life. Unlocking the magic of the everyday*. Ambrosia.

Buber, M. (1970). *I and thou* (W. Kaufmann, Trans.). Scribner & Sons.

Buhner, S. H. (2010). *Ensouling language. On the art of nonfiction and the writer's life*. Inner Traditions.

Capra, F. (1996). *The web of life*. Anchor Books.

Hasebe-Ludt, E., Chambers, C., & Leggo, C. (2009). *Life writing and literary métissage as an ethos for our times*. Peter Lang.

Hauck, D. W. (1999). *The emerald tablet: Alchemy for personal transformation*. Penguin.

Holling, C. S., & Gunderson, L. (2002). *Panarchy: Understanding transformations in human and natural systems*. Island Press.

Jung, C. J. (1953/1968). *Jung, psychology and alchemy. Collected works of C.G. Jung* (Vol. 12, R. F. C. Hull, Trans.; Bollingen Series XX). Princeton University Press.

Kimmerer, R. W. (2013). *Braiding sweetgrass. Indigenous wisdom, scientific knowledge and the teachings of plants*. Milkweed.

Kingsnorth, P. (2017, January/February). The axis and the sycamore. *Orion*, 34–45.

Lazlo, E. (1996). *A systems view of the world: A holistic vision for our time.* Hampton Press.

Leighton, H. (2014). *Wild (re)turns: Tracking the epistemological and ecological implications of learning as an initiatory journey toward true vocation and soul* [Doctoral dissertation]. University of Victoria, BC.

Levinson, E. J. (2018). Conservation through creative writing. *Green Teacher*, Fall.

Lionnet, F. (1989). *Autobiographical voices: Race, gender and self-portraiture.* Cornell University.

Lowan-Trudeau, G. (2015). *From bricolage to métissage: (Re)thinking intercultural approaches to Indigenous environmental education and research.* Peter Lang.

Macy, J., & Brown, M. Y. (2014). *Coming back to life. Practices to reconnect our lives, our world.* New Society.

Meyer, M. A. (2013). Holographic epistemology: Native common sense. *China Media Research, 9*(2), 94–101.

Neumann, E. (1969). *Depth psychology and a new ethic.* Harper & Row.

Noble, M.-A., Leighton, H., & Dale, A. (2021). Stepping toward a sense of place: A choreography between natural and social science. In W. Leal Filho, A. Lange Salvia, & F. Frankenberger (Eds.), *The handbook on teaching and learning for sustainable development* (pp. 406–417). Edward Elgar.

Pinar, W. (2004). Foreword. In R. Irwin & A. de Cosson (Eds.), *A/r/tography. Rendering self through arts-based living inquiry.* (pp. 9–25). Pacific Educational Press.

Richardson, L., & St. Pierre, E. (2005). Writing. A method of inquiry. In N. Denzin & Y. Lincoln (Eds.), *Handbook of qualitative research* (2nd ed., pp. 959–978). Sage.

Shaw, M. (2011). *A branch from the lightening tree. Ecstatic myth and grace in wildness.* White Cloud Press.

Tempest Williams, T. (2009). *Finding beauty in a broken world* [Audio file]. Sounds True.

Thompson, F. (2012). The mistress of vision. In D. H. S. Nicholson & A. H. E. Lee (Eds.), *The Oxford book of English mystical verse.* Apocryphile Press. (Original work published 1917)

van Manen, M. (1990). *Researching lived experience. Human science for an action sensitive pedagogy.* SUNY.

Weller, F. (2011). *Entering the healing ground: Grief, ritual and the soul of the world.* Wisdom Bridge Press.

Yunkaporta, T. (2020). *Sand talk. How Indigenous thinking can save the world.* Harper One.

Zak, P. J. (2015). Why inspiring stories make us react: The neuroscience of narrative. *Cerebrum: The Dana Forum on Brain Science, 2015*, 2. https://www.ncbi.nlm.nih.gov/pmc/articles/PMC4445577

CHAPTER 6

Currere as a Wayfinding Process of Writing the Learning Self

Lucrécia Raquel Fuhrmann

Learning is a wayfinding process and, as such, it is challenging. When we add a new language to this process, it is necessary to develop a new way to address questions like *who am I?* and *how do I make meaning from my learning experiences in a new environment?* Guimarães Rosa, *um autor brasileiro*, wrote *Grande Sertão: Veredas* in which he plays with words and meanings, two important things in my learning journey. In that book, he said "*o correr da vida embrulha tudo, a vida é assim: esquenta e esfria, aperta e daí afrouxa, sossega e depois desinquieta. O que ela quer da gente é coragem*"[1] (Rosa, 2016, p. 290). I am living what he expressed in those words since I moved from *Brasil* to Canada almost three years ago to study.

To make sense of this experience, I draw on *currere* writings and insights from writing weekly blog postings, which were valuable opportunities to reflect on my trajectory as a researcher in the new milieu; both were proposed activities in a course in my PhD course schedule. The first one challenged me to participate in Pinar's *currere* process and to read *Solid Broken Changing*, a recent novel for young people by Ellsworth (2019), which is attuned to Pinar's ideas. During the writing process, I studied Pinar's *currere* method, and there were moments in which those reflections were shared with classmates who helped me to better understand the process. I also collaborated with peers to create a reflective atmosphere, an important step in shaping those writings (Beierling et al., 2014).

Weekly blog posting was a writing process that challenged me to post on the course's blog a picture a week, for 10 weeks, and to write about it. The objects or situations that I pictured could be ordinary frames, not necessarily related to learning, but the way I had looked at them should be different. From this process of *currere* and blog writings, I noticed that words and their sounds are important aspects in my curricular understanding; this helped me to discover my voice in a new environment, a process I call wayfinding, based on Ellsworth's idea (2019). What emerged from this process was an understanding of individuals' learning processes as important components in re/centering human being in education (Lyle, 2021).

© KONINKLIJKE BRILL NV, LEIDEN, 2022 | DOI:10.1163/9789004521186_006

The *Currere* Process

Currere, the lived experience of *currículo*, is a way to make sense of our *autobiografia* in terms of our formal studies' perspective (Pinar, 1975). I used it as a way to explain my connections to English language learning and to understand the struggle to have voice during this process. In the practice of writing from the perspective of *currere*, I went through the four phases of that method. In the regressive, I chose an episode from my first year at the elementary school in *Brasil*. For the progressive phase, the depicted event was related to the defense of my comprehensive exams. In the third phase, I described a moment I lived in a Canadian school where I was filling in for someone else. For the analytical phase, I analyzed the previous three papers in order to investigate some specific aspects of *currículo* as I lived them (Pinar, 1975). I was also able to find connections between Ellsworth's (2019) book, the blog postings, and my *currere* writings.

In this new experience, *saudade* is a feeling that is embedded in my readings, writings, and sensations in the new country, and the connections I am able to make with *Brasil* and the experiences I lived there. I have been learning that identity is something that is also built on *saudade,* a word that does not have translation in English. That word expresses the complex feeling of missing someone or something, mixed with sadness and melancholy, and sometimes sweetness and tenderness. It is something that really hurts. *Saudade* is also an important component in my wayfinding journey.

When analyzing my writings from *currere*'s perspective, I could see someone who was built through lifelong learning and who is not done learning *porque é interessante como sempre tem alguma coisa que eu não sei. Isso nunca termina.*[2] I have been forged throughout my practice, and I think I have never paused to think of that kind of *currículo* as the writings provoked me to do. I also discovered what it means to live with/in a wayfinding process, struggling to bridge the gap between voiced and unvoiced moments, those moments related to being able to express my ideas and those when I was silenced by the fear of exposing myself. At this point in my writing and studies, I was living in Canada for a year and a half. I learned the *idioma* back home and that was the first time I used it to communicate with people who did not understand *português brasileiro.* As my laptop asks me to add *as palavras brasileiras* in this text to its dictionary to be part of a new repertoire, I was adding new experiences to my *currículo.*

While finding my footing in this new land, I had been teaching for more than 20 years in *Brasil;* however, *toda a experiência acumulada em mais de 25 anos de profissão, em várias turmas, escolas e níveis de educação diferentes, não contavam, porque além de meu irmão e família e uma outra família brasileira de amigos, ninguém sabia quem eu era,*[3] as I wrote about it (Fuhrmann, 2020). It is similar to what Onită expresses in her poem *dragă anita* (Lafferty & Onită, 2021) when she also felt powerless and voiceless in an academic context. I am a language teacher, one whose whole life to this point had been built in *português brasileiro*. My way of thinking and writing was—and still is—molded by my *língua materna*. Coming to a new country made me feel *inexperiente*, then being pushed to compare myself to others, which is also attuned to as Onită's feelings in the academic world (Lafferty & Onită, 2021).

On the other hand, in my regressive writing, I realized that the struggle for finding voice is also present within the writing that shows a little girl who could not talk in *português brasileiro* to her teacher in a literacy class in *Brasil*. The feelings associated with that writing were shame and embarrassment, as I was unable to go to her and ask for help, a familiar feeling in my present condition. As the next step in my synthetical writing, I looked more closely at Canadian experiences, first as someone who was unable to talk to a student's parent and, then in my progressive writing, as someone who wants to impress her thesis committee. This helped me to understand that my struggle to find voice occurred in both my native language and in English, and it is interesting how I am learning these things from my wayfinding process as an English speaker.

All of the moments depicted in my *currere* are related to language in its words and sounds; however, I call them *unvoiced moments* because although I was surrounded by words, I was unable to speak. When I look back upon the weekly blog and *currere* writings, I see how words exercise influence on me; I am interested in them—in their sounds and meanings. I am surrounded by sounds, and they really matter to me. They affect my position in the world, and they are parts of my inner voice and the ongoing struggle to have voice.

The Struggle to Find a Voice: Sounds and Language in the Learning Self

When analyzing the *currere* process, the first writing shows someone who is attuned to her inner voice, but it also shows someone who cannot voice her thoughts to others. The writings show I am both a voiced and a voiceless person; there is a gap here that might be filled during the wayfinding process I am in. This process encompasses both the daily life and the academic journey, so I am in a position in which having voice means to survive not only in the country, but also in the academic context. In this situation, being able to express my ideas and stand up for them is crucial. This is connected to my personal agency (Anya, 2017). The writings demonstrate how I try to think of my present and connect it to my past and future lived experiences of *currere* in a way that shows *currículo* is not linear. It allows me to understand my lived experience as my *currere*, which means to realize my struggle to find voice is something that really speaks volumes to my wayfinding journey throughout my life.

Kally, the main character of *Solid Broken Changed* (Ellsworth, 2019), has a similar experience when her world is turned upside down after an experience she had with her father. They were sailing when a wave caused an accident with Home, their boat; then they were rescued by a family who was vacationing on a nearby island. Until that point, everything seemed nice and smooth in Kally's life; the wreckage caused not only the boat destruction, but upended her life, as she was imprisoned on that island. There, she met Stuart, a member of the rescuing family, and they started a relationship that helped them to survive in the new milieu. As the plot develops, the reader starts to understand what is happening is not just local but also a major environmental change. In that changing world, Kally is a wayfinder as she works to understand what does not make sense (Ellsworth, 2019). She is experiencing what the Spanish poet Machado (2003) says *Caminante, no hay camino, se hace camino al andar.*[4] I am in a similar situation. I am both Kally and the *caminante*; I am making *meu caminho* by walking and trying to make sense of what is happening while it is happening, and *currere* helps me to look back to the past and to connect it to my present and future, giving me a sense of wholeness.

This meaning-making process is a nonlinear way of thinking of the *currere* of my life. This is similar to the writing process of a novel, which has flashbacks and glimpses of the future to help the reader better contextualize the character's point of view. I am both the reader and the character of my wayfinding story. I am moving *autobiograficamente*, not only linearly, in a multidimensional way (Pinar, 1975) to find my new way.

In my wayfinding process of finding voice, it is crucial to be attuned to survive in the new world. Attunement, based on Pinar's studies of Grant's ideas, is to bridge the gap between our world and what is outside it; however, attunement cannot be used as a tool as it is not an instrument (Pinar, 2019). Like revelation, attunement cannot be possessed or invoked; it is necessary to wait, to be open, and to listen to what lies beyond what we can perceive. "Attunement is listening, feeling, thinking, sometimes separated, sometimes fused attentiveness to what is revealed to—and what is withheld from—us" (Pinar, 2019, p. 289). Attunement is as multimodal as language is; when I perceived myself attuned to sounds, words, utterances, as showed in the excerpt from my *currere*, I engaged in a part of analytical currere:

> *That class was planned for me. They have learned the sounds for 'oa' as in 'boat'; 'ai' as in 'pain'; 'ie' as in 'tie,' 'lie,' 'died.' Another thought came to my mind: when I heard lie, died, it reminded me there is a song by* REM *where they repeat*

try, cry, why, try…It happens a lot when I hear some words, or even phrases and sentences. It makes me think "oh, those words really exist in real life."

My inner voice appears in my writings; this is the thread that connects the dots and helps me to mend the gap (Pinar, 2019) I have been experiencing. I am tentative about making meaning or sense in a holistic way, trying to apprehend the wholeness, and to be attentive to my inner source (Pinar, 2019), which is my inner voice—myself and *meu eu*—as compounded by my mind, my mood, and my knowledge so far. That is the point between fighting to find the right words and feeling voiceless or speechless, and the voiced moments; attunement to it is another way of working in this frustrating gap.

From this perspective, I have come to find there are a variety of *estímulos* in this new environment, which drive me to look at everything as if it were brand new. It also appears in my synthetical writing, as I am in a literacy classroom in Canada, learning the language with the students, as the excerpt also shows. A word, a sound, almost anything can trigger a thought, an image, or an idea that helps me relate it to learning and to fill in the gap. I can learn by creating connections, and they appear everywhere in my writings. I can call it attunement as well, as it emphasizes attentiveness to what is not necessarily visible, imaginable, thinkable (Pinar, 2019), and analogies are good ways to connect knowledge to beyond what is logical.

The experience of being an immigrant and an academic student both at the same time are lived experiences that help me be more attentive to words and sounds that surround me. All this process is a return to *português brasileiro* as well because my inner voice still falls back on it to understand and interpret the world I have been learning. In this regard, Boroditsky (2017) has shown that language shapes the way we think and affects our perception of the world. Although my writings were in English, I used *português brasileiro*, which is still shaped as inner voice, to be attuned to the new situation. It appears not only in my *currere* process analysis, but also in the present paper, and it speaks volumes to the lived experiences so far. Although the idea is to think in English, to better express myself in English, there is a component that can never be supressed: my lived experience as a *português brasileiro* speaker, and the materiality of it also appears in my *currere* writing process.

Language and the Materiality of Teaching and Learning

Another point that sticks out from those *currere* writings is the material conditions of the school environments both in *Brasil* and Canada. I think that material conditions are strong components in the learning process, especially when it comes to language learning. The material condition in schools is something that crosses both countries' *currículos* and my practice. It does affect teaching, from the material conditions of voice, as well as the ability to speak the language and vocal health, to objects and equipment available for planning and conducting class activities. They also influence what type of content we are going to teach to whom.

Because of that, I think of what Ellsworth (2004) proposes when she states that "places of learning explore what it might mean to think of pedagogy not in relation to knowledge as a thing made but to knowledge in the making" (p. 1) Ellsworth says that "by focusing on the means and conditions, the environments and events of knowledge in the making, it opens an exploration into the experience of the learning self" (pp. 1–2). It is what happened in my progressive *currere* writing, as it is shown below.

> OK, breathe into the count of four, hold to the count of three, breathe out to the count of five. Again, breathe in, hold, breathe out...again...OK, it is working...Let's do it! All the people are here. I am so nervous! I am sure I cannot remember what I have to say...And I have to focus on my pronunciation, sometimes people do not understand me...And I need to remember to say that fancy word, it could impress someone...OK, breathe in, hold, breathe out...Do it again...Where is my water bottle? Here, drink it slowly...I am shivering, trembling, or is it shaking? I can't even describe my feelings...OK, OK, you can do it...Slow down, you have done all the work, you know your stuff...

Having voice, being able to express ourselves in our native language, is intertwined with the conditions in which teachers have to teach and in which students have to learn. I think it is also related to attunement to the lived experiences students bring with them when they come to school. Pinar (2019) says listening, like attunement, is multimodal, because we not only listen to words, but also the melody of the voice, the posture and gesture of the body (Lipari, 2014 as cited in Pinar, 2019), and so on. Our most inner thoughts are permeated with words from outside and are affected by the verbal and nonverbal languages we speak (Boroditsky, 2017). Attention to words plays an important role in my *currículo* as lived experience.

Finally, all my writings are about school scenarios. They are a sort of first experiences, maybe because I am always starting over; I think I prefer to build experiences than lean on them. Simultaneously, I try to change all the time, which brings discomfort, because I am constantly struggling to accommodate voiced and unvoiced moments. It seems I learn better when I am out of my comfort zone; it forces me to pay attention to instructions, to the environment, to people, to words, and to sounds.

Final Considerations

The *currere* writing process helped me understand my struggle to find voice in a different milieu. As a result, the lived experiences I have built during the wayfinding process allow me to rely on knowledge that is interconnected to my learning journey. In this way, the wayfinding process and *currere* are important contribution to understanding students' lived experiences. I think that understanding *currere* as lived experience may help to answer the epistemological questions such as *what is knowledge?* It even points to axiological ones, like *what knowledge is of the most worth?* These questions at the end of this text might be the beginning of a new one, and it could start by saying that I as teacher/student am trying to achieve knowledge and make meaning of it with flexibility (Ellsworth, 2004). Rosa (2016) reminds me that this flexibility requires courage. I extend this courage to include Machado's (2003) *caminante*. We are all *caminantes* wayfinding and making meaning of the mixing of life in a process that is always new, as Chacal,[5] *um poeta brasileiro* explains

o tempo em que marx explicava o mundo
tudo era luta de classes
como era simples
o tempo em que freud explicava
que édipo tudo explicava
tudo era clarinho, limpinho, explicadinho
tudo muito mais asséptico
do que era quando eu nasci
hoje rodado sambado pirado
descobri que é preciso
aprender a nascer todo dia

Notes

1 The flow of life mixes everything, life is in this way: it heats up and cools, it squeezes and loosens, it calms then disquiet. What life wants from us is courage.
2 It is interesting how there is always something that I do not know. It never ends.

3 All the experience I had gathered throughout 25 years as being a teacher, in different classes and schools, have no worth in a new environment, because nobody but my brother and his family knew me.
4 Traveler, there is no path, the path is made while walking.
5 In the time when Marx explained the world/ everything was class struggle/how simple it was/in the time when Freud explained/that Oedipus explained everything/everything was very clear, very clean, very explain /everything was more aseptic/than it was when I was born/ today rotated samba crazy/I've realized that it is needed/learning to be born everyday

References

Anya, U. (2017). *Racialized identities in second language learning: Speaking Blackness in Brazil.* Routledge.

Beierling, S., Buitenhuis, E., Grant, K., & Hanson, A. (2014). "Course" work: Pinar's *currere* as an initiation into curriculum studies. *Canadian Journal for New Scholars in Education, 5*(2), 1–9.

Boroditsky, L. (2017, November). *How language shapes the way we think* [Video]. TED Women. https://www.ted.com/talks/lera_boroditsky_how_language_shapes_the_way_we_think/footnotes?language=en

Chacal. (2007). Como era bom. In Chacal (Ed.), *Belvedere (1971–2007)* (p. 12). Cosac Naify.

Ellsworth, E. (2004). Introduction. In *Places of learning: Media, architecture, pedagogy* (pp. 1–13). Routledge.

Ellsworth, E. (2019). *Solid broken changing*. Dragon Tail Books.

Fuhrmann, L. R. (2020). Sobre as voltas que a vida dá [About the turns that life takes]. *Expressão Digital, 11*(23). http://gaia.liberato.com.br/expressao_digital/?p=12117

Lafferty, A., & Onită, A. (2021). Gently stomping with K'onį Nátsę and Nădejde: A poetic duoethnography between a Ts'élî-Iskwew and Româncă in academia. In E. Lyle & S. Mahani (Eds.), *Sister scholars untangling issues of identity as women in academe* (pp. 93–104). DIO Press.

Lyle, E. (2021). Call for proposals: *Re/centring lives and lived experience in education.*

Machado, A. (2003). *Campos de Castilla, 1907–1917* (14th ed). Cátedra.

Pinar, W. F. (1975). *The method of currere* [Paper]. The annual meeting of the American Research Association, Washington, DC.

Pinar, W. F. (2019). Attunement. In *Moving images of eternity: George Grant's critique of time, teaching and technology* (pp. 261–322). University of Ottawa Press.

Rosa, G. (2016). *Grande Sertão: Veredas [The devil to pay in the backlands]*. Globo.

CHAPTER 7

(Re)centring Our Presence in Education with Story

Experiences of Ts'élî Iskwew and Dinjii Zhuh Scholars

Anita Lafferty and Crystal Gail Fraser

Our Stories as Essence

Story is how we situate ourselves as Indigenous Peoples, especially in our connection to Land.[1] How we relate to our Lands, and the stories about Land, forms our innate connection to our Homelands. When we think of the Land, we think of how we are collectively connected as humans in relation to all things. (Re)[2]centering both individual and collective understanding in education requires us to seek *what centres us*. From our perspectives as northern Indigenous scholars, we have learned that Land is what centres us. We know our stories carry the history of generational wisdom where "story is methodologically congruent with [Indigenous] knowledges" (Kovach, 2009, p. 35). Through storying our inherent experiences, we answer the *call* of (re)centering our lives as we seek to find connections of *presence* as two dynamic, Indigenous scholars, living and learning in different places but connected by northern relationality. We ask: *what does it mean for us to be in relationship with the Land, while we are not on our Homelands?*

First, we must situate ourselves and our relationship to each other and the North. The kinship ties Anita stems from are abundant: she is a ts'élî iskwew (Dene Cree woman) and a direct descendant of the Łíídlı̨ı̨ Kų́ę́ First Nation in Northwest Territories. She carries the wisdom of her matriarchs through the distinct learning experiences from strong Dene women who have helped shape her worldview. Crystal's Dinjii Zhuh Homelands span what is now northern Alaska, northern Yukon, and the northwestern part of the Northwest Territories. Her ancestors and kin have been there since Ts'ii Dęįį, the earliest days of the Land (Heine et al., 2007). Nanhkak Thak—a relational concept in Dinjii Zhuh Ginjik meaning "the whole country around here, or our country"[3]—is currently situated in the Gwich'in Settlement Area in the Western Arctic. Crystal also has Scottish ancestors who arrived in 1773 in what is now Canada.

As we revisit our *presence* on Land, we feel this sense of urgency where the (re)centring of our stories (re)connects us to our ancestral places. This urgency not only brings forth an embodied understanding of what the North means for

© KONINKLIJKE BRILL NV, LEIDEN, 2022 | DOI:10.1163/9789004521186_007

us but also rematriates the voices of matriarchal wisdom in a way that honours our grandmothers' voices. Crystal looks to the wisdom of her late grandmother, Marka (Bullock) Andre, and great grandmother, Julienne The'dahcha, and Anita looks to her late granny, Elizabeth Lafferty (Tonka), who lived in this world to the age of 93. We are conscious of their voices as we recollect stories of generational wisdom. Through this storying relationship, we are (re)centring our storied lives by framing what it means for us to be *thinking with the Land*, embracing new ways of *walking with the Land*, sharing how we *honour kinships*, and finding solace in the *(re)embodiment of matriarchal wisdom* as we begin to *(re)connect with our grandmothers' songs* as a way forward in how and what we teach.

Our connection to the North is deeply related to the Land; the Land sustains us, envelops our knowing, and situates our kinship ties and relationships. Thinking about Land and the knowledge, histories, and stories it carries is crucial in our relationship with ourselves and others. Although we come from different sovereign Indigenous Nations, our interconnected histories are based on northern Indigenous cultures, relationality, kinship, and Land. We also share collective trauma through both ancestral and lived experiences of colonialism, including the institutionalization of immediate family members at Indian Residential Schools and Indian Sanitoria.[4] Stories that once denied our *presence* are now present in our daily lives. These stories uphold our existence, resilience, and determination as we (re)cover the essence of our grandmothers.

Here, we embrace the practice of *turning inward* as we are contextualizing the lives we seek to represent as Indigenous women scholars. We both write from the perspective of Indigenous Northerners living in Alberta. Anita moves between Treaty 6 and Treaty 7 Territories, while Crystal has been a guest on Treaty 6/Métis Nation Lands, skirting Amiskwacîwâskahikan,[5] for nearly 20 years. Being physically disconnected from ancestral northern landscapes has evoked a strong desire to find solace in the heart of our stories.

Thinking with Land

We find ourselves in this notion of becoming wakeful to our *presence*, our situated selves, and negotiating ways to (re)connect to the Land that defines us and embodies our kinship relations. We understand that "accountability to our relationships is what would be considered the shared aspect of an Indigenous axiology and methodology" (Wilson, 2001, p. 7). By bringing together our voices, we reimagine intersections of northern matriarchal knowledge as we highlight the many shifts we are encountering as we are (re)awakening our conscious minds back to the Land in connection to our identities as ts'élî-iskwew and dinjii zhuh. As Indigenous women, our teachings about *memory* situate our oral histories that connect us to our past. Through the simultaneous engagement with story and memory, we are (re)connecting with our northern Homelands as they bring us back to these teachings.

Land-based stories and teachings from our grandmothers have been absent from our formal educational experiences for far too long. For us, we have had to reclaim these stories and our roles as matriarchs. We envision our place on the Land as a place that situates our grandmothers' wisdom and stories that continue to guide us in education. Thinking through our (dis)connection to Lands is intimately connected to our complexity as Indigenous Peoples, given that Land has been at the centre of colonialism for centuries. As educators, we (re)conceptualize teaching and learning through a practice of exercising complex personhood. Gordon (2008) describes the essence of complex personhood where "the stories people tell about themselves, about their troubles, about their social worlds, and about their society's problems are entangled and weave between what is immediately available as a story and what their imaginations are reaching towards" (p. 4). We are beleaguered by contradiction; our experiences are relational yet fiercely personal, emotive, and sensory, and we perceive different truths based on our situation and social setting. We see Land "as centre" in a different way.

At the forefront of these experiences is how we embody our status as matriarchs, practice our culture, and use our senses to understand our worlds. There is a fragility that sits with us but also a fragility in how we, as two Indigenous scholars, find security in a world that seems to want to tear us apart or negate a separation. Barnett (2000) discusses fragility within our world as "a fragility brought on not merely by social and technological change; it is a fragility in the way that we understand the world, in the way in which we understand ourselves and in the ways in which we feel secure about acting in the world" (p. 257). We now refuse to be fragile in the ways we understand this world and challenge this colonial system that consistently demands us to "prove" our storied history. Million (2009) states that "because the emotional knowledge of our experiences is an alternative truth, it is challenged ferociously" (p. 64); therefore, we counteract this challenge as we know truth lies in our historical accounts. In her discussion of felt theory, Million (2009) explains that as Indigenous Peoples, we not only think our histories but "we *feel* our histories" too (p. 54). The *feeling* of our histories can be manifested by a bodily sympathetic response of goosebumps when we recall the words of our great grandmothers speaking to us or when we observe and feel the presence of our oldest ancestors on our Lands: the animals and spirits. It is these untold or often lost narratives that shape who we are as we seek to find ways of (re)connecting to stories of our oldest ancestors. As we reflect, we are challenging our understanding of identity and action in places we inhabit, where how we feel secure in the world is our connection to Land.

Walking with the Land

As we navigate the Land, we place history at the centre of our stories where the voices of our oldest ancestors are visible. Nurturing our relationship with Land is like learning to walk again. We continue walking, knowing we may fall here and there; we get up again with the help of family, community, and ancestors. We are learning that being active on the Land has a purpose whereupon paying close attention to our surroundings, relevant teachings are present. Staying close in our relationship with the Land and notion of *home* characterizes our actions within the context of our daily lives. These actions lead us to "the wild places, [where] we are audience to conversations in a language not our own" (Kimmerer, 2013, p. 48), but where we are beginning to recognize it again as the language of our grandmothers.

Presently, we are isolated and constrained in our immediate surroundings and left with feelings of silence and sacrifice. This notion of silence has forced us to slow down, allowing for the ceremony of silence to exist as we renegotiate our understanding of our relationship with self and Land. While we walk the Land with familiar yet unfamiliar steps, we focus on fostering renewed identities and (re)imagining meanings of nationhood. It is the silence that brings our footsteps back home and our footsteps that bring us back in relation to our ancestors. There is learned comfort in the silence as we walk the Land. The physical aspect of being on the Land brings forth questions about matriarchal and Land knowledge. We are reminded of the ability to learn and value nonverbal communication, found beneath the language of the tongue as the language of the Land, language of the heart, and language of relationships. When walking the Land, we seek to acknowledge our relationships with all creations.

Honouring Kinships

As we begin to understand more about who we are as Northerners and why identity is important in our understanding of the Land, we start to unravel our stories that (re)centre our relationships.

anita ᐊᓂᑕ (*there at that place*)

I am the granddaughter of Dene strength, where courage and love are embossed within my heart as the wisdom of generations embodies me as I walk the Land. I live the stories of being on the Land, taught to me by my matriarchs: my grandmother; my mother; and my aunties. I am also Cree, with a name that translates to "there, at that place," or "place" as though I was always meant to be in relation to place in a way that honours the Land relations.

Today, as I walk among the spruce, I am reminded of their silent gifts that appear, the ones that bring with them life medicines, and ones that resonate with my connection to home. The North. A place that sits idly in my thoughts and movements as I walk upon the Land. I think of home, of the sights, sounds, smells, and touch of dii ndéh (Earth). It is where the sun meets the sky, and the vibrancy of nature sits upon the waters. There is nothing else like it that speaks to my heart. Having travelled to many places across Turtle Island, the North is a place of great wisdom and purity, a place that transcends the knowledge of my ancestors like a ripple effect that continues to grow within me.

Today, as I sit here in silence with the Land in a ceremony of self-reflection, I think of my Homelands, I think of the abundant knowledge that conveys generations of Dene wisdom and philosophies that existed long before written text. This time away from my Homelands, especially during this time of going inward, has also brought with it fear—fear of the unknown, of placelessness, where I know the ground under my feet is not Home. Negotiation within my spiritual praxis brings me to waver in my understanding of Home as I reveal the in-between perspectives that have shaped my understanding of borderlines.

Even though I sit here on the Traditional Territory of Treaty 7, I am still connected to my relatives in the north through the modes in which I interact with my environment; through a multisensory conversation with place (anita). The Land allows me refuge from what has confined me from Home, and a place where I find the strength of my grandfathers and grandmothers as their wisdom lives within me. Even though I sit in discomfort knowing I cannot go Home at this time, I am growing and learning on this Land. I sit with the knowledge of nationhood that Dene relatives are still near me, that the Land still sits close to my heart and that my relations are safe upon my Homelands.

Nationhood is not a matter of physically being in my nation, for I carry the language and culture with me as I engage with the Land. This is embodied nationhood. My sacrifice of being away from Home is a vital sacrifice. I was told that I will bring strength to my Homelands upon my return. I am like a cartographer of the Land, embracing people and places along the way, emerging from inherent knowledge of my ancestors. The presence of my matriarchs is revealed with each step forward. My grandmother's hands guide and lift me as I (re)center my relationship with place and self. (*anita* ᐊᓂᑕ)

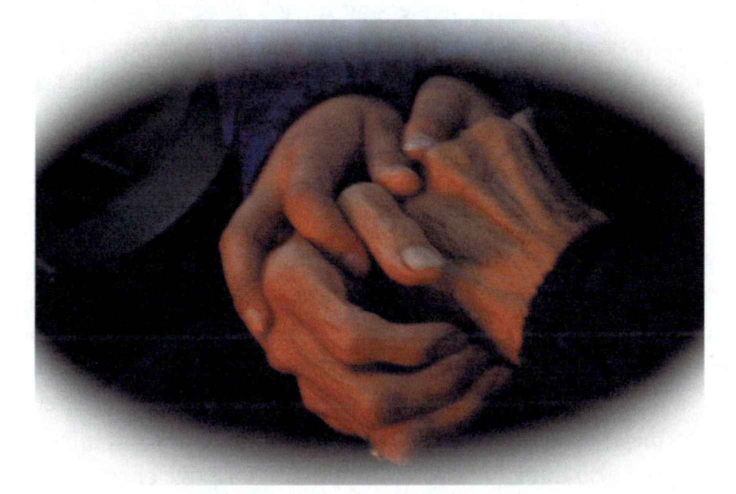

Grandmother's hands (Photograph by A. Lafferty, © 2019, used with permission)

crystal t'aih (*ancestral strength*)

> As a child, I never stayed anywhere else except with my Momma….I remember all the things my Momma did" —Marka Andre Bullock, Crystal's grandmother. (McCartney & Gwich'in Tribal Council, 2020, p. 551)

I sat on the rocky embankment, twirling one of my pig tails around my index finger. "Ugh, when will Gramma let me go play?" I thought to myself, rolling my eyes. "Surely the birds will not steal anything," as I eye-balled the fish strips on the stage.

I was seven years old, at my family's fish camp on the Mackenzie River, Dachan Choo Gę̀hnjik. I was alone, with my grandmother, Marka Andre

Bullock. She was a strong Gwichyà Gwich'in matriarch and had learned the ways of fish camp from her mother, Julienne The'dahcha (Andre). Marka was my mother's mother and that held special significance: since our culture was matrilineal—and especially as the first-born grandchild—I was at fish camp to absorb every teaching from here. Even the ones that seemed insignificant at the time.

"Oh shit!" I exclaimed, my voice slowly trailing off at the end as I wondered if Gramma heard me or not, particularly the swear word. I had turned my attention elsewhere, neglecting my job as guardian-of-fish-strips for a moment; it was just long enough to check out the gut bucket to see if there were any whitefish scales I could salvage for evening art projects. But the seagulls and ravens had won again, having made off with several fish strips. I stretched my neck up to see if Gramma had noticed. I exhaled heavily with relief.

The coney strips were particularly popular with our feathered friends. You know, the ones that glisten in the sun and drip with fat. I never had a problem letting those cony strips go; they gave me heartburn. I never understood how anyone could eat cony. Or goose, for that matter. Today, as a matriarch-in-training and tenure-track professor, I wonder how these fatty animals sustain us and have nourished the bodies and minds of our ancestors. I also think of how fat dripping is reflective of colonialism: how have our people been subjected to and lived the outcomes of genocidal policies at the hand of the settler state? And seemingly—in most cases—lived to tell stories about the last century of genocide.

Even though, as Gwichyà Gwich'in, we are a matrilineal society, women are often absent from conversations about colonialism and its effects such as addiction, domestic violence, abuse and deaths at Indian Residential Schools, and a myriad of other factors. Our mothers and grandmothers are not absent because of informed decision-making practices but are often occupied with the background noise of colonialism. These are the screeches and disruptions that only some of us can hear and respond to. Every day, my generation asks the Creator to make the violent melodies of colonialism quieter and quieter so our families can continue to heal, and matriarchs can assume their rightful places on the Land.

Crystal at Dachan Choo Gę̀hnjik (Photograph by E. Debastien, © 1987, used with permission)

(Re)embodiment of Matriarchal Wisdom in Education

We had to (re)centre our stories and lives to include the stories of our grandmothers. This is something we did not learn from the typical classrooms we have encountered in Eurocentric educational contexts; this is something that we had to (re)learn. As we are both rooted in matriarchal cultures, the embodiment of the living concept of Land shapes our everyday lives as cis-gendered Indigenous women. Like the women who came before us—our matriarchs, leaders, and mentors—we hold our Indigenous teachings close to our hearts and spirits.

Wilson (1998), an Indigenous Studies scholar also known as Waziyatawin, writes "the stories handed down from grandmother to granddaughter are rooted in a deep sense of kinship responsibility, a responsibility that relays a culture, an identity, and a sense of belonging essential to [our] lives" (p. 27). Stories from our grandmothers ground us in our work as educators, academics, mothers, and matriarchs. The strength and persistence of our stories remind us of who we are as we learn from each other. Our stories remind us that *turning inward* was also part of our grandmothers—and their grandmothers' lives.

McAdam (2019) reinforces our understanding of autonomy as Indigenous Peoples writing, "nationhood is primarily about land, language, and culture" (p. 25) directly linking to our sovereignty and distinction as nations within nations. This knowledge was not transferred in the school systems we attended as students. We recognize that our grandmothers' stories carry oral histories and are written on the Land in ways that only our people understand—through memory, Land use, animal movements, weather patterns, economies, and social movements. As we (re)learn matriarchal ways of knowing, we (re)embody their teachings as we (re)centre the meaning of education through a decolonial lens. As northern matriarchs, we understand that, in education, we must continue the stories of Land. These stories shape and (re)centre matriarchal wisdom leaving a strong presence where no presence was acknowledged before.

(Re)connecting with Our Grandmother's Songs

Kinship creates a song that sings to both of us, harmonizing our experiences as relatives and descendants of the North. As we call attention to the matriarchal stories that sit within us, we are embracing the knowledge of generations once stolen from us. By reconnecting to these stories, matriarchal wisdom lives on in the ways we live, learn, and teach. Collectively, our hearts sing the songs of our grandmothers, as we are granddaughters of the North, emerging from legacies of strength and courage. These stories are like the drumbeat—strong and central to our Nations. Without the drumbeat, the song sits idle and, without the song, the drum sleeps. As we cultivate a balanced relationship in places that are not our Homelands, we are finding *presence* in the knowledge dexterity of the Lands where we are situated as a way to negotiate our experiences in new ways.

The Land is our new classroom. It connects us and repositions knowledge in a contextual framework where our ancestors now sit at the forefront of our stories. The Land provides us with the capacity to advance our relationality with all beings. We are learning and growing together in a harmonious way that embodies the connection we share as Northerners, as knowledge seekers, as Indigenous women. We let what we learn guide us in our understanding of self, place, and *home* while listening to the heartsongs of our grandmothers who continue to guide us as we think, walk, and (re)embody our kinship relations with self and Land.

Heart Song

the silence echoes
where the heart knowledge
of our grandmothers (re)center our lives
no disruption can defeat
the wisdom we embody
upon Lands that
sing the heart songs of our grandmothers

where complex personhood
entangles and weaves stories
of imaginations gone wild
where felt theory embraces our songs
as narratives of the heart
where axiology and methodology
collide in a harmonious wonder
as Eurocentric theories frame our work, like barb wire
found incapable of fully encapsulating our feelings of Land
we know
it is where the silences
and stillness
sing the heart songs of our grandmothers

we feel our grandmothers' hearts
supporting our words and ways forward
encouraging us—Indigenous women—
to push and to persist
to feel and to connect
where the road North
reverberates with each step,
on ground that holds stories
of wisdom, of old ancestors
as our lives may be disrupted
the matriarchs (r)center us and
sing the heart songs of our grandmothers.

Notes

1. We capitalize certain words to acknowledge their importance. We use "capitals where conventional style does not. It is a deliberate decision" (Younging, 2018, p. 77).
2. In using parentheses around (re), we emphasize and call attention to a "looking backward notion" where remembering is an act of decolonization. Bhabha (2012) explains that "remembering is never a quiet act of introspection or retrospection. It is a painful re-membering, a putting together of the dismembered past to make sense of the trauma of the present" (p. 90).
3. Gratitude to dinjii zhuh Elder Agnes Mitchell for this translation.
4. Indian Sanitoria were racially-segregated medical institutes that operated across Canada during the late 19th and 20th centuries, and treated Indigenous Peoples who were ill, often with tuberculosis.
5. Beaver mountain house, also known as Edmonton.

References

Barnett, R. (2000). Supercomplexity and the curriculum. *Studies in Higher Education, 25*(3), 255–265.

Bhabha, H. K. (2012). *The location of culture*. Routledge.

Gordon, A. (2008). *Ghostly matters: Haunting the sociological imagination*. University of Minnesota Press.

Heine, M., Andre, A., Kritsch, I., & Cardinal, A. (2007). *Gwichya Gwich'in Googwandak: The history and stories of the Gwichya Gwich'in*. Tsiigehtshik and Fort McPherson, NWT.

Kimmerer, R. W. (2013). *Braiding sweetgrass: Indigenous wisdom, scientific knowledge and the teachings of plants*. Milkweed Editions.

Kovach, M. (2009). *Indigenous methodologies: Characteristics, conversations, and contexts*. University of Toronto Press.

McAdam, S. (2019). *Nationhood interrupted: Revitalizing Nêhiyaw legal systems*. Purich.

McCartney, L., & Gwich'in Tribal Council. (2020). *Gwich'in K'yee Gwiindandài' Tthak Ejuk Gòonlih, our whole Gwich'in way of life has changed*. University of Alberta Press.

Million, D. (2009). Felt theory: An Indigenous feminist approach to affect and history. *Wicazo Sa Review, 24*(2), 53–76.

Wilson, A. C. (1998). Grandmother to granddaughter: Generations to oral history in a Dakota family. In D. A. Mihesuah (Ed.), *Natives and academics: Researching and writing about American Indians* (pp. 27–36). University of Nebraska Press.

Wilson, S. (2001). What is an Indigenous research methodology? *Canadian Journal of Native Education, 25*(2).

Younging, G. (2018). *Elements of Indigenous style: A guide for writing by and about Indigenous Peoples*. Brush Education.

CHAPTER 8

Feeling Connection and Belonging

Factors for Veteran Students' University Success

Lorrie Miller, Tim Laidler, Eric Lai and Benjamin Hertwig
(with contribution from McKenzie Robinson)

> Watching the Taliban once again sweep across the country has dragged Mr. Laidler back in time with an unnerving intensity. "It's triggering all the memories," he said. "It puts your body into a high level of alert. It feels like I'm back overseas on operation again. There's this level of stress, this cortisol pumping through my blood—I can feel it. ...Our minds are so preoccupied, we don't even have time to grieve what's happening to the country. We're still in crisis mode."
>
> MERCER AND ANDREW-GEE (2021)

∴

Crisis mode is something that veterans know all too well and, yet, when they leave active service and enter post-secondary institutions, crises rise from new causes. To better understand who these students are and how institutions of higher education can support them, we tap into recollections and experiences of veterans who have experienced both post-secondary education and active military service. Three of the co-authors are veterans, and all of us have been, or are currently involved with the University of British Columbia's Institute for Veteran Education and Transition (IVET). It is our goal to shed light on the realities of veteran students, their challenges, and hopes. We also hope to highlight the value of transferable skills from a military context in to a university environment and make recommendations for post-secondary institutions in Canada.

© KONINKLIJKE BRILL NV, LEIDEN, 2022 | DOI:10.1163/9789004521186_008

Who Are Canadian Military Veteran Students and What Should We Know about Them?

Veterans can be some of the humblest yet experienced and worldly students in a classroom environment. Even so, they often have to advocate for themselves for resources to support mental and physical wellness even as they struggle to redefine their identity. We need to consider this as they enter our institutions. Not all veterans will offer first-person insights into their experiences, and not all academic environments will provide opportunities to highlight veteran students' strengths. However, the classroom has potential to provide rich cross-training and learning that permits all individuals to shine. This is particularly relevant to stigmas and cultural misunderstandings of the veteran population. Some veterans yearn for opportunities to grow beyond their prior roles and trades they held in the military. So, while in the university setting, it is important that instructors, university administration, and staff members understand that veterans are more than the last hat or helmet they wore.

We believe that when we support veteran (re)education, we create opportunities for them to be more connected with their environment and school community as they work to shed psychological armour and redefine themselves as *civilian*. This is where mentorship and academic networking sessions come into play. A tailored briefing of the academic landscape would support the lack of academic pedigree that is typical of front-line, non-commissioned Members/Officers (NCM/Os), and combat-arms veterans.

The military recruits young Canadians from across Canada. Recruits, as young as 17 (with parental consent), are accepted into the Canadian Militia and, once they complete their high school credentials, they can join the Reserves or Regular forces. Though no longer the case, for many years, only Grade 10 was required to join the Canadian Armed Forces (Blatchford, 2019). Regardless of who new soldiers are or where they come from, the military aspires to treat all soldiers as equal with promotions based on dedication and measurable skills. Young people are trained from the ground up, from how to make a bed, to marching, to leading others in battle. At the end of a military career, a once unskilled person has leadership skills, self-esteem, and a get-it-done attitude. Canadian Armed Forces is an institution of social mobility, but we ask, *are universities*?

Universities have extremely competitive entrance requirements where traditional students (those entering directly from high school) enjoy an array of social, familial, and institutional supports as they begin their freshman year (Accamando, 2017). This stands in stark contrast with the Mission and Values espoused by many universities—to be inclusive and diverse as they promote academic excellence. The dualling principles of excellence and inclusion are on display with university entrance requirements. "Institutional efforts to address equity, diversity and inclusion in educational settings have been often met with overwhelmingly critical accounts pointing towards well-intentioned attempts that have reinforced exclusion and inequity" (Tamtik & Guenter, 2019, p. 41).

Training and Learning: Cultural Differences between Military and Universities

There are very different education cultures between military training and university education: the emphasis in a military education is on *training* and skills where the university focus is on *learning* and critical consciousness. Another significant difference is regarding the onus of responsibility: in the military, educational outcomes are often regarded as a reflection of the success of the curriculum and, thus, the curriculum is often adjusted to maximize the success of the students. In the university culture, students are largely responsible for their success and have little voice in a changed curriculum. Given these significant differences, we need to consider the experiences of veteran students coming to a university campus where the onus of their success rests entirely on their own shoulders without any consultation. This cultural transition is often quite a shock to students (Taylor & Francis Group, 2019). It also chafes against many of their values, as veterans often have held leadership positions by the time they retire, on average in their mid-forties (Van Til et al., 2017). They hold the university and professors accountable for failing to teach students rather than the *student failing to learn properly*. The communication of expectations and protocols within the university setting may be assumed by instructors, but not necessarily clear or obvious to all students. For instance, when a student is called on for duty, they may leave their studies and deploy without informing the university, resulting in a *F* on their transcript. Whereas, active duty is an approved leave from study, and they can be withdrawn (regardless of add/drop deadlines). If an instructor does not know that their student is also part of the reserve forces, they would not even know to allow for such accommodation. Likewise, if a student who is a reservist does not know that there is no academic penalty for leaving studies for deployment, it is unlikely they would request accommodation. Bridging these gaps in expectations is important. Here we consider the lived experience of veterans within the post-secondary institution and explore what we can do to improve the quality of education for this underserved group of students.

Humanizing Stories through Personal Narratives

In crafting this chapter, we turn to the military veteran students' (MVS) experience in the form of collaborative narrative inquiry based on first-hand account. We understand the value of such narratives as the data for inquiry. "Sharing the stories helps to legitimize, validate, and further the research and its objectives," (Abraham et al., 2005, p. 110). Dougherty (2015) states that MVS have several skills and dispositions that will help with a transition into post-secondary. In particular, Dougherty found that, "(a) veterans were experienced with group collaboration; (b) veterans held high expectations of themselves; (c) veterans were organized and task oriented; (d) veterans were experienced learners; and (e) veterans had experience and ability to work with others" (p. 2). Drawing on Dougherty's work, we consider ways to re/centre the MVS in the learning experience at this university and beyond. To bring about such change, we must first care, listen, understand, and act. As such, we are drawn to narrative reflections and observations in connection with current MVS literature to provide a way to better understand the veteran reality with the hope of improving the post-secondary experience for veteran students. Such well-crafted personal accounts help us to understand an alternate perspective so that we might challenge preconceived assumptions. Writer, poet, veteran, and scholar, Benjamin Hertwig's reflections also provide illumination here.

Benjamin Hertwig

In my work as a poet, I have visited with thousands of primary school students across Canada and have learned that few of these students know little, if anything, about the war in Afghanistan. Most are entirely unaware of Canada's longest war. In their defence, all these students were born after September 11, 2001, and they were infants when Canada withdrew from Afghanistan. Even some of their teachers were born in the late 1990s and have no direct memories of the day itself and even fewer of the wars that followed. I provide this statement with neither glibness nor sadness nor defensiveness, though the time I spent as a soldier in Afghanistan remains the single most influential six months of my life. In the national memory, however, 13 years of war in Afghanistan does not even seem to register as a wound. The memory of Afghanistan is the faintest of scars, only seen in certain lighting, and only if you are looking for it. The question is *who is looking for it?*

As Catherine Savage Brosman (2020) says in *The Functions of War Literature*, "no other literary rendering of human experience has exercised such an extensive influence on human beings" (p. 85). A war starts and a war ends and life, for many, goes on. But for those whose lives were shaped by war—soldier, civilian, parent, spouse—the war continues long after the weapons and the politicians are silent. When I agreed to teach a course to a group of Canadian veterans and soldiers, I was trying to offer the care and educational understanding I was searching for when I returned from Afghanistan in 2006. In both my undergraduate and graduate studies, I never met a fellow veteran in the classroom. In fact, I did not consider my military experience as being relevant to academia. During these years, I tried not to think about the war, but the suppressed memories—suicide bombings, the death of a friend, the suicide of a fellow soldier—all re-emerged in my life. I found healing by writing about the war and eventually decided to apply for Ph.D. programs. I wanted to research the literature of the war in Afghanistan, which was what I was doing when offered the opportunity to teach veterans.

Teaching the course was difficult, but it was also good. As I continued to unpack my own traumatic memories, I was learning about the trauma of others. We analyzed the parts of speech and the structure of a sentence as we listened to each another's stories. We read historical narratives and developed narratives of our own. We did not always agree with one another, but we agreed to learn from one another. Veterans do not need to be coddled, but they deserve to be heard. I left the classroom each night completely exhausted and grateful. I drove home the slow way, against the ocean, the tall trees dark against the deep purple of the night sky.

McKenzie Robinson

McKenzie Robinson was a student in Benjamin's course and shares how Benjamin immediately developed a relationship with the class and provided a space for the military students to learn and share personal stories with fellow military students. Benjamin, a Ph.D. candidate, Parachute qualified, Reconnaissance qualified, and Afghanistan veteran knew his audience. He carefully selected literature for the course that would relate closely to the students' experiences. McKenzie writes, "I personally found my imagination going wild during class readings. Overall, the course was successful because the instructor (Benjamin) knew that military students don't just open up to any instructor."

Eric Lai

I grew up in the suburbs of British Columbia's Lower Mainland and did not want to mimic the typical paths that I witnessed, so I volunteered to join the Canadian Armed Forces. For me, it was not about financial accumulation and self-fulfillment. I saw 9/11 newscasts playing the entire day on the televisions within the halls of Rockridge Middle School. This stuck with me and, in my senior years of high school, I started taking the extra-curricular cadet program and physical conditioning seriously. I wondered how I could contribute with my innate strengths—one of which was athleticism. At 18 years old, I signed-up at the Vancouver recruitment office and never looked back.

Trained as Combat Engineer, I eventually specialized in Explosive Ordinance Defusal, which was exactly what I wanted to do since it directly helped to save lives and limbs, especially in the context of Afghanistan. During my second tour in Afghanistan, I was injured with friendly fire and medically released from the military. All at once, I had to redefine who I was and what I wanted to do, while coming to grips with my capabilities and limitations. I was left with internal injuries and external scars but internalizing new limitations was the most humbling of all.

Still, I felt like I have been given the gift of another life. I realized I had the potential to do so much more and began to wonder what I might do in *my second life*. In a sense, it was like a rendition of the *Miracle Question* described by De Shazer (1988) where the client is asked how their life would change if they woke up one day with the main problem facing them having vanished. Conceptualizing a way forward from this mental space created possibilities from the limitations and, years later, I still hold the same mentality as I examine other salient issues that beg for increased attention.

At first, I was proud in letting my student peers know that I was a Canadian veteran with the lived experience of frontline overseas deployment. However, I eventually learned that stepping off with that foot led to more difficulty in building peer relationships. It was from the multiple moments when student peers responded with "oh…," I knew I had to hold back, as this would immediately and notably change the perception of who I was. I've learned to reveal my history of service only after there has been some trust-building. In retrospect, I have come to realize that sometimes we, as veterans, do not recognize that our lived experiences and stories are so unique that they drop jaws.

> The risk of death creates a deep rift between the soldiers and the rest of the population and, in their view, cuts them off from the society from which they come and which it is their mission to defend. The fact that death is ever present makes the front an 'island,' it creates a world apart. (Cecil et al., 1996, p. 223)

Going back to school after deployment and recovery made it difficult to recognize the underlying similarities among my classmates. But there is a profound appreciation born of confronting life-threatening contexts, and they create avenues to connect—it is true what they say: *the sun is warmer, the air is fresher, and the flowers more fragrant.*

A memorable moment in my business communications class occurred when the instructor encouraged me to share my unique story and perspective. “Wow!” I thought, “Here’s someone who cares about individuals and cares to hear my unique perspective with lived experience!” It is classes like this that make the most of in-person learning experience. Here, I came to understand that my past experiences had translatable value into the academic sphere. Here, I saw how important it is to allow the space and time for students to listen to each other carefully, intentionally, and with deep respect.

I was the only veteran in my class, and I often felt small, insignificant, and uncomfortable in the larger auditorium classes. There were classes where I felt and acted like a fly on the wall; however, this nudged me to ask myself where I would find my next fraternity. Then while attending finance and social enterprise conferences, I realized that I had most in common with people studying social enterprise.

A pivotal experience for me was attending the Sauder Social Enterprise Kenya in 2016. While volunteering in this culturally-rich experience, my memory was triggered with a *felt sense* (Berkovitz, 2020) of why I joined the regular force military after September 11th (Levine et. al., 2018). Having the pleasure of meaningfully interacting—looking into the eyes, seeing the smiles, hearing their songs—and being inspired daily from the local Kenyan students was what redirected my trajectory into the realm of social impact. It reminded me how much we re/learn together despite our cultural and geographical differences.

This immersion allowed me to improve my academic knowledge and enjoy the delights of travel. There, I did things that I did not get to do in my early twenties because I was either training to be deployed or deployed. Like me, other young veterans sometimes miss the important personal exploratory stage of development that adolescence permits, in exchange for fast-track, first-hand learning about the realities of combat, war, inequality, and international development.

Recommendations

In consideration of co-authors’ observations and reflections based on their lived experiences, we summarize these experiences into recommendations and identify other areas for further inquiry. In response to a review of research, and as a result of listening to veterans, the University of British Columbia has launched a comprehensive program to make its campus *veteran friendly* to address the needs of this under-represented group of students. In addition to founding the Institute for Veterans Education and Transition (IVET), we have created a new certificate program to support MVS in their transition post service: *Veterans Transition Certificate in International Development and Human Security*.

We recognize that there are many ways to support students during an important life transition, and we hope that this chapter with its veteran-student and veteran-instructor experiences can inform others. Life and work in the military is not just a job: it is a way of life; a culture; and a deeply embedded set of values. Although each veteran student comes with their own unique circumstances, tailored student supports with knowledgeable instructors who are willing to begin where the student is can have a profound impact. The gap we identify is not just one of research to better understand veteran students within a Canadian context, but also the gap of action. Here we call for inclusive and responsive actions to meaningfully serve the students who have served us all.

References

Abraham Radi, D., Hildebrandt, P., Martin, J., & Peters, B. (2005). *First experiences of four PhD students in collaborative narrative inquiry research: ArtSSmarts Research Project.* https://www.umanitoba.ca/faculties/education/media/Hildebrandt_et_al-2005.pdf

Accamando, D. (2017). *Determining the specific transition needs of military and veteran students (MVS), a qualitative/mixed methods study* [Doctoral dissertation, Duquesne University]. Duquesne Scholarship Collection.

Berkovits, P.-C. (2020). *The client's bodily felt sense: A phenomenological study* [Doctoral dissertation, Staffordshire University]. ResearchGate.

Blatchford, C. (2019, April 19). The Canadian FORCES jobs where only women need apply. *SaltWire.* https://www.saltwire.com/halifax/news/canada/the-canadian-forces-jobs-where-only-women-need-apply-303663

Brosman, C. (1992). The functions of war literature. *South Central Review, 9*(1), 85–98. https://doi.org/10.2307/3189388

de Shazer, S. (1988). *Clues: Investigating solutions in brief therapy.* WW Norton & Co.

Dougherty, J. (2015). *The impact of military experience on the higher education experiences of veterans* [Doctoral dissertations, Illinois State University]. ISU ReD: Research and eData.

Fowler, L. (2006). *A curriculum of difficulty: Narrative research and the practice of teaching.* Peter Lang. https://www.peterlang.com/view/title/58617

Freire, P. (1972). *Pedagogy of the oppressed.* Herder and Herder.

Mercer, G., & Andrew-Gee, E. (2021, August 13) As the Taliban retakes Afghanistan Canadian military veterans look on. *The Globe and Mail.*

https://www.theglobeandmail.com/canada/article-as-the-taliban-retakes-afghanistan-canadian-military-veterans-look-on/

National Defence. (n.d.). *Training development officer*. Training Development Officer | Canadian Armed Forces. https://forces.ca/en/career/training-development-officer

Peterson, A. F. (1997). Facing armageddon: The First World War experienced. *History: Reviews of New Books, 26*(1), 8. doi:10.1080/03612759.1997.10525251

Semer, C., & Harmening, D. (2015). Exploring significant factors that impact the academic success of student veterans in higher education. *Journal of Higher Education Theory and Practice, 15*(7), 31–43. http://digitalcommons.www.nabusinesspress.com/JHETP/SemerC_Web15_7_.pdf

Tamtik, M., & Guenter, M. (2019). Policy analysis of equity, diversity and inclusion strategies in Canadian universities – How far have we come? *Canadian Journal of Higher Education / Revue canadienne d'enseignement supérieur, 49*(3), 41–56. https://doi.org/10.7202/1066634ar

Taylor & Francis Group. (2019, April 26). Veterans suffer from 'culture shock' when returning to university. In *ScienceDaily*. www.sciencedaily.com/releases/2019/04/190426100341.htm

Van Til, L. D., Sweet, J., Poirier, A., McKinnon K., Sudom K., Dursun, S., & Pedlar D. (2017). *Well-being of Canadian regular force veterans, findings from LASS 2016 Survey*. Veterans Affairs Canada. https://www.veterans.gc.ca/eng/about-vac/research/research-directorate/publications/reports/lass-2016#fn30

CHAPTER 9

Perform(actively) Sacred

Rehumanizing Learners through Ritualized Embodied Inquiry

Steven Noble

> Between what we do in class and what I am able to take with me to the practicum, it is like my body remembers what I should be doing, even when I might panic in the moment.
>
> PRACTICUM STUDENT (personal communication, 2015)

∴

Habitus, Ritual, and Performance for Learning

When I think of schooling, it's the people who come to mind—teachers, students, parents, and administrators. Ironically, in recollecting the spaces in which learning occurs, I see rows of desks, boards at the front, students folded into chairs with bodies locked in place. Within the quotidian spaces that make up schools, the focus is on mental work, while bodies tend to be simply transporters of minds. In the taken-for-granted routines of classrooms, bodies are sorted, folded, categorized, shaped, controlled, and put in place. Over months and years, learners are unconsciously conditioned to fit their bodies into spaces in order for various authorities to focus on controlling and manipulating brains. Bodies and minds are monitored, measured, and managed in taken-for-granted ways that inform learners where to be and how to think, dehumanizing learners a little bit each day in the process (Illich, 2000).

The product of set, systematic, and internalized norms and expectations that function as a kind of shorthand between individual subjectivities and broader constraining social structures that envelope interactions often result in somnambulistic living or one's habitus (Maton, 2008). The collection of daily habits, routines, and ways of being create an approach or practice with regard to a particular life activity. Within this writing, the practice is that of teaching/learning. Schools are places of cultural reproduction where physical presence and social imagination are closely policed through daily interactions

© KONINKLIJKE BRILL NV, LEIDEN, 2022 | DOI:10.1163/9789004521186_009

(Bourdieu, 1977). When divergent thinking is experienced or bodies are expressed in unfamiliar ways, the experience can be shocking and disorienting. Those moments are powerful instances of learning. This routinized way of living becomes the status quo of daily life.

Related to the notion of habitus are the twinned terms of ritual and theatre. Ritual theorists (Bell, 1997, 2009; Grimes, 2005; Turner, 1982, 1996) have suggested that rituals emerged from very early African religions usually connected with spring rites of fertility that included music, chanting, and dance. In contrast, it is thought that ancient Greece held the earliest forms of theatre. Theatre and ritual drama are considered to be related, but separate, with distinct dynamics that I rely upon within this chapter (Bell, 2009). Theatre is seen as secular. There is a division between performers and spectators, the spoken text is more variable (though much of modern theatre is scripted), and the purpose of a theatre is to entertain (Sidebottom, 2018). On the other hand, ritual drama remains rooted in religion, audience members and actors are seen as co-participants, the choral text is fixed, and the purpose is to conjure a particular effect of reverence (Sidebottom, 2018).

In popular theatre, performance is more inclusive and far-reaching to re-engage with some of the tenets of ritual. For example, Boal (1992, 1993), has written about "spect-actors" who witness a performance and engage directly in the performance. In addition, there are other elements of ritual added into popular performance, so as to blur the lines between theatre and ritual. This blurred space is a liminal home where much of my work resides. I draw upon ritual and theatre in the service of learning within the context of contemporary lessons and social struggle (Belliveau & White, 2010).

The rest of this chapter will interrupt normalcy by imagining the power of ritual and the centrality of student materiality and embodied learning. The process will begin with imagining a learning space that can be used for a ritual of growth that begins in emptiness and possibility (Brook, 1968). Once that ground is prepared, the discussion shifts to how a ritual of learning reimagined could bring learning bodies to the fore. Upon completion of those explorations, there is a mindful closing of the ritual container in order to return to the habitus of everyday, routine profane life. The dissonance realized within the ritual will be integrated and explored in the ordinariness of life. Finally, the writing explores the rippling legacy of body-memory within habitus. Before any ritual of learning can begin, there is an intentional and mindful preparing of the environment, within which education can occur. There has to be intentional and mindful co-involvement (Fels, 1998) of all participants to collaborate in the co-creation of this liminal environment.

Preparing for the Liminal Learning Space

Often spaces for learning are simply considered to be extensions of everyday environments. However, in my classroom teaching practice, I see things very differently. Several years ago, a friend of mine (Chapman, 2002) completed research involving master teachers. One of the dynamics she revealed was that master teachers often think of their teaching approaches in terms of an analogy. She asked me what I thought of when I prepared each class. My response was immediate: a dinner party. Before guests arrive, I have to arrange the meal (my agenda and class offering), the dinner table (the classroom space), and timing (same for both dinner party and class). Central to my planning for both events are the bodies of those present. Every dinner party, like every class, has a different energy signature, so planning has to happen each and every time. There is a sacredness to the preparations of this liminal space (Palmer, 1997), a separateness from the profane everyday.

Liminal spaces are often physical spaces but, more importantly, they are emotional, intellectual, and psychic spaces that allow for the focussing of the mind on the body in play-full moments allowing for the unfolding of free expressions and explorations to "interstand" among and through bodies (Fels, 1998; Linds, 1998, 2001). The critical lesson is the transformation of understanding (Taylor & Cranton, 2013; Taylor & Tisdell, 2013) to interstanding the meaning between and through bodies in action. The key to liminal spaces is that they are spaces or places that are not used how or when they would be used in their habitual ways. The result is what people are doing in a space and place is off-putting, strange or unfamiliar and unsettling—a dynamic (Barba, 2002, 2021; Okus, 2020) called "extra-daily." Liminal spaces are not meant to be comfortable; they are meant to encourage participants to move out of their comfort zones together to explore and become aware.

With my practice of performed ritual as a way to engage learning, every group—whether community setting or post-secondary program—starts with participants who are typically entering the space, pre-liminality, distracted with the detritus of incomplete tasks, moments of worry, undone plans, future unsettled relationships, and so on. Because of these distractions, there needs to be a ritual to help bring participants' bodies and minds into focus. The opening ritual is done in three phases: a general round of conversation occurs to see how people are feeling and what they are thinking about currently as they enter the space; this conversation is followed by an autogenic exercise, which is both meditative and physically relaxing; this ritual is rounded out by the larger group being divided into smaller groups of five to six people to have each group, without talking, create a body sculpture, called a tableau. The goal is to engage their bodies to come up with four to five frozen images of how the group is feeling (Grant, 2017). These tableaux are presented to the rest of the class for critical comment, physical engagement, and general observation. Once, this has been achieved, the group has become wholly centred in the liminal space and a sacred "container" has been created, within which the group can explore a wide variety of messy, challenging, risky, and inspiring explorations (Butterwick & Selman, 2020).

Embodied Learning Contained Rituals

What happens within this liminal time is guided by the needs of the students. I have done a social geography mapping of a city with a group of homeless people to make sense of how they viewed an urban setting in ways most people see the space of a home (Vaughan, 2018). I have worked with a group of psychiatric survivors as they found ways to tell their stories in embodied ways. I have also worked with practicum students as they analyzed and unpacked their practicum experiences, so that what occurred made deeper sense and had a stronger impact on their learning. This post-practicum experience is the context within which I will talk about more embodied learning with physical emotion taking priority.

For several years, I taught in a teacher education program in the areas of social justice, sociology of education, global education, and equity of education. One of the challenges students had involved making sense of their experiences after returning from their practica. There would be much dialogue about what happened among the students, but there was no deeper sense made of their experiences. In my sociology of education class, I had already been doing the "dinner party" preparations each class—including students taking turns bringing in snacks for the rest of the class. After a particularly stressful practicum period, I thought performatively exploring experiences could help unpack the socio-physical-emotional-psychological awareness (Butterwick & Selman, 2012; Summers-Effler, 2006).

Forum Theatre

The group opened the class with the collective, liminal container-building activity, and then students suggested that we look at some of the practicum experiences—especially the more challenging ones. Drawing from Boal's (1992, 1993) forum theatre approach, the group began its explorations. Boal, a Brazilian popular theatre practitioner, developed a number of exercises and approaches to engage learning through the performing bodies of those who were experiencing oppression to find ways toward Freire's (1993) concept of conscientization. The class broke into small groups to playfully create two to three short 1-minute scenes that highlighted those challenging practicum moments. Rather than find answers, these were problem-posing scenes where no answer was given. Only the complexity of the situation was portrayed up to the point of crisis, including the common challenge practicum students faced: being considered only guests in a school, with no power to intervene. In forum theatre, the group presented the scenes once non-stop and then repeated the performance. The second time, however, the rest of the class—Boal's (1993) spect-actors—could stop the action when audience members saw something that was oppressive or troubling that needed to be rectified (Gőgőkdağ, 2014). However, rather than just shouting out a suggestion, an audience member yelled "stop" and then stepped into whatever role that was causing the problem in the vignette being performed. So, instead of telling the performers what to do, the audience member switched from spectator to actor. People relied on their bodies, through their physical expression, to offer a suggestion. The conversation was physical, rather than verbal.

One example of what was presented ended up being quite challenging. The example was of a physical education practicum student teacher who, with his gym practicum teacher, walked into a boys' changeroom to see two Grade 9 boys holding hands and embracing. Also portrayed was how the gym practicum teacher responded, which was widely understood to be insensitive and demeaning—even homophobic. What was a practicum student to do? In every offer or suggestion, others in the class would take the initial suggestion to a conclusion that presented a whole set of unforeseen repercussions. The two scenes totalling four minutes in length lasted for well over an hour as offer after offer was made. Many were good suggestions; none was perfect. This kind of learning is focussed on *what if, so what,* and *now what* (Fels, 1998)—a deep curiosity to interstand.

Environmental Theatre

The second example was a town hall scenario. A practicum student helped organize a parent–teacher townhall involving the start-up of a program for teenaged mothers (recent moms and those who wished to return) in the school. This scenario was based on Schechner's (1994) concept of environmental theatre. Everyone was given a role (a short background detail) to play in the townhall. No one knew the character of anyone else, but each was given a physical action or attribute they needed to incorporate into who they were, such as "always crossed arms," "always crying and sniffling," "always pacing" (Schechner, 2013). Adding a physical attribute kept each participant aware of their bodies through the scene (Boal, 1992). The townhall was completely improvised with only the agendas of each person being the impulse for their actions. The room was set up in a townhall fashion. There were typical townhall refreshments (doughnuts, juice, muffins from the cafeteria downstairs.) available. Reports were handed out to the audience and each person asked questions based on their persona and agenda. Just like the previous scenario, there was no clear answer as to what needed to be done, but there were many questions raised that had not been pondered previously. This was embodied problem-posing learning that challenged taken-for-granted norms (Linds, 2001).

Sacred Play-full Bodies

Because of the time taken to set up this space as separate and liminal, there was an innate sense of permission to take the action wherever it needed to go, knowing that what was done here in this space stayed here when the participants ventured back into their everyday lives. A fairly low level of self-censorship was evident, and people took on their roles and responsibility with deep seriousness, yet with a high level of playfulness (Turner, 1996).

After each of the groups had each taken its turn, we realized that the 3-hour class had lasted five hours. Such was the concentration and focus that had gone into the explorations. Before we ended the ritual of our learning by closing the sacred container, we went around the room to have each person draw the three insights they were taking with them out into their practice and habitus. No names were attached to the drawings. All were posted on the walls with a short phrase to title each picture. Then, like an art gallery, the students moved around the space in silence to take in the insights that were gained from the experience. Once done, it was time for the group to take its leave from this in-between space and close this collaborative learning container.

Drawing a Close

To ensure that our time together remained separate and sacred (Palmer, 1997) within the larger often profane world, there needed to be a ritual of closure. So, once the tour of insights was achieved through walking around and reviewing the drawings, individuals returned to their seats or to a space on the floor. Quiet music or sounds of nature filled the space as participants closed their eyes to focus, once again, on their bodies through autogenics. This form of self-talk (HealthLink BC, 2020) is a whole-body meditative or mindful relaxation exercise meant to focus each individual on the insights gained within the learning container that was now being drawn closed. Near the end of the meditation time, I asked everyone to think about their experience in the class and ways that their insights could be integrated into their broader lives, whether work, home/family, recreation, or other areas of their lives. This entire phase of mindful reflection took approximately 15 minutes. At the end of this time, I instructed the group to slowly conclude their thinking about this time together. This was the closing of the ritual or the container, keeping this unique experience relatively separate from their profane, everyday worlds. Everyone was invited to stand up to circulate around the room and shake hands, hug, or simply say thank you to each other for their part in their learning. Always, the class left in complete silence because of the focussed work and the remaining thinking that continued as they left the physical room and the ritualized space.

Body/Memory

Ritualized and performative learning places learners' bodies in a centralized focus to work on and through them. Ritual is an embodied action and a form of practice relied on to apprehend the world and make sense of it. The ritual exercised within the learning described within this chapter could be construed as a ritual of transformation, ritual of communication, or a ritual of storytelling (Butterwick & Selman, 2020; Summers-Effler, 2006).

Within the learning space, participants use their bodies in ways that would be considered "extra-daily" or outside the normative of their respective habitus (Bourdieu, 1977; Okus, 2020). Because using their bodies is more expressive, in emotionally communicative ways, there is the striking unfamiliarity of embodied use that becomes more memorable (Bourdieu, 1977). Importantly, the key connector between ritual and habitus is the concept of practice. For the purpose of this chapter, practice is an activity that is situational and strategic, and therefore intentional, in order to reconfigure power relations in the world (Bell, 1992). There is a sense that this kind of learning is redemptive of oppression by changing the story (Belliveau & White, 2010; Butterwick & Selman, 2020).

Further, within learning that is both ritualized and performative, there is a highly symbolic attitude within the process. Ritual, while being highly symbolic of power, is also the exercise of power through embodied communication that individuals internalize in significant ways (Bell, 2009). Words are strategically chosen and are relatively few. Instead, the use of bodies to communicate is employed much more expansively and expressively than one would use within one's habitus. Rather than communicate in a more quotidian fashion, rituals communicate situations and implicate relationships of power and meaning—much as the practicum students did when they enacted their challenging stories that oppressed.

Importantly, within broader society, rituals are used to control and manipulate populations, typically from the perspective of social elites. Institutions today are rooted in rituals of long ago. Thinking of education, there were rituals involved in educating long ago that have, since, become incorporated in schools replete with their own system of rites and rituals that are used to categorize and control behaviours (Bell, 1997; Turner, 1982). Pushing back against formal structures in society within a ritualized vessel is called "communitas" or something that is an antistructure filled with intense, focused emotion when compared to those everyday structures of habitus (Turner,1996). Using ritual to liberate rather than oppress, teachers and learners can co-create educational rituals to reimagine and reconstruct social worlds.

Parting Ways: Returning to the Profane

The ritual of learning is a time of transition, of liminality, when everything that was true in one moment becomes initially suspended and then changed following the end of each of the group's time together. The interconnectedness of knowledge is that the relationships of beliefs and insights shift, even minutely. This chapter explored one way of thinking of teaching and learning by placing learning bodies and their materiality more centrally than simply focussing on learners' mental abilities. By creating a container where special time and place can be conjured through the collective efforts of educators and learners alike, a unique threshold moment provides an opportunity to explore, rehearse, and integrate insights in a playful way that is outside the normative tendencies of an individual's habitus.

By intentionally creating a separate space and time to explore, learners can find a freedom that may not exist in the same way within a more everyday environment. Co-creating insights, through free and playful queries, allows problem-posing to arise. The centrality of the body and reacquainting learners with the ability of making bodies expressive creates an opening for being in the world differently. A whole-body ability allows individuals to become more holistic, so that body language can play an equal and even more important role than speech alone.

The examples included in this chapter of using two different types of theatre, forum theatre and environmental theatre, allow teachers and learners to re-imagine bodies in spaces of collaborative *make-believe* that help explore *the real*. By dismissing the power of rituals to dis(en)courage control, teachers are affecting exploration and autonomy. Education has enormous capacity to recentre learners through embodied approaches that cultivate greater autonomy and self-efficacy along with deeper creativity and critical thinking.

References

Barba, E. (2002). The essence of theatre. *The Drama Review, 46*(3), 12–30.

Barba, E. (2021). First hypothesis. *Journal of Theatre Anthropology, 1*, 45–51.

Bell, C. (1997). *Ritual: Perspectives and dimensions.* Oxford University Press.

Bell, C. (2009). *Ritual theory; Ritual practice* (2nd ed.). Oxford University Press.

Belliveau, G., & White, V. (2010). Performer and audience responses to ethnotheatre: Exploring conflict and social justice. *ArtsPraxis, 2*(1), 29–48.

Boal, A. (1992). *Games for actors and non-actors* (2nd ed.). Routledge.

Boal, A. (1993). *Theatre of the oppressed.* Theatre Communications Group.

Bourdieu, P. (1977). *Outline of a theory of practice.* Cambridge University Press.

Brook, P. (1968). *The empty space* (2nd ed.). Simon & Schuster.

Butterwick, S., & Selman, J. (2012, Summer). Embodied knowledge and decolonization: Walking with theater's powerful and risky pedagogy. *New Directions for Adult and Continuing Education, 134*, 61–69.

Butterwick, S., & Selman, J. (2020, Spring). Community-based art making: Creating spaces for changing the story. *New Directions for Adult and Continuing Education. 165*, 35–47.

Chapman, V.-L. (2002). Teaching as a site of re-presentation. Metaphors, tropes, and texts. *International and Multidisciplinary Perspectives, 3*(2), 191–204.

Fels, L. (1998). In the wind clothes dance on a line. Performative inquiry: A (re)search methodology. *Journal of Curriculum Theorizing, 14*(1), 27–36.

Freire, P. (1993). *Pedagogy of the oppressed.* Continuum.

Gőgőkdağ, E. (2014). Augusto Boal's the joker system. *ÌDÌL, 14*(3), 27–37. doi:10.7816/idil-03-14-03

Grant, D. (2017). Feeling for meaning: The making and understanding of Image Theatre. *RIDE: The Journal for Applied Theatre and Performance*, 1–16. http://dx.doi.org/10.1080/13569783.2017.1286977

Grimes, R. A. (2005). Ritual studies. In *Encyclopedia of religion.* https://www.encyclopedia.com/environment/encyclopedias-almanacs-transcripts-and-maps/ritual-studies

HealthLink BC. (2020). *Autogenic training: Topic overview* [Blog]. Healthwise. https://www.healthlinkbc.ca/health-topics/ta7045spec

Illich, I. (2000). *De-schooling society.* Marion Boyars.

Linds, W. (1998). A journey in metaxis: Theatre of the oppressed as enactivist praxis. *NADIE Journal, 22*(2), 71–85.

Linds, W. (2001). *A journey in metaxis: Been, being, becoming, imag(in)ing drama facilitation.* [Unpublished doctoral dissertation]. University of British Columbia.

Maton, K. (2008). Habitus. In M. Grenfell (Ed.). *Pierre Bourdieu: Key concepts* (pp. 48–64). Acumen.

Okus, D. (2020). Eugenio Barba and extra-daily scenic behaviour: Influences of Stanislavski, Meyerhold, and Grotowski. *Journal of Theatre Criticism and Dramaturgy, 31*, 23–43.

Palmer, P. (1997). *The grace of great things: Reclaiming the sacred in knowing, teaching, and learning* [Keynote address]. Spirituality in Education Conference, Naropa Institute.

Schechner, R. (1994). *Environmental theater* (2nd ed.). Applause Theatre and Cinema Books.

Schechner, R. (2013). *Performance studies: An introduction* (3rd ed.). Routledge.

Sidebottom, D. (2018). *Distinguishing ritual from theatre: An update and expansion of Richard Schechner's efficacy/entertainment braid* [Unpublished master's thesis]. Queen's University.

Summers-Effler, E. (2006). Ritual theory. In J. E. Stets & J. H. Turner (Eds.), *Handbook of the sociology of emotions* (pp. 135–154). Springer.

Taylor, E. W., & Cranton, P. (2013). A theory in progress? Issues in transformative learning theory. *European Journal for Research on the Education and Learning of Adults, 4*(1), 33–47.

Taylor, E. W., & Tisdell, E. J. (2017). Patricia Cranton and transformative learning theory: An integrated perspective. *Adult Education Quarterly, 54*(4), 1–10.

Turner, V. (1982). *From ritual to theatre: The human seriousness of play.* PAJ.

Turner, V. (1996). *The ritual process: Structure and anti-structure.* Routledge.

Vaughan, L. (2018). *Mapping society: The spatial dimensions of social cartography.* Universal College London Press.

CHAPTER 10

Our Relationships with Water

How Student Lived Experience Helps Reorient Inquiry into Water Issues

Carmen Schlamb

> Subjective introspection is often viewed as complementary to—or a reversal of—objective, scientific methods. The apparent incompatibility of these approaches has produced a long-standing tradition of keeping them relatively independent of one another. Yet we know—irrespective of how firmly we seek to draw a dividing line—they are intimately intertwined.
>
> BORDEN (2014, p. XVII)

∵

Water, and its management, is undoubtedly one of the most important conversations taking place on the planet today. As a professor of environmental and sustainability studies, it is inevitable that water finds a prominent place in the curriculum I teach. What is also inevitable is the eventual storytelling that occurs among post-secondary students when exploring scientific data that speaks to water issues such as scarcity, pollution, and access. Filled with eye-witness accounts and first-hand experiences with water, these exchanges happen spontaneously amidst a delivery of biological, chemical, and physical data intended to represent an objective look at the critical issues facing global and local water.

Students' spontaneous injection of the subjective is why I stumble when someone asks if my courses are *science-* or *arts-based*. Environmental problems are notoriously complex and *sustainability*, as many have come to realise, is not an easy term to define as it lacks the neat boundaries of traditional disciplines we have come to rely upon when organizing and categorizing post-secondary course offerings. This dichotomous approach (science or art) to what is taught, and assumptions on how information will be learned, may also encourage a divisiveness of the self, in both teacher and learner, significantly limiting the inquiry space within which we explore the world.

© KONINKLIJKE BRILL NV, LEIDEN, 2022 | DOI:10.1163/9789004521186_010

Driving this structural and logistical divide further, is how we think about the ecological emergency facing the planet. Emergencies, by necessity, demand an abandonment of all superfluous priorities to attend to the critical nature of what it means to survive. This type of survival approach to sustainability and environmental studies usually places an emphasis on the value of hard data; it often also privileges the mantra *we're all in this together* where the focus on the individual journey of the learner is less important than the collective destination.

This concentration on a perceived end goal is often made at the expense of the student who might benefit from pedagogy that "extends beyond the specific agendas of 'environmentalism' and 'sustainability'" to adopt a more human ecological perspective that "[scratches] the surface of a far deeper reorientation" (Borden, 2014, p. 8). As an educator, a rethinking of how I approach human/environmental interactions in the curriculum, and how I support that approach (objective or subjective methods), could make a vastly important difference to the learner in my class who has life experience with water that may or may not be reflected in the course content. It is the juggling act that occurs here, between what is taught and what has been experienced, that I believe leads to deeper inquiry and potential reorientation regarding a subject originally thought of as purely objective.

This chapter highlights the outcomes of a research project dedicated to infusing storytelling in a post-secondary, online, science-based general education course in local and global water issues. Purposefully muddying the waters between science/art and qualitative/quantitative, the project adopted a human ecological approach to the curriculum (orienting away from a strictly scientific lens), and asked students to consider their lived experiences with water alongside scientific data. Utilizing narrative inquiry as both methodology and method by which students generated data, the project created an opportunity for students to post their thoughts, feelings, and attitudes associated with water experiences. How students connected water to their lived experiences and what those connections could mean in a reorientation of their study of water is explored here.

The Research Project: Student Perceptions and Reflections of Water-Related Issues

It is very common for professors to receive student work that either directly reflects the teaching of the curriculum (as is necessary in a specific skills-focused course), or indirectly reflects how we lecture our material within the course. As much as we try, it can be near impossible to convince a group of students that what they think matters and that, if they disagree with what we lecture, that we welcome that conversation. The perceived threat of losing grades for not mirroring the professor's point of view is very real for some students who are reluctant to risk a good grade for a chance to have an opinion heard. This worry can be particularly strong for students in a science-based course where it is often assumed that the data presented is inarguable.

With this concern in mind, the aim of the research project was to invite student participation in storytelling rather than require it, and to build a forum through which student perceptions and reflections of water-related issues were shared and understood as valuable data entries that only students could create. Details of the course that housed the project, the intent, and parameters of the project, and influences on the data are examined below.

The Course

The Blue Planet is a natural science, general education course offered to college students completing a 2-year diploma program. The online course delivers curriculum pertaining to local/global water resources and issues, and it covers themes such as aquatic species at risk, water scarcity, the water economy, and water conservation and innovation. A wide range of contemporary topics are explored in the course including the impact of climate change on water, water conflicts between nations, the bottled water industry, and utilizing recycled water where resources are scarce.

Students enrolled in the course come from all over the world including places of water abundance (e.g., North/ South America), water scarcity (Africa, Middle East), and water management challenges (e.g., South/ East Asia). Ranging in age from 18 years to late adulthood, students from a variety of programs (nursing, business, aviation, fire protection, fashion, and early childhood education, etc.) complete the course as part of their general education options. The diversity of students in this course provides a unique opportunity to share perspectives and vastly different lived experiences from around the globe and from many walks of life.

The Intent of the Project: Formalizing Anecdotal Data

I have taught *The Blue Planet* both in-person and online for the past four years. In this course, it was not unusual for either me or the students to spontaneously share a story in response to the curriculum being presented. Water, as a life-giving and life-taking entity, has a way of creating instant community. During these times of sharing, water became more than a subject of scientific interest to us; it took on the role of villain, saviour, teacher, and friend in the stories we told. Storytelling during the class became the conduit through which we began to better understand each other and the role water played in our lives. It was this consistent, informal engagement with storytelling that spurred the formation of this research project.

It is prudent for me to mention as a researcher in this work that I live and work narratively (Schlamb, 2021). I value storytelling for its generation of rich, descriptive data (Denzin & Lincoln, 2000) and see narrative inquiry as a way of understanding phenomena (Pinnegar & Daynes, 2006). I have often incorporated narrative inquiry methods into my teaching where I felt they fit well with the qualitative nature of a course. However, the question of why I did not automatically incorporate these methods in my predominantly science water course as well became of particular interest to me when I reflected on how powerful the sharing of stories had been in class. It was "thinking from within experiences" that led me to conceive of this project as a first step in what is a larger exploration about "deeply held ways of being" driven by a "critically informed curiosity" (Bolton, 2001/2010, p. 14).

This research project attempted to investigate formally what I have felt viscerally for years teaching this course—that the act of sharing lived experiences helps place students at the centre of environmental/sustainability learning and expands their capacity not only for broader inquiry that is both contextual and relevant, but also for reorientation of a deeper kind.

The Project Parameters

The Blue Planet is comprised of online learning modules dedicated to delivering provocative data concerning water quality, quantity, and management. In addition to these modules, the research project embedded a weekly invitation to students to access an online space called the *Reflective Forum* and to contribute a post. Each week, the *Reflective Forum* would contain a new probing question in connection with the topic of the module. Questions such as: *what is your relationship with water*; *do you know the water near you*; and *have you ever experienced a water shortage* were just a few threads explored by students in the forum. *Reflective Forum* posts had only three criteria: (a) that the post be "research-free" and without citation in an attempt to identify the student's baseline thinking on the topic; (b) that the post be a first-person narrative using an *I* instead of a *we* statement that is so common in environmental writings; and (c) that the post answer the probing question presented.

Influences on the Data

Student narrative posts from the *Reflective Forum* comprise the data for this research project. The project was conducted over the 2021 spring semester, and participants were students who consented to be a part of this anonymous study. The number of participants in the study fluctuated week to week depending on student interest in answering the probing question posted for the module. A maximum of 30 and a minimum of 22 students participated in the study at any one time within a single week.

The data had some influences worth noting. While posting to the forum was an optional exercise and not worth formal grades, students did receive bonus points in the course for contributing to the learning community (posting anonymously was an option). The probing questions I posted in the forum were provided with some context as to their meaning and intent, so students had guidance in what was being explored. Otherwise, the narrative exercise was left open without word counts or other requirements beyond the three criteria already mentioned for acceptable posts. As faculty, I declared the forum to be a safe space, where all posts would be accepted as long as they met with college student conduct guidelines. I also posted my own responses to the questions in the early stages of the forum to model the kind of *vulnerable* inquiry that encourages the richest kind of sharing (Brown, 2012).

In the *Reflective Forum*, students posted about their perceptions, reflections, and attitudes, regarding water and its management. These posts were collected and examined with two considerations in mind: (a) How were students connecting water to their lived experiences? and (b) Were students allocating meaning to those connections? In the analysis of the data, meaning was assigned when a student demonstrated an ability to inquire inward about the self, outward towards society, backward to include history, or forward to project on the future (Clandinin & Connelly, 2000). The ability to extend inquiry beyond the course curriculum, and to make that inquiry meaningful and relevant, is the foundation upon which a reorientation can occur regarding how we approach complex topics like water.

Taking a Step Back: Why a Human Ecological Approach and Why Narrative Inquiry?

There have been many successful attempts at blurring the lines between science and art in the classroom. Creative educators have displayed imaginative ways of teaching course content such as using music in astronomy, art in math, and baking in chemistry. As a writer, I am drawn to narratives, particularly stories of human/environment interactions that I believe become landmarks on our individual identity landscapes and influence the way we receive, interpret, and utilize environmental information (Schlamb, 2017). It is because of my past work that I chose to pursue this research using narrative inquiry and a human ecological approach.

A Human Ecological Approach

Human ecology is the study of humans and their interactions with their environment—how they live within it, use it, celebrate it, revere it, fear it, and love it. Because the scope of human/environmental interactions is "nearly boundless" (Borden, 2014, p. 113), a human ecological approach to inquiry is helpful when considering complex environmental issues like water. A human ecological perspective is all at once inclusive and all-encompassing because the ways in which we interact with the environment break the boundaries of traditional academic disciplines and demand "a multiplicity of perspectives in search of connections among otherwise segregated ways of knowing" (Borden, 2014, p. 113). The transdisciplinary nature of the approach provides the important "reorientation" (Borden, 2014, p. 8) we require today, when our current ways of being and doing have failed the planet and we are in desperate need of "the know-how of non-specialists," the important "creative contributions of open collaboration," and the most critical ingredient, the "role of imagination" (Borden, 2014, p. 147). This approach values the lived experience of students as curriculum itself (Dewey, 1938), and places the student at the centre of learning where they become "each other's teachers" and "counsel" (Borden, 2014, p. 155) generating "a self-designed curriculum and a well-developed sense of purpose" (Collins, 2014, p. xv).

Narrative Inquiry

I believe all people are natural storytellers; they only require an interested audience with which to explore this skill. In addition, I believe stories never come as originals; rather, they are manifestations of often unconscious alternate ways of knowing of the past (Abram, 1996; Butala, 1994/2004; Davis, 2011) that surface in the present day to bring attention once again to a "storied earth" (Abram, 1996, p. 154) and the way of "many-eyed seeing" (Kelly, 2012, p. 154).

Narrative inquiry is storytelling presented as "a distinct form of discourse" with the intent to concretize and sort lived experience as a way of granting and understanding meaning (Chase, 2011, p. 421). In this way, new knowledge is constructed by the student rather than taught by the teacher, and educators become the providers of opportunity for engagement rather than providers of lessons (Ültanir, 2012). When students share lived experiences with others in class, the "learning and understanding [that comes] through dialogue and reflection" (Doll, 1993, p. 156) creates the opportunity for self-organization where an individual becomes unique in their ability to negotiate information coming from themselves, others, and the curriculum of the course.

How Students Connected with Water and What Those Connections Might Mean

Student posts in the *Reflective Forum* revealed a number of ways students were connecting water to their own lived experiences. The summary presented here is not intended to be exhaustive of what was shared in the forum; rather, it is intended to highlight the extraordinary ability of students to think beyond water as a mere resource for survival, and to inquire deeply about its importance when provided with the opportunity to share in class.

David Orr (1991) calls upon educators to challenge the "foundations of modern education…enshrined in myths we have come to accept without question" (p. 2). By presenting an open forum in an otherwise positivist curriculum, I am hoping to do just that and respond to the question "What is education for?" (Orr, 1991, p. 1). When left to their own devices, students produced far more connections to water through personal inquiry than I could have lectured about in class. They also revealed a surprising depth in such a short inquiry time, a sign of "meaning-making" (Ültanir, 2012, p. 1308) and self-organization that comes from "the shaping and ordering of experience" (Chase, 2011, p. 421).

The following student writings regarding connections with water highlight what Orr (1991) celebrates as a new pedagogy based in direct experience, responsibility to others, the value of examples, and a greater emphasis on the way we learn. These threads are valuable in their support of greater inquiry into environmental and sustainability learning and the possibility of reorientation when it comes to considering environmental problems.

Connecting Water to Building Relationships

> Since the stream was…close to my school, my *friends* and I would often eat right beside it…during our lunch break. The…stream was one of the things that allowed my friends and I to build strong relationships…

> Whenever I see any water body, it reminds me of precious times when me and my *mother* went for a walk on the side of the river.

> When I was a kid my *father* always brought me to the beach. He taught me how to swim. It's our bonding time. Now that I have kids I want them to learn how to swim too.…I taught them how to swim like…my father taught me.

> I liked fishing with my *grandfather* when I was little. There was one time, my grandfather hunted a huge red lobster…he found there were tons of

> lobster eggs on the back of the tail. He explained to me, this lobster was going to have babies, we should let [her] go and give…birth. And next year, we could hunt her babies.

In these posts, students inquire backward to the past and forward to the future to connect water with building important relationships. Rooted in these lived experiences is the act of learning, wonder, and belonging, driven by contact with water. The realization of the importance of human/water relationships on human/human relationships provides students with a foundation to consider the ways in which environmental information is shared, the importance of acts of sustainability, and how water management decisions deeply affect communities.

Connecting Water to Well-being

> Whenever I am stressful or nervous, I go there and feel *calmness* by looking at the blue and calm water.

> One of the thing[s] which I liked the most is, there are no motors allowed in the…River making this place very calm and peaceful. That is why, in my opinion, this is the best place to do…*introspection*.

> I used to walk to the water in my tumultuous teen years and sit at the water's edge. The site, feel and smell of the lapping water always *calmed* my active mind and nerves. With technology now it's perhaps easy to take these moments by the water for granted, but I never lived far from the water since.

These postings demonstrate inward inquiry to the self and backward inquiry to the past. There is no question that student life these days is stressful, and posts containing feelings of support and reprieve in connection with water were common. Student writings connected water to the importance of mental health, the need for quiet places, and the ability of water to help heal.

Connecting Water to Self-Discovery

> There is a small pond across the road from where I live. Despite walking by the sign for years, *I've never checked* to see what its name is…

> When I was younger, I always thought that water was a basic resource to find…I simply *assumed* that everyone had access to water.

> I have *never really thought* about my relationship with water, it is just something I have taken [for]granted. I realize the true importance of water when it is not available.

> ...when we moved back to India after having lived in Europe...As a teenager that was a *big adjustment* for me...Soon I learned to bathe using just one bucket of water, which included washing my hair...I remember being so proud and boasting to my parents about it.

These student posts inquire inward to the self, outward to society, backward to the past, and forward to the future in this connection. Self-discovery can be profound for the learner and when assisted by narrative inquiry, which is experiential by nature (Clandinin & Connelly, 2000), it can help reorient a student to see previously hidden things like privilege, resiliency, and obliviousness (all critical explorations for a sustainable future).

Connecting Water to Loss

> When I visited the river I grew up with I was *shocked* by the change...My grandfather told me the river is getting smaller and smaller in the last ten years.

> People in my home nation of India...have recently been affected by floods...They witnessed truly appalling situations. All of their homes, fields, and livestock were *washed away* in the flood.

> Now I really feel a sense of *crisis*.

> The seasons in my country have become more severe and *unpredictable*.

These posts are short, but they say a lot. They inquire inward to the self, outward to others, and backward to the past. They speak of changing times, and of uncertainty, with a general sense that the earth is shifting, and things are out of sync. This connection to loss is likely one of the most influential drivers when considering the need for reorientation in environmental learning.

Conclusion

In one of the forums this semester, a student wrote "the river raised my family." The short phrase stopped me cold and caused me to reflect on all the ways the river that backed onto my childhood home had also raised me. With those words, I could see that as two individuals we shared one understanding of water. Others in the class also shared moments like this, and I witnessed the power of narrative inquiry to move students beyond the curriculum into a space of reorientation that not only allows, but encourages, students to author their own curriculum with their lived experiences as valid data.

It is our job as educators to create the environment within which this reorientation is possible. If I had not run the *Reflective Forum* this semester, I am certain that students would leave the course with knowledge of water quantity and quality issues, climate change impacts on earth's water resources, and water as a sold commodity. But I am not so certain that they would leave the course knowing themselves better and where they fit into the water conversation.

Upon completion of the course, I surveyed the students to determine if they felt that the narrative exercise had been time well spent. From the responses, 88% of students strongly agreed that the *Reflective Forum* helped them better understand water issues and 84% of students strongly agreed that classmate posts in the forum surprised them, granting them better understanding of how their peers thought.

Science needs stories. The sharing of individual stories contributes to a greater, collective narrative that reorients not only the learner but the learning community as a whole and lays out a path forward that is not divided between what we learn and how we feel, but rather is widened to create room where all forms of knowing and learning are honoured. As educators, we just have to create space for that exploration.

References

Abram, D. (1996). *The spell of the sensuous*. Random House.

Bolton, G. (2010). *Reflective practice: Writing and professional development* (3rd ed.). Sage. (Original work published 2001)

Borden, R. J. (2014). *Ecology and experience: Reflections from a human ecological perspective*. North Atlantic Books.

Butala, S. (2004). *The perfection of the morning*. HarperCollins. (Original work published 1994)

Brown, B. (2012). *The power of vulnerability: Teachings on authenticity, connection, and courage*. Sounds True.

Chase, S. E. (2011). Narrative inquiry: Still a field in the making. In N. K. Denzin & Y. S. Lincoln (Eds.), *The Sage handbook of qualitative research* (pp. 421–434). Sage.

Clandinin, D. J., & Connelly, F. M. (2000). *Narrative inquiry*. Jossey-Bass.

Collins, D. (2014). Foreword. In R. J. Borden, *Ecology and experience: Reflections from a human ecological perspective* (pp. xiii–xvi). North Atlantic Books.

Davis, W. (2011). *The wayfinders: Why ancient wisdom matters in the modern world* (CBC Massey Lecture). Anansi Press.

Denzin, N., & Lincoln, Y. (Eds.). (2000). *Handbook of qualitative research* (2nd ed.). Sage.

Dewey, J. (1938). *Experience and education*. Macmillan.

Doll, W. (1993). Changing paradigms. In W. Doll (Ed.), *A post-modern perspective on curriculum* (pp. 1–17). Teachers College Press.

Kelly, V. (2012). A Métis manifesto. In C. Chambers, E. Hasebe-Ludt, C. Leggo, & A. Sinner (Eds.), *A heart of wisdom: Life writing as empathetic inquiry* (pp. 363–368). Peter Lang.

Orr, D. (1991). *What is education for?* The Learning Revolution (IC#27). http://www.context.org/iclib/ic27/orr/

Pinnegar, S., & Daynes, J. G. (2006). Locating narrative inquiry historically: Thematics in the turn to narrative. In D. J. Clandinin (Ed.), *Handbook of narrative inquiry: Mapping a methodology* (pp. 3–34). Sage.

Schlamb, C. (2021). When curriculum disrupts: A case for gratitude after decades of being surprised. In C. Shields, A. Podolski, & J. J. Guiney Yallop (Eds.), *Influences and inspirations in curriculum studies research and teaching: Reflections on the origins and legacy of Canadian scholarship* (pp. 45–51). Routledge.

Schlamb, C. (2017). On the practice of narrative landmarking: Navigating an ecological identity through self-study. In E. Lyle (Ed.), *At the intersection of selves and subject: Exploring the curricular landscape of identity* (pp. 41–52). Sense.

Ültanir, E. (2012). An epistemological glance at the constructivist approach: Constructivist learning in Dewey, Piaget, and Montessori. *International Journal of Instruction*, *5*(2), 195–212.

CHAPTER 11

The Art of Rebraiding

Re/centring Self to Humanize Praxis

Jennifer Blue and Ellyn Lyle

Unravelling

Our lived experiences shape our understandings, yet education systems too often abstract self from subject and, in so doing, marginalize the self in teaching and learning contexts. As both a learner and an adult educator, I have experienced this abstraction and felt the effects of dehumanizing pedagogies. Working in health sciences where care for human life is central, I feel conflicted in spaces that prioritize the scientific over the human. This is a new revelation for me as, prior to entering graduate school, I tended to dwell in and privilege these same scientific ways of knowing and being.

Once I began my advanced studies, though, something in me stirred. As I learned about re/centring lived experience, I began to wonder what was missing from my practice in relegating the personal to the periphery. I came to understand how the self and subject necessarily intersect. Re/integrating these marginalized parts of myself helped me to feel more whole (Yoo, 2019). From within this emerging wholeness, I recognized the toll taken by fragmented and dehumanized approaches to learning, leading, living, and being.

tied (to old ways)
i am coming undone even as i am bound
once held together so tightly—so safely
i am slowly unravelling
only frayed ends in sight
i grab for old ways (of knowing)
welcoming the tug of the strings.

the dark dance begins again
here, in the shadows,
hidden from myself
unable to see the light

Bound (Photograph by Jenn Blue, used with permission)

© KONINKLIJKE BRILL NV, LEIDEN, 2022 | DOI:10.1163/9789004521186_011

Despite the heartbreakingly common marginalization of self, “our humanness is integral to teaching and learning” (Lyle, 2017, p. 121). The act of bringing myself and my experience into my practice is proving to be (en)lightening and renewing. As a mid-career woman responsible for the leadership, oversight, and efficacy of a multihospital healthcare team as well as an Infection Prevention and Control program, I am responsible for both clinical instruction and epidemiological issues. Working to emerge from a physically, mentally, and emotionally challenging pandemic, I find myself feeling unraveled and frayed. Desperate to uncover a path back to (my)self, I also wonder how I can positively impact the lives of others suffering similarly within my professional context. Increasingly, as I lead my team in patient education through a global health crisis, I am coming to understand the centrality of engaging the whole human as we work to foster wellness. This shift has led me to explore the potential of re/centring lived experience as a way to humanize praxis.

all eyes on me—
ears hanging on my every word
but i cannot speak

my head is screaming from lack of sleep
desperate to quit
to run away and never look back
to save myself

no end in sight

Statues (Photograph by Jenn Blue, used with permission)

Rebraiding

I have experienced profound resonance in the practice of re/centring lived experience in education—in understanding the impact of the abstraction of self and exploring pathways to reintegration. Motivated and inspired, I aim to make apparent the importance of including lived experience in clinical education contexts and explore how opening up critical dialogue with each other supports humanized praxis. In engaging with an inquiry such as this, I turn to post qualitative inquiry and rely on photopoesis as method.

Post-Qualitative Inquiry

As I sort through my frayed ends looking for threads to rebraid, I am drawn to Elizabeth St. Pierre’s (2018, 2019) scholarship on the living theory of post-qualitative inquiry (PQI). Instead of posing a traditional research question and applying predetermined research methodologies, PQI invites me to engage in an encounter with an emerging curiosity (St. Pierre, 2018, 2019). In living the theories, I learn to trust myself and "do the next thing, whatever it is—to experiment—and keep moving" (St. Pierre, 2018, p. 605). I take up PQI to open my mind to new ways of thinking that might help me to understand different ways of existing within the world (St. Pierre, 2018). Elizabeth St. Pierre (2018) challenges me to attend to the surprises that come up along the way and to "follow the provocations that come from everywhere in the inquiry that is living and writing" (p. 603).

As I engage with the *unpredictability of always becoming*, I resist methodological bracketing in favour of attending to the profoundly personal aspects of being present in my practice (St. Pierre, 2018). I seek the freedom to make meaning from the process of writing so that discovery and creativity can occur. Drawing on Elizabeth St. Pierre's (2019) reassurance that writing is a means of inquiry, I find resonance in Graham Badley's (2019, 2020a, 2020b) work on post-academic writing. He says that academic writers too often produce material that is difficult to relate to and devoid of authenticity (Badley, 2019). Through post-academic writing, I can relate more meaningfully as I examine lived experience through *organic writing* that resonates (Badley, 2019, 2020b).

As I begin to write, I re/centre myself in the discussion and the subject. This humanizing practice gives me confidence to resist ways of knowing that historically favour predictable processes and de/humanizing approaches. This allows me to take a more creative approach to writing that is personally meaningful and authentic (Yoo, 2019). As I engage in this practice, I realize that organic writing calls on me to navigate "intense situations and effects that linger" (Yoo, 2019, p. 355). This becomes especially apparent to me as I work to examine my unraveling and begin the work of rebraiding.

fingers shaking

belly full of butterflies

not enough—never enough

deep breath—steady heart

release the butterflies

freedom

Vulnerability (Photograph by Ellyn Lyle, used with permission)

In re/centring myself, I feel something shift—a sigh—a letting go or relinquishing of practices that distrust the humanness that ought to be so fundamental in health care settings. In this shift, I begin to understand the significance of integrated ways of being and consider how I might re/humanize professional contexts so that others may also benefit.

take all the mistakes,
missteps,
misunderstandings,
miscommunications
lies.
set them on fire
watch them burn
rise up from the ashes
the embodiment of fierce grace

Phoenix (Photograph by Ellyn Lyle, used with permission)

Photopoesis

Photopoesis "opens up the space for the visceral imagination, and in this place wonder is born" (Wiebe & Snowber, 2011, p. 102). Poetry and other arts-based forms have long been used as means of inquiry and understanding because engaging with these practices involves bringing us "closer to the finely nuanced textures of our experience" (Wiebe & Snowber, 2011, p. 103). Sean Wiebe and Celeste Snowber remind me that poetry, in particular, is well suited to our storied lives as it allows us to reveal insights into our understandings; it also leaves behind a trace of felt experience with which we can connect. Through photopoesis, I find an opportunity to create new self-understanding (MacKenzie, 2012).

Photopoesis offers a way of attending to both my wonder and my praxis, offering space for learning things that otherwise may not make sense to me

the struggle to outrun
a ridiculous attempt
to sound
to look
to feel

competent in chaos

my mind screams,
you don't know how to do this

my heart begs me not to listen

Into the Unknown (Photograph by Jenn Blue, used with permission)

(Lyle & Snowber, 2021). It cultivates a living space of visual and textual literacy that leads to transformational understanding (MacKenzie & Wolf, 2012; Yoo, 2019). When I explore my lived experience this way, I access deeper insight about how I might humanize praxis.

Re/humanizing Praxis

When I initially encountered the notion of *praxis*, I found it elusive. It wasn't until I was introduced to the scholarship of Paulo Freire that it began to come together. In 2005, he wrote that "there *is* no true word that *is* not at the same time *a praxis"* (p. 68). He defined praxis as "reflection and action upon the world in order to transform it" (p. 51). The need to braid together reflection and action is important as it has an overarching goal of achieving transformation (Freire, 2005). Investigating my own experience with praxis, I realized that my understanding was more closely aligned with Eastern philosophies. Having trained in and taught martial arts since I was young, I spent most of my days in a dojo studying traditions tightly bound to principles of respect. Masking emotion, fighting through pain, and demonstrating physical and mental discipline were foundational expectations. Each day I would militantly lead groups using a mantra that bound us together. Until I was in my mid-twenties, these beliefs lived within me uninterrogated and formed the foundation of an unexamined praxis.

although the word master
makes the hair on the back of my neck stand on end
you were exactly what i needed
your ways became the stronghold of my life
like a dog-eared page from a favourite book
welcoming my return—
reliable traditions and trusted discipline
nose flattened across my face
taste of metal filling my mouth
target sharply in my sights
flying feet and striking fists
i would have followed you anywhere...

Meditative me (Photograph by Jenn Blue, used with permission)

I have come to understand praxis as the intersection of theory and practice with the aim of creating change (Freire, 2005; Lyle, 2017). Said another way, praxis is *practicing theory* and *theorizing practice* (Lyle, 2017). As I engage with this process, I work to develop critical consciousness that will help me support others who look to me for guidance in this arena. Praxis, as I have come to learn, is only possible through deep knowledge of self and self-in-relation, both of which I access through photopoetry.

two truths and a lie—

a childhood game i used to play

to centre others
to obscure myself

fearing rejection
living to please

seen and not heard

not even really seen

Mirror, Mirror on the Wall (Photograph by Jenn Blue, used with permission)

My work in health care has led me to look for re/humanizing possibilities as I have witnessed their implications for well-being. As I wonder about the capacity of centring lives and lived experience to humanize praxis, themes emerged regarding vulnerability, reflexivity, attunement, and resilience.

Vulnerability

Vulnerability is a struggle for me. My reluctance to live vulnerably has defined my life because I fear judgement by others. My personal work in learning to embrace vulnerability, although difficult, continues to be exceptionally rewarding as it allows me to explore what I hold onto in a way that I can untangle issues and address them. Photopoesis helps me to be vulnerable in a way that I haven't been before. Brené Brown (2013) reminds me that, although vulnerability and emotional exposure feel risky, they also hold potential for greatness. Leveraging a creative process to embrace vulnerability has provided me with an opportunity for personal exploration within an intentional and creative process. Through this practice, I am learning that vulnerability is integral to teaching, living, and being. This realization continues to inform me as I work to cultivate spaces for humanized praxis.

bottled up
squeezed back in the fetal position—
preconsciousness—

too tight to breathe
filling what space there is with lies
created to appease others
designed to assure myself
here
no one hears the noise i make
to cover up the truth

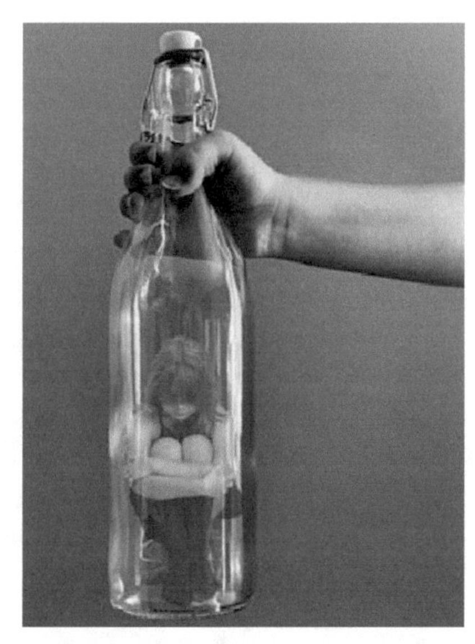

Bottled up (Photograph by Jenn Blue, used with permission)

Reflexivity

We can only make sense of our experiences by storying them somehow (Lyle, 2017). How the storying occurs is not where the importance lies; rather, the significance is found in the reflexive awareness of the storying process (Abbott, 2008). Photopoesis allows me to be reflexive as I story my experience. It helps me to develop praxis in creative and imaginative ways by encouraging me to engage in critical introspection in the moment as well as after it (Lyle, 2017). As I create images and partner them with words that, together, engage critical consciousness, I reflect on the experience in a way that allows me to be critical data within the research process (Lyle & Caissie, 2021).

Attunement

I have continuously found myself in systems that encourage compartmentalization, and I have found that this separation of self from my educational and professional contexts has contributed to an overarching sense of fragmentation. As I seek to humanize praxis in a way that creates opportunities for wholeness, I reconnect with (my)self in a meaningful way that encourages insights that extend to those in my professional contexts. I think of this emerging intimacy of awareness as *attunement* (Lyle & Snowber, 2021). This way of being speaks to me as it works with my subconscious to unlock things deeply held. The more I engage in this type of inquiry, the more I feel able to re/humanize praxis.

the light breaks
encouraging the suspended state of
winter
to let go
to give way to possibilities of rebirth

new growth reaching through the ice
for the warmth awaiting
in possibility

Refracted possibility (Photograph by Ellyn Lyle, used with permission)

Resilience

Resilience reflects how well we pick ourselves up, dust ourselves off, and return to lives lived fully after suffering a setback. Photopoesis has become one such means of resilience for me as it allows me to study challenges from different angles and perspectives.

the vast space that holds old ways of being
sheltering the shit and shame that surrounds me
covering my mouth
compelling me not to speak
creating a self-imposed paralysis of ruminating thoughts

Silenced (Photograph by Jenn Blue, used with permission)

Engaging photopoesis helps me to investigate tribulations in a new way as I problematize meanings that I have historically attached to them. It exposes ways that I am complicit in my own imprisonment so that I might identify more helpful and healthy ways of being. In centring myself equally in both problems and solutions, I create agency and am better able to imagine ways to humanize praxis.

inner voice needing to shift
from it to me
from blindness to see
to release this burden
and acknowledge the lightness underneath
and give it space to take flight

Resilience (Photograph by Jenn Blue, used with permission)

Significance of Research

Teaching and learning are human endeavours that require us to move beyond process efficiency toward a place that values individual and collective humanity. Parker Palmer (1997, 1998, 2004, 2017) has said repeatedly that that there is no room for education systems that abstract self from subject—that in doing so, we deny humanity and perpetuate a hegemonic culture of disconnection and fear. Purposefully including lived experience in praxis creates capacity for connectedness (Palmer, 1997, 2017). The experience of engaging this type of inquiry has opened me to a more human way of learning and teaching, and it compels me to consider leveraging this learning to cultivate re/humanizing spaces for those who look to me for direction.

like a door opening to fresh air
after a hundred years of suffocation,
tiny tendrils reach toward the light
yearning for more
reaching for renewal

Expansiveness (Photograph by Ellyn Lyle, used with permission)

In/Conclusion

Joanne Yoo (2019) tells me that "the threat of ending can spark new beginnings" (p. 354). As I situate myself within the unbracketed space of PQI and engage organic writing in the form of photopoesis, I recognize the frayed and threadbare elements of a self too long relegated to the periphery. Re/centring self continues to open me to possibilities for fostering more robust personal wellness, and it has led me to examine what I might cultivate for others if I were to incorporate re/humanizing pedagogies into my own praxis. As a leader of a team of healthcare professionals, I am responsible for maintaining a level of resilience in both myself and my team. Having found restorative spaces in re/centring self, I eagerly return to the field where I will work to integrate this humanness within (my)self even as I encourage it in others. This writing, then, has become the experiment—the adventure (St. Pierre, 2018). My hope is that, in sharing my experience, I am offering space for others to live and work in more humanized ways.

the trees part
their protective canopy gives way
to luminescence
i am drawn to this light
my eyes close
as i raise my face to the sun
feeling its warmth deep inside me
I see this for what it is
both the end and the beginning

Lighting the way (Photograph by Ellyn Lyle, used with permission)

References

Abbott, H. P. (2008). *Cambridge introduction to narrative*. Cambridge University Press.

Badley, G. F. (2019). Post-academic writing: Human writing for human readers. *Qualitative Inquiry, 25*(2), 180–191. https://doi.org/10.1177/1077800417736334

Badley, G. F. (2020a). Why and how academics write. *Qualitative Inquiry, 26*(3–4), 247–256. https://doi.org/10.1177/1077800418810722

Badley, G. F. (2020b). We must write dangerously. *Qualitative Inquiry*, 1–7. https://doi.org/10.1177/1077800420933306

Brown, B. (2013). *Daring greatly: How the courage to be vulnerable transforms the way we live, love, parent and lead.* Portfolio Penguin.

Davidson, S. (2018). Responding aesthetically: Using artistic expression and dialogical reflection to transform adversity. In E. Lyle (Ed.), *The negotiated self: Employing reflexive inquiry to explore teacher identity* (pp. 86–102). Sense.

Freire, P. (1972) *Pedagogy of the oppressed.* Penguin.

Freire, P. (2005). Education for critical consciousness. In *Education and Conscientizaco* (pp. 37–51). Continuum. (Original work published in 1974) http://abahlali.org/wp-content/uploads/2012/08/Paulo-Freire-Education-for-Critical-Consciousness-Continuum-Impacts-2005.pdf

Furman, G., (2012) Social justice leadership as praxis: Developing capacities through preparation programs. *Educational Administration Quarterly, 48*(2), 191–229.

Lyle, E. (2017). *Of books, barns, and boardrooms: Exploring praxis through reflexive inquiry.* Sense.

Lyle, E. (2018). Untangling sel(f)ves through a/r/tography. In E. Lyle (Ed.), *The negotiated self: Employing reflexive inquiry to explore teacher identity* (pp. 1–11). Sense.

Lyle, E. (2020). Unprivileging dividedness: In favour of undivided ways of knowing. *Advances in Research on Teaching, 34*, 119–128. https://doi.org/10.1108/S1479-368720200000034007

Lyle, E., & Caissie, C. (2021). Re/humanising education: Teaching and learning as co-constructed reflexive praxis. *LEARNing Landscapes, 14*, 219–230.

Lyle, E., & Snowber, C. (2021). Walking as attunement: Being with/in nature as currere. *Journal of the Canadian Association for Curriculum Studies, 18*(2), 6–20.

MacKenzie, S. (2019). (Re)acquaintance with praxis: A poetic inquiry into shame, sobriety, and the case for a curriculum of authenticity. *Journal of Curriculum Theorizing, 34*(2), 72–89. https://journal.jctonline.org/index.php/jct/article/view/mackenziedawson.pdf

MacKenzie, S. K., & Wolf, M. M. (2012). Layering sel(f)ves: Finding acceptance, community and praxis through collage. *Qualitative Report, 17*.

McGarry, K. (2019). Reflexivity as a process for coming into knowing. *LEARNing Landscapes, 12*(1), 155–170. https://www.learninglandscapes.ca/index.php/learnland/article/view/985

Palmer, P. (1997). The heart of a teacher: Identity and integrity in teaching. *Change, 29*(6), 14–21.

Palmer, P. (1998). *The courage to teach.* Jossey-Bass.

Palmer, P. (2004). *A hidden wholeness: The journey toward an undivided life.* Jossey-Bass.

Palmer, P. (2017). *The courage to teach.* Jossey-Bass.

Richardson, L. (1997). *Fields of play: Constructing an academic life.* Rutgers University Press.

St. Pierre, E. A. (2018). Writing post qualitative inquiry. *Qualitative Inquiry, 24*(9), 603–608. https://doi.org/10.1177/1077800417734567

St. Pierre, E. A. (2019). Post qualitative inquiry in an ontology of immanence. *Qualitative Inquiry, 25*(1), 3–16. https://doi.org/10.1177/1077800418772634

Wiebe, S. (2015). Poetic inquiry: A fierce, tender, and mischievous relationship with lived experience. *Language and Literacy, 17*(3), 152–163.

Wiebe, S., & Snowber, C. (2011). The visceral imagination: A fertile space for non-textual knowing. *JCT (Online), 27*(2), 101–113.

Yoo, J. (2019). A year of writing 'dangerously': A narrative of hope. *New Writing, 16*(3), 353–362. https://doi.org.10.1080/14790726.2018.1520893

CHAPTER 12

Centring the Lives and Lived Experiences of Girls of Colour in Mathematics

Mahtab Nazemi

Changing Mathematics Instead of Changing Our Selves

Mathematics has been most accessible to students who are from historically privileged groups, such as those who identify as White men (Battey & Leyva, 2016). Equity-seeking students, in this case, at the intersection of gender and race, are often expected to leave parts of themselves and their experiences at the classroom door to engage with and succeed in mathematics learning that is not in line with their lives and identities (Varelas et al., 2013). This segmenting of identity and experience does not work, since who we are has everything to do with how we learn as students and how we teach as teachers.

Equity is often a stated goal in school mathematics yet, outside of providing vague statements such as having high expectations for students, sharing resources equitably, and accommodating differences, there has been little inquiry into exactly *how* to support all students to participate substantially in mathematics. As racialized girls and women, learning mathematics must provide us with opportunities where we are allowed and encouraged to draw upon our own personal and cultural ways of knowing. Gutiérrez (2012) calls this *re-humanizing mathematics*, where students' identities are affirmed in the context of learning critical and equitable mathematics. Centring the voices and experiences of girls of colour who are learning mathematics attends to a multitude of identities: students' gendered and racialized identities and students' academic identities, both as doers of mathematics and within the context of learning mathematics. In looking at identities in this way, we find evidence through students' narratives that supports students' ongoing negotiation of their identities—racially and mathematically—as they participate in learning mathematics (Nazemi, 2018; Varelas et al., 2013). Simply put, as equity-seeking educators, we want to shift from trying to keep mathematics the way it is and fit students into it, toward changing mathematics so that it centres students' lives. Equitable and humane mathematics teaching needs to be responsive to students and their cultures, as well as affirming to students' identities both academically and socially.

© KONINKLIJKE BRILL NV, LEIDEN, 2022 | DOI:10.1163/9789004521186_012

An important aspect to affirming students' identities and rehumanizing mathematics is putting students and their sense of selves back at the centre of learning. In fact, exploring experiences amongst students of colour in mathematics can "reveal how and why some students maintain positive mathematics identities despite external constructions of their abilities" (Martin, 2012, p. 53). Martin (2012) suggests that paying attention to historically underserved groups of students proves to have more merit than attempting to attend to *all* students. To date, much important mathematics education research centring students on the basis of their racial and gendered identities has to do with African American boy students. In this chapter, I hope to look to students who identify as girls and across different *of-colour* identities, a standpoint that is unique and under-represented in mathematics education research. To do this, I look at the identity-affirming classroom of an experienced, race conscious, White middle-class, ciswoman mathematics teacher, from the perspective of her girls of colour students. In adopting a sociocultural lens towards learning and identity, and in centring race and the process of racialization through critical race theory, students are re/centred through interviews. Through these counter-narratives, we learn what constitutes mathematics teaching that re-centres, rehumanizes, and re-affirms these students' lived experiences and their multitude of identities—social and academic. Specifically, we explore the advice that these girls of colour have for (white women) teachers on how to relate to students and teach to their identities and needs.

The Context of Mathematics Learning

As an Iranian woman who graduated as a mathematics major who now researches the experiences of historically under-represented peoples in education and educational institutions, I bring a particular understanding of my positionality to the collection and interpretation of this data. My subjectivity encourages me to develop nuances and complex understandings of mathematics, mathematics learning, and educational institutions more broadly, as socially exclusionary spaces, experiences, and processes. My woman of colour identity allows me to partially relate to some of the feelings raised by these girls of colour participants. Specifically, I understand worrying about assumptions and judgements made about me and how I learn and what my capabilities are based solely on the colour of my skin and other markers of identity such as (in my case) my name. Additionally, having the sense that to succeed academically in mathematics, white ways of learning and knowing are privileged and centred, such that sometimes without realizing it I am participating in futile attempts of performing whiteness as best and closely as possible, and engaging in colour-blind and meritocratic ontological assumptions. A shared experience as women and girls of colour participating in AP mathematics allowed an intersubjective stance that helped me build positive rapport with all my participants. At the same time because of my experience as a mathematics instructional coach, I approached the school, classroom, and participants with a strong familiarity of their learning environment and an ongoing visibility to student participants during teacher candidate observations and debriefs with teacher candidates and mentor teachers. This allowed me to use "my multiple identities as an interaction quality" (Berry, 2008, p. 472), which helped my connection with student participants and the classroom teacher so that they felt they could share and reflect on their experiences.

For this chapter, I am drawing from a six-month study that explored how six girls of colour (Carlin, Gena, Jane, Leilani, Lia, and Mya) navigated and negotiated their identities while learning mathematics within an AP Statistics classroom, with a race-conscious White woman teacher who employs equity-driven forms of instruction. The overarching goals of the study were to understand how these girls of colour felt their racial identities played a role in their learning mathematics, how they viewed themselves in relation to other students in their classroom, what sort of racialized narratives persisted in spite of the equitable forms of instruction taking place, and how these racialized narratives reflected or ran counter to dominant neoliberal ideologies.

I employed qualitative interview study methodology and drew upon standpoint theory and critical race theory (CRT) along with sociocultural theories of learning and identity, to ensure that I was centring the stories of these girls of colour to understand their experiences in their own words. The major data sources for this study included eight hours of interview data, with focal girls of colour and their classroom teacher, and field notes based on 23 hours of classroom observations. Students were asked about their racial and ethnic identities and responded with various racial self-identifications. They identified as "*South Asian, Cambodian*" (Jane) and "*African American*" (Leilani), or "*Mixed*" (Lia), "*Mixed Race*" (Mya), and "*Multiracial*" (Carlin). Gena's self-identification stood out in that, while she identified as Filipino, she first listed all the ways in which she did not identify yet was assumed to by others (Nazemi, 2020). Because of the sensitive nature of asking people about their racial identity, I accepted the language that students provided and respectfully probed for further clarification when given the opportunity. For example, Lia identified as "*Mixed*," and she expanded on this term to say: "*My, umm, my mom is White and Black, and then my dad is Black.*" Yet, when I asked Mya about her racial identity, she said, "*Pretty much like mixed race*," and throughout our conversation it never felt appropriate or respectful to probe further to know the specifics behind her chosen racial identification.

Overall analyses took place in two phases: student data was first examined to explore and centre their racialized narratives; and then classroom observation data helped describe classroom instruction as well as how students interacted with one another, their classroom teacher, and the curriculum. The second phase of analysis also situated students and their classroom within the larger social context in which these people and places are located—in order to explore how students' narratives ran in support of, or counter to, greater discourses of institutional racism and neoliberalism. This study grew out of my work as a mathematics instructional coach in a secondary teacher education program in the Pacific Northwest. I first came to know the classroom teacher, Ms. Williams, through her and her school's partnership with my university. I observed and learned quickly that, unlike any other teacher I had met, Ms. Williams' attention to her students and their identities—both academically and racially—was something unique and worth understanding more closely. This, in addition to the AP Statistics classroom being racially diverse in ways unlike any other upper level mathematics classroom I had seen, made for a phenomenon I wished to further explore. This means that in some ways, this classroom was typical of other large urban classrooms in the United States (Nazemi, 2020), given the White and woman identifying teacher and the majority of students being of colour. At the same time, this classroom was atypical for an upper level mathematics classroom in terms of the racial composition of students, making it a useful site for exploring the experiences of students of colour in mathematics (Bol & Berry, 2005).

Critical Race Sociocultural Theory, Centring Students' Identities in Mathematics

I connect sociocultural theories of learning and identity to critical race feminist theories to guide my inquiry. While sociocultural theories of learning have helped researchers to situate learning as embedded within a social, cultural, and historical context, and connected to one's identity or sense of self, these theories do not begin with the underlying assumption that recognizes the endemic role of race and power in all everyday contexts. In an aim to push scholarship around equitable and (re)humanized mathematics education further than sociocultural theories of learning have taken us before, I consider that all contexts of learning are racialized spaces in which power and privilege are at play.

Recently, scholars have focused on racialized and gendered identity experiences of students learning mathematics through a sociocultural lens of understanding learning and identity (Esmonde et al., 2009; Leyva, 2016; Nasir et al., 2013; Oppland-Cordell & Martin, 2015; Zavala, 2014). Concurrently but separately, recent scholarship in mathematics education has employed CRT to begin with the understanding that all spaces are racialized and to centre and share the counter-narratives of students of colour (Berry, 2008; Esmonde et al., 2009; Leyva, 2016; Martin, 2012; Nasir et al., 2013; Shah, 2016; Zavala, 2014). Of these works, only Esmonde et al. (2009), Leyva (2016), and Zavala (2014) employed both CRT and sociocultural theories of learning and identity. Drawing on CRT in conjunction with a sociocultural perspective allows us to consider processes of learning and the learner's identity as interconnected. In this way, we identify the mathematics classroom (nested within larger contexts) as a site both for learning mathematics and for identifying (or not identifying) with mathematics content and/or others (the teacher and peers) within that context. In this chapter, I consider mathematics learning as a sociocultural experience in which students' identities are supported (or not), affirmed (or not), shaped, and negotiated within the context of learning in the mathematics classroom.

Girls of Colour Offer Advice for White (Women) Teachers

This chapter draws on interview data where students were asked about the characteristics of the best mathematics teacher they have ever had, and students were also asked what kinds of advice they would offer to White woman teachers that worry about relating to students of colour. I have organized the following by varying themes and pieces of advice taken from students' responses to the abovementioned questions from their interviews.

Connecting with Students and Getting to Know Their Lived Experiences

When I asked students what advice they have for White teachers who are worried about relating to students of colour, Gena was insistent that teachers need to understand students and the lives that they bring into the classroom with them. She describes here the importance of understanding students' situations and taking the time to sit with students and help them with their problems, mathematics and otherwise.

> You have to understand where [students] are coming from. Some kids take the situation from home and they bring it to school, you know? And

> then how do you deal with a student that has problems from home and brings it to school and is having more problems from school? It's kind of like one big problem. So, I think…you have to kind of like, if you see the problem, sit down with your student, to understand and…like help them.

For Gena, she saw students' home lives and school lives as connected, meaning that it is important to take the time to notice what students bring to school from home and offer to help students with their problems. Jane adds that being understanding of students' lives is important for how teachers plan lesson and assign homework to students.

> [Teachers need] to be understanding of the students' lives and their schedules so they plan their lessons around what the students will be able to handle. I've had teachers that give loads of homework and all that stuff, but with Ms. Williams…[gives] us time to work on homework and get help that we needed instead of just handing it to you and giving us a due date.

It is essential that teachers consider students' lives outside of class and school and offer students support—academic and otherwise. All the students I spoke with had busy lives. They juggled family and home responsibilities, as well as jobs (sometimes even full-time jobs), on top of their demanding schoolwork. When teachers recognize their out-of-school lives and responsibilities, students feel their identities and lived-experiences are being affirmed in the classroom. In this way, classroom teachers are able to know their students and affirm their lived experiences and identities, both academically and personally.

In addition to getting to know students' lives, students felt that good teaching meant finding ways to connect with students and build relationships with them. Jane was adamant that it is important that teachers are invested in their students rather than coming in just to teach them. Specifically, she said: "I feel like there should be a relationship, like instead of just coming here to teach the students and having them go off, you should just if you care about your students you should have a really good relationship [with them]." When it came to giving teachers specific advice, Jane felt that taking the time to connect with students and recognizing that students learn differently is what's most important. She described that "To be a good teacher, I feel you should connect with your students and understand…that everyone learns differently, that everyone has their own stories. To be understanding is the best thing you could be as a teacher." Jane's description of some characteristics of a good teacher are very much in line with what we know of rehumanizing mathematics, as she describes the importance of seeing students wholly, for who they are, how they learn, and what backgrounds, experiences, and stories they bring to the classroom with them.

While Mya and Lia adopted colourblind ideologies when it came to race, the other four students of colour had complex advice specific to White teachers. Jane suggested that while there is a recognition that White women teachers might have a hard time relating to students of colour, sharing parts of one's identity is not a necessity for relating to and connecting with students as a teacher. She said, "I don't think it matters. Cuz, I've had teachers who are from the same background that I didn't connect with as much as other teachers who weren't. It's all about the teacher itself, not the race." Jane recognized that connecting with students has little to do with a shared racial identity and has more to do with the teacher and the efforts they make. For example, she felt that Ms. Williams was "passionate about racial equity," while Jane recalled that even when she's had teachers from the same background as her, it was not necessarily the case that she connected better with them. Much like Jane, Leilani felt that "Ms. Williams takes the time to connect with students that identify differently than her." Leilani felt that Ms. Williams "always like encourages us. She used to do, like talk about like racial stereotypes among people, and she's always like talks to me about that because she knows I'm really into like writing about like racial topics." Leilani and Jane both felt that their White woman teacher took the time to connect with them in ways that resonated with their lived experiences and interests.

Carlin gave similar advice. She described a time when Ms. Williams told her an anecdote about her own experience and commented on the importance of connecting with students and trying to relate to their experiences. She explained that it shouldn't be hard to find ways to connect to others, "not just as a White woman, but like as a person who grew up and is experiencing life." Carlin added that it was important to connect to students with "emotions and different feelings instead of just the obvious out appearance, but like getting more like inside and understanding where they're coming from."

In regard to relating to students, Leilani is the only student who brought up mathematics content as part of a teacher connecting with students. Leilani described the single most important attribute of a good teacher as "involving real life scenarios" and "real life topics that relate to students and the math" that they are studying. She described an assignment that Ms. Williams gave "where we're having to [administer] a survey based on [a topic in our lives that] we want to [look at more closely using statistical methods]. She involves real life topics, and relates them to the math we do." Students in this class were given the unique opportunity to explore something in their personal lives using statistical methods. While Leilani is the only one to have explicitly given this curricular example, all students felt that in order to relate to students of colour, teachers could and should find things that connected them to their students, regardless of their differences in identities and experiences.

Knowing Stereotypes Operating in Your Classroom and Schools

Leilani is the only student who specifically advised that teachers should think carefully about race and their racial prejudices in relation to test scores and disciplinary measures. Leilani recalled that, as part of recent labour disputes and a recent strike in the school district, teachers had been asking for more professional development around talking about race and dealing with racial issues in their classrooms and schools. Just as she appreciated Ms. Williams' attention to racial justice, Leilani described here that by being aware of trends vis-à-vis students' racial identities, teachers can work to make sure to improve the condition of their classrooms for all students.

> Well I know now they're doing [professional development] classes that were taught around how to deal with races and they talk about like suspension rates and all that and I know that they have classes around that. I think that's a start because I think it's very important to analyze the disproportion of suspension, disproportion of um maybe test scores, and just see how you can do better in that.

Leilani suggests above that White teachers need to work to become aware of racial stereotypes that they hold—perhaps through examining test scores and suspension rates. In her own schooling experience Leilani noticed that sometimes White teachers were anticipating that there would be disciplinary issues with Black students.

> Some of the classrooms with like White teachers, …they already hold stereotypes so they were on edge about like how you would act. Like they think you're going to act out and like they're going to have to call the security on you and stuff like that. Like suspension rates for Black students is, so that's like in their head. So they're thinking "Oh I'm going to have to call the security today."

Leilani reiterates above that having stereotypes in your head about students makes you (re)act to them based on the assumptions you have about them. In the case above, some White teachers that Leilani has encountered assumed that because the suspension rate is highest for Black students, they would have a disciplinary issue just based on there being Black students in the class. Leilani suggested that teachers could work to find alternative ways to discipline a student rather than suspending them, or better yet, "find out what's going on with them, rather than being like reactionary." In other words, Leilani wanted teachers to find the root cause of a student's issues and to be less reactionary and reliant on suspensions.

Leilani and Gena both felt that White teachers need to examine their own prejudices in order to work towards eradicating them. These two focal students are the only ones that brought up the "Asians are good at math" stereotype, positioning themselves very differently with respect to the stereotype. Gena was noticeably upset that teachers and students alike assumed her to be excelling in mathematics because they saw her as Asian, whereas Leilani's concern was that because of the way Asian students are seen as smart, her racial identity as African American is marked in contrast to that as less smart and incapable of succeeding in mathematics.

Leilani described here the way that the stereotypes teachers hold about students affects how they view, treat, and teach students.

> I think that you have to acknowledge that um there certain stereotypes that you have in your mind about who's going to do better in certain things and you have to kinda eliminate those, because like I said about the Asians in math, you feel like already like "oh they're gonna do good in math" and then you like the Black kids they're not going to do as well then this is something that's already going to be established in you and it's going to cause you to do, maybe teach and treat them differently, even though that you don't see that you're treating them differently…, it doesn't matter because kids see it so I think it's important for you to acknowledge what stereotypes you already have and to eliminate them.

Gena and Leilani both described how the stereotypes that teachers hold about students affects all students negatively. In the case described above, Leilani tells us that holding stereotypes about students affects how you treat students, something that teachers can't always notice is playing out, yet students do notice. Gena's feelings were that it's hard to feel validated as an Asian person who does not find mathematics easy. "People are just like 'Asians can do math,' and I'm like no, not all Asians can do math, cuz I know a lot of us don't know what the heck is going on!"

Students' descriptions of the characteristics of good mathematics teachers, as well as advice for White teachers, are both in line with what it takes to rehumanize mathematics. Finding connections with students based on experiences and expressing compassion towards others is both humane and necessary for an environment in which learning takes place. Remembering that students' lives and the relationships with students are at the centre of learning mathematics in humanizing ways, it is clear to see that being aware of stereotypes one holds towards students and working to eliminate those stereotypes can help us more wholly see, understand and include students and their sense of selves in the mathematics classroom.

Concluding Remarks

More research is needed to know how students experience other aspects of the classroom (such as interactions with peers, teachers, instructional activities, discipline), especially since as Leilani said teachers' stereotypes have an impact on students even if the teacher doesn't realize it. This chapter is the start of a long journey to find out from students, in their own words and through their own narratives, more about what it takes to affirm and support students' identities and experiences in the classroom. Relating to students and seeing them as they identify and want to be seen allows for this necessary shift towards rehumanizing mathematics where students and their lived experiences are at the centre, and they are seen and understood for who they are and the complexities around the identities that they bring to class. Let's work to change mathematics so that it is centred around our students' lives.

References

Battey, D., & Leyva, L. A. (2016). A framework for understanding Whiteness in mathematics education. *Journal of Urban Mathematics Education, 9*(2), 49–80.

Berry III, R. Q. (2008). Access to upper-level mathematics: The stories of successful African American middle school boys. *Journal for Research in Mathematics Education*, 464–488.

Bol, L., & Berry, R. Q. (2005). Secondary mathematics teachers' perceptions of the achievement gap. *The High School Journal, 88*(4), 32–45.

Esmonde, I., Brodie, K., Dookie, L., & Takeuchi, M. (2009). Social identities and opportunities to learn: Student perspectives on group work in an urban mathematics classroom. *Journal of Urban Mathematics Education, 2*(2), 18–45.

Gutiérrez, R. (2012). Embracing Nepantla: Rethinking "knowledge" and its use in mathematics teaching. *Journal of Research in Mathematics Education, 1*(1), 29–56.

Leyva, L. A. (2016). An intersectional analysis of Latin@ college women's counter-stories in mathematics. *Journal of Urban Mathematics Education, 9*(2), 81–121.

Martin, D. B. (2012). Learning mathematics while Black. *The Journal of Educational Foundations, 26*(1/2), 47.

Nasir, N. I. S., Snyder, C. R., Shah, N., & Ross, K. M. (2013). Racial storylines and implications for learning. *Human Development, 55*(5–6), 285–301.

Nazemi, M. (2018, June 1–5). Des discours racialisés persistants postent une nouvelle demande d'équité pour la formation des enseignants. In J. Holm & S. Mathieu-Soucy (Eds.), *42nd Actes de la Rencontre Annuelle 2018 du Groupe Canadien d'Étude en Didactique des Mathématiques.* Squamish, British Columbia, Canada.

Nazemi, M. (2020). Persisting racialized discourses pose new equity demands for teacher education. In L. Jao & N. Radakovic (Eds.), *Borders in mathematics preservice teacher education* (pp. 245–266). Springer.

Oppland-Cordell, S., & Martin, D. B. (2015). Identity, power, and shifting participation in a mathematics workshop: Latin@ students' negotiation of self and success. *Mathematics Education Research Journal, 27*(1), 21–49.

Shah, N. (2016). Race, ideology, and academic ability: A relational analysis of racial narratives in mathematics. *Teachers College Record, 119*(7), 1–42.

Varelas, M., Martin, D. B., & Kane, J. M. (2013). Content learning and identity construction: A framework to strengthen African American students' mathematics and science learning in urban elementary schools. *Human Development, 55*(5–6), 319–339.

Zavala, M. D. R. (2014). Latina/o youth's perspectives on race, language, and learning athematics. *Journal of Urban Mathematics Education, 7*(1), 55–87.

CHAPTER 13

Re/centring Families

Principal as School Landscape Architect

Debbie Pushor and Esther Maeers

Debbie's Narrative: A Landscape Project

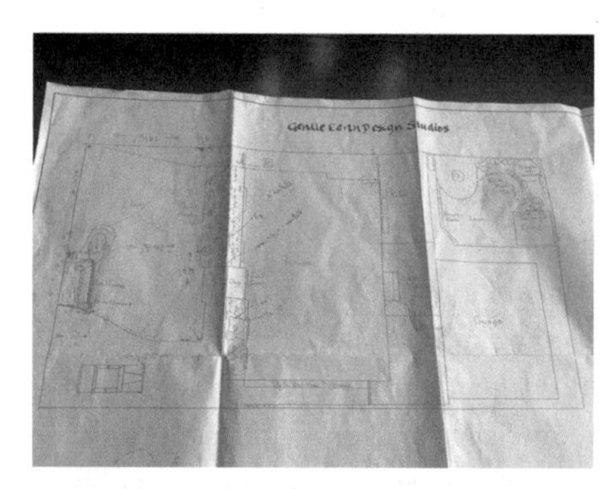

Yard blueprint (Photograph by Debbie Pushor, 2021, used with permission)

As I sit on the loveseat in the corner of our backyard, landscape plans laid out across the fire table in front of me, looking at where we are in our yard's redesign and redevelopment, I give thanks to Mother Earth. I marvel at how her gifts of earth, water, fire, and wind are emerging in this piece of land that we call home. Her spirit has been generous through the many years of work in which our landscape project has been in the making.

Redesigning a landscape in ways that bring the lives of humans together with the life of the land itself is a more complex and contextualized process than I realized when my partner, Laurie, and I first decided to work with a landscape architect. Janet, our landscape architect, helped us to think about our yard in ways that attended to the physical, mental, social, emotional, and spiritual elements of the space. As we talked together, imagining people in our yard and various events unfolding—family dinners, evenings around the fire, open play space for children, quiet places to read, relax, or just think—it became easier to determine the things we wanted to create in each of those areas. Working with design ideas on onion skin paper, placing them on the blueprint of our yard's current footprint—shifting them, removing them, adding new ones—it became possible to visualize how the elements of earth, water, fire, and wind might combine to create a holistic vision for a built landscape in harmony with Mother Earth.

Then, with our design in hand, we sought out people with the expertise and resources to help us realize the elements of earth, water, fire, and wind that we

© KONINKLIJKE BRILL NV, LEIDEN, 2022 | DOI:10.1163/9789004521186_013

Backyard 1 (Photograph by Debbie Pushor, 2021, used with permission

were wanting to honour and foreground. We visited landscape and sprinkler companies; we talked with carpenters and electricians; we made decisions about materials such as plants, stones, mulch, and wood. There were so many decisions, so much to manage as we worked to integrate elements and maintain harmony. It became clear that there was a rhythm to this landscaping process, often with multiple things needing to be done at once, yet in thoughtfully scaffolded phases.

As we proceeded, our learning deepened in significant ways. When we bought our house, we were not awake to the force of the wind that blew directly out of the North toward our front face, nor were we aware of the originally marshy land on which our house was situated. As we grew in this knowledge and as we learned more about our planting zone and the amounts of sun and shade the various areas of our yard received, we discussed and selected plantings reflective of the growing conditions of our urban lot. As we became more attuned to ecological sensitivities at play all around us, sometimes subtle and yet always important, we worked more in partnership *with* the living world, bringing human and environmental life forces together.

And now, here I sit, relishing our relationship with Mother Earth and the landscape that has emerged. I love the feel of the sun in my face, the sound of the water trickling, the smell of the herbs, and the beautiful lushness of the new growth. I look forward to the family dinner we will have tomorrow at our big table. I naively thought we would be done our landscaping by now. It makes me smile; I know now that it will never be done. Change and growth in the landscape, in us, and in our family, all will call us to respond continually, as landscape architects do, to our fluctuating lives and to the shifting environment.

Debbie and Esther's Narrative Inquiry

A School, Too, Is a Landscape

Immersed in our research into systematic parent engagement at the same time that Debbie is immersed in her backyard landscaping, we are drawn ever more strongly to the conceptualization of a *school landscape*, first developed by Clandinin and Connelly in 1995. They consciously used this metaphor to step away from the language of *school culture* that was (and is) commonly used in writing and thinking about schools. Because the word *culture* is used pervasively in so many disciplines, they felt people came to the word with deeply embedded, predetermined, and perhaps unquestioned understandings. They were seeking a fresh perspective in thinking about lives lived in schools, for themselves and for others (personal email communication, 2001). What Clandinin and Connelly (1995) were drawn to is that, when considered in the context of schools, "a landscape metaphor…has a sense of expansiveness and the possibility of being filled with diverse people, things, and events in different relationships" (p. 5). Intended to capture place, space, and time in its conceptualization, it is a landscape of relationships, of knowledge and ideas, of interactions and emotions (Pushor, 2001). This landscape of relations makes it, then, as stated by Clandinin and Connelly (1995), "both an intellectual and moral landscape" (p. 5). Building from this notion of a landscape of relationships as moral, we frame our understanding of a school landscape using Ermine's (2017) conceptualization of *ethical space*. Ermine stated that "ethics entertains our personal capacity and our integrity to stand up for our cherished notions of good, responsibility, duty, obligations, etc." (p. 195). In an ethical space, then, we acknowledge and honour the crucial lines that protect an individual's, a family's, a community's, and a culture's personal, moral, collective, relational, and principled boundaries. It is in the "sacred space of the ethical" (p. 196) that we are able to balance considerations that are trans-boundaried in any one of many possible ways. In this 21st century, with the particular challenges facing the planet, it is more critical than ever that the school landscape is shaped in moral, ethical, relational, and intellectual ways to re/centre lives and lived experience—to more equitably honour and embrace diverse ways of interpreting the world and multiple understandings and interpretations of learning, living, and relating.

A School Leader, Too, Is a Landscape Architect

We draw a parallel between the work of Janet, Debbie and Laurie's landscape architect, and that of Linda, Vice Principal at Edgeview School, our research site. Linda, too, was a landscape architect—but on a school landscape. The metaphor of a vice/principal as a school landscape architect arose for us as we engaged in our study, using both participatory action research (PAR) and narrative inquiry. PAR is a methodology characterized by collaboration between community, staff, and academic participants, mutual learning and education, and resulting educational, social, and policy action (Elwood et al., 2012, p. 109).

As we engaged collaboratively, living and working relationally alongside members of the school and community, we captured the lived experiences of individuals engaged in the research using narrative inquiry, through gathering field notes, artifacts, photographs, and recording conversations with participants. As we captured stories of their experiences, the participants shared both what they knew and how the particularity of the context shaped their knowing. It was in participants' accounts of their experience with parent engagement that fine-grained insights added to our learning, allowing us to focus on the human *beings* in education (Lyle, 2021) and led us to the conceptualization of Linda, the Vice Principal, as a school landscape architect.

Let us take a minute and turn back to Janet's role. In designing a plan with Debbie and Laurie, and in relation with their space, Janet spent much time with them, learning about who they are, where they live, and how to foreground Mother Earth's elements of earth, water, fire, and wind in order to bring their living together with that of the land on which their home is situated. Throughout this time, Janet was engaged in creative practice to plan and design an outdoor space of a certain scale, creating attunement between people and environment (Canadian Society of Landscape Architects, n.d.). Janet's work was centred around three key aspects that define the work of a landscape architect. As together they layered and worked with multiple ideas overlaid on the blueprint of Debbie and Laurie's yard, using possibilities sketched on onion skin paper, Janet was establishing a *strong design* (Abbott, 2018) that honored their particular landscape. As Janet provided ideas for a natural water feature, with supporting technical information, and as she sourced materials and services—stone columns and river rock, she engaged in the critical act of *resource management* (Nawre, 2016). As Janet taught Debbie and Laurie about soil composition, drainage, wind patterns, and planting zones, she awakened them to the *ecological sensitivities* (Young, 2019) of their particular city plot and to the considerations to which it was important that Debbie and Laurie stay awake.

Now, let us explore Linda's role. Linda was appointed as Vice Principal of Edgeview School to co-lead an elementary school in the development and implementation of a systematic approach to parent engagement. Such a systematic approach was intended to move parent engagement from "random acts" (Gill Kressley, 2008, as cited in Weiss et al., 2010, p. 1) occurring only when individual educators valued the knowledge parents hold, to a philosophy and pedagogy through which parent engagement became integral—an aspect of everything that happened on the school landscape. Linda was selected purposefully for this assignment. Like Janet, Linda was tasked with the *creative practice* of supporting an elementary school staff and community in *planning and implementing a strong design* for the engagement of parents in teaching and learning, both on and off the school landscape. She was also responsible to *manage, monitor, and maintain the resources* of the school, a context in which time and people are truly the greatest resources. Further, she was called to act thoughtfully in regard to the *human ecological sensitivities* of the moral, ethical, relational, and intellectual aspects of the school landscape.

Introducing Linda

Meeting Linda today, you would be introduced to a proud and vivacious Michif woman, married to a Cree man, and mother to six beautiful children. Her history, though, continues to live below the surface of her current self, as she did not grow up with this pride in her identity. Sobbing with the pain of recollection, Linda shared a story of being asked to draw a self-portrait when she entered school. As her teacher circulated around the room, she arrived beside Linda's desk. Pausing, she made the hurtful comment that Linda looked like a potato in her drawing. The significance of this moment was lasting as Linda, from that moment on, drew herself with the peach-colored crayon that all other children were using (Keynote address, *Walk Alongside Parent Engagement Forum*, June 1, 2018). Attending predominantly all-white schools in elementary and high school, Linda continued to hide her Michif heritage and identity. With fair skin, Linda could *pass* as white. Wanting opportunities for her and desiring to remove racial barriers she may face, her parents raised her without immersion in her culture, language, or ceremony. Not knowing who she was growing up, Linda faced challenges as a youth and young adult common to many Indigenous individuals trying to find a place in the world. Finally, there came a time when she was ready to begin her learning journey.

> Y'know, I carry a bundle, I go to Sweat, I go to Sundance…There's an article that I've read that said, "At Sundance, you cannot tell the difference between who are the First Nations and who are the Métis because they were all doing the same thing and they were all dressed in the same way." So, I'm figuring my way and I feel good about who I am and I have to trust that the Creator is guiding me to believe that I am Métis enough. (Recorded conversation, March 3, 2020)

When Linda stepped into Edgeview School as a leader, she brought her worldview to that role, in profoundly personal, heartfelt, and centred ways.

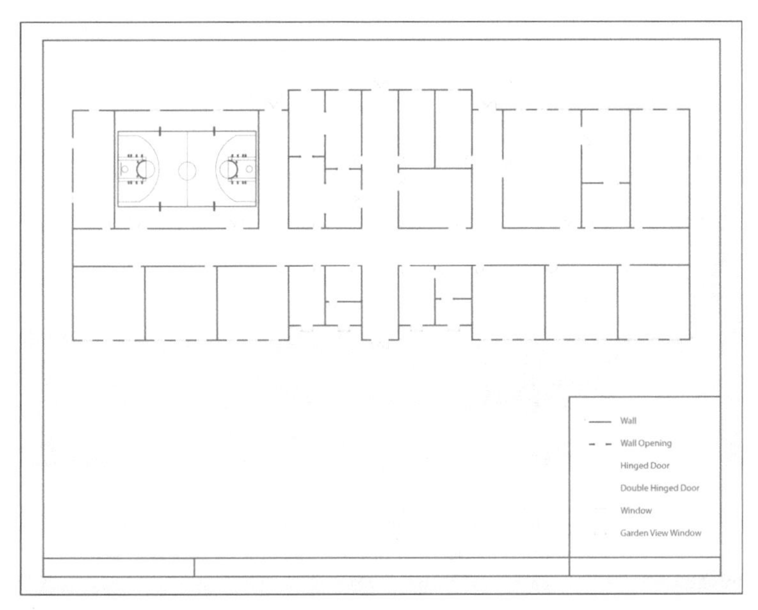

School landscape architect blueprint (Photograph by Debbie Pushor & Esther Maeers, 2021, used with permission)

Linda's School Landscape

Linda entered a PK–8 public school with three distinct communities comprising the whole—one third of the population was majority Canadian, one third Indigenous, and one-third newcomer from various places in the world. A context of economic poverty, low literacy rates and levels of education, English language needs, and unemployment and under-employment were challenges presenting themselves at Edgeview. Both because of the diversity within the area and the life challenges many members faced each day, the Edgeview community was not a cohesive and integrated community.

Further, Linda entered a landscape to work with a White female principal, new to her role and new to a philosophy and pedagogy of parent engagement, although not new to Edgeview School. Linda joined a staff, many of whom were also White, returning members of the Edgeview staff, with established relations with one another, and demonstrating resistance to the move toward systematic parent engagement. Her task, as challenging as it was, was to work toward re/centring those historically marginalized—whether students, parents and families, or staff—to create a new understanding of school landscapes as places for both teacher knowledge and *parent knowledge* (Pushor, 2015).

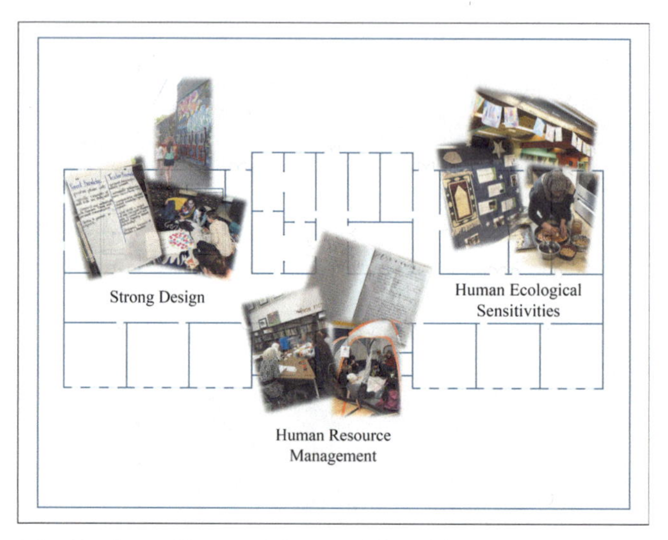

School landscape blueprint (Photograph by Debbie Pushor & Esther Maeers, 2021, used with permission)

Linda as School Landscape Architect

As a school leader, Linda became a school landscape architect in all the ways that Janet was a landscape architect for Debbie and Laurie's front and backyard redesign and redevelopment. Linda's role as school landscape architect was to assist in developing a shared vision for the school community, strengthening school and community cohesion, and embedding practices that created place and voice for parents in their children's teaching and learning. Awake to the contextual nature of this human-built educational landscape, Linda's role encompassed attending to the particularities of the many people who were envisioned to be spending time on the school landscape and to the places and things in which they would be engaged.

Strong Design

Strong design, to create a harmonious space and voice for diverse people, both staff and community became a starting place for Linda. Linda explained:

> Part of the idea behind that was that we wanted to model for our staff what we wanted the staff to model for our families, and how we wanted them to engage with families. So, we thought about different ways to know our families, and something new to lots of our community was getting to know our Indigenous population, as well as our newcomer population, because most of our staff are majority Canadian. And we recognized the richness within our families and wanted to bring that to our staff.

> One thing we did was a community walk during one start up school day, and we wanted to bring a welcome gift to each of our families too. … So, we did create a little paper bag gift for each of the families. And the staff went around and delivered them, and we just modeled and practiced home visiting on the doorstep, kind of getting to know, a first introduction, and walking through the community. So, just getting to know the different areas and kind of the socio-economic status of our families. Giving staff a better understanding of who's going to be in their classroom. (Recorded conversation, March 3, 2020)

As well as facilitating a community walk with staff, Linda worked to orchestrate home visits to staff members' residences with the principal, personal sharing of meaningful artifacts by staff to provide a sense of their identity and values, and lunch hour cooking and storytelling sessions in the homes of parents from diverse cultures to foster a sense of connection and cohesion.

What we see in the strong design of Linda's first week back to school for staff is a huge departure from what is typically done by school administrators in those first non-instructional days with staff. Linda, as a school landscape architect, chose to make central the lives of the staff and families of Edgeview School, sharing and creating lived experiences that shaped both who they were in that moment and how they might continue to live out a meaningful, equitable, and representative story in relation to the Edgeview school landscape.

Resource Management

A school's resources are approximately 85% human, with the majority of a school budget taken up through salaries. Resource management for a school principal, then, becomes primarily a task of education and development with leaders, teachers, staff, and parents—*human* resource management. Toward this end and given that people are the greatest resource on a school landscape, Linda facilitated experiential and relational education and development for leadership, teachers, staff, and parents. She reflected:

> We started to look at how we wanted to be holistic in the school, and I brought in the holistic framework. That was building on our beliefs, moving away from a list of rules to a holistic belief of the staff where we were all invested in the same thing. I think the question was something like, "What do we believe about children or children and learning?" After [staff] categorized their ideas in the four domains, I think they wrote a "We believe…" statement about each of the four domains. And we all had a voice in it. We had our educational assistants (EAs) with us as well, even

> though the school division wasn't paying for EAs to be at staff meetings anymore. At our school, we gave them time in lieu to be a part, so that we could build a strong community. (Recorded conversation, March 3, 2020)

The holistic framework as a means of evoking deep thinking about a desired school landscape, Linda was living her Indigenous philosophy of "being holistic…, process-oriented, and firmly grounded in a particular place" (Little Bear, 2000, p. 78). Linda foregrounded the importance of each of the four domains: physical, mental, emotional, and spiritual, and how she believed, when these domains are in balance, the result would be an integration of beliefs and practices.

Human Ecological Sensitivities

Every landscape, as an ecological system, has sensitivities that require attention if the landscape is to thrive. Debbie spoke earlier of how Janet took into account the force and patterns of the north wind when suggesting plantings for their front beds. Further, it ended up that the particularity of their drainage and soil conditions demanded the installation of a sump pump to avoid pooling water and potential flooding. School landscapes, filled with people, things, and events in interaction, have their sensitivities as well.

As *human* ecological systems, *human ecological sensitivities* arise in response to environmental changes caused by external and internal factors (Rossi et al., 2008; Zhang et al., 2012, as cited in Özhanci & Yilmaz, 2018). New to the school landscape, Linda had much work to do to learn the human contours of the school, the subtleties of existing relations between people, allegiances forming with her and/or with the school principal, and a sense of the story carried by those who had been at Edgeview School for some time.

Recognizing the very tenuous nature of establishing trust and relationships, Linda committed time and contact each day to build the connections she valued and to live her stated beliefs in action:

> I started to take that time to go into every classroom every morning, and just say good morning to each of the students, and say good morning to the teacher, and just engage that way. And [one of the teachers] emailed me and was like, "That is so meaningful that you come and check in." I was just trying to re-establish those relationships and show them that there was somebody there that cared about them.…And then I could maybe discuss the work or have those conversations informally. You know, about meeting parents in the hallway and stuff like that. (Recorded conversation, March 3, 2020)

As Linda walked the halls and was visible in the school throughout the day, she could be seen greeting Muslim staff in their language, addressing all students by name, and having informal conversations with teachers and parents. Linda often joined in on Wednesday Conversation Circles where parents were learning English, staying to play a language game with them, and taking the time to get to know the many members of the school community.

Linda interacted with staff, parents, and students in ways that honoured and valued who they were and invited them into the circle. As she stated, "If I tell people the circle is strong when we're all there, it's my job to make sure everybody's brought in" (Recorded conversation, March 3, 2020). Linda, in re-centring lives and lived experience through attending to human ecological sensitivities, embodied the values of respect, reciprocity, and relationality (Wilson, 2008). She engaged in "deep listening and hearing with more than [her] ears" (Wilson, 2008, p. 59), and worked from a "connection between [her] logic of mind and the feelings of [her] heart" (Wilson, 2008, p. 59). Linda invested herself fully—mentally, emotionally, physically, and spiritually, building trust and relationships as she demonstrated her unwavering commitment to the Edgeview school community.

Attending to the Moral, Ethical, Relational, and Intellectual

Our research to implement a plan to systematically engage parents on a school landscape arose from five decades of research in the field (Mapp, 2013) that attests to the fact that when parents are engaged in their children's teaching and learning, children do better, stay in school longer, and like school more (Henderson & Mapp, 2002). With this evidence available to us, it becomes a moral, ethical, relational, and intellectual imperative to act on it. Linda certainly embraced and lived that imperative.

Backyard 2 (Photograph by Debbie Pushor, 2021, used with permission)

Linda recalled that, in the schools she went to as a child, "Everybody was *Mr.* and *Mrs.* and there was no kinship or family. You know, you went into school, you sat in your desk, you did your work" (Recorded conversation, March 3, 2020). Linda was adamant that she did not want to be that kind of leader; embodying an Indigenous worldview of kinship relations, she wanted to create a school community where students felt comfortable to call her *Auntie* and parents felt that their children were being cared for. In Cree (nêhiyaw),

> relationship terms convey a job description, and the focus is on the role, relationship, and connection—the action and the verb. For example, ...[a child] may have many aunties or grandmothers who may or may not be blood-related—their connection is determined by how they fulfill those roles in the life of the child. (Makokis et al., 2020, p. 50)

Reflective of this knowledge, Linda expressed, "Somehow, I'm walking the way I know that our Ancestors would've. And I think the idea of being called *Auntie* was also thinking about, 'How best do we treat kids?'" (Recorded conversation, March 3, 2020).

Linda's passion for the particular success of Indigenous children in schools was a further aspect of her moral, ethical, relational, and intellectual pursuit with 18 years of lived experience as an educator with both Indigenous and public sectors; Linda knew and embodied what is at stake given her position as a mother and a Michif woman. In a keynote address, Linda shared data showing that on-time graduation rates for Indigenous high school students rested at just above 40% in her province. As a mother of five children at the time of her comment, Linda wept, "Do you understand that you are talking about my children? That this statistic predicts that only two of my five children may graduate high school?" (Keynote address, *Walk Alongside Parent Engagement Forum*, June 1, 2018).

Foundational to Linda's holistic work as a school landscape architect was her commitment to engaging staff and parents in an examination of their beliefs and assumptions about each other, about the work of a school, and about the place and voice of parents in their children's learning and development. Then, to act on this reflective work, Linda consciously and concretely promoted the development of trust and relationships, and a sense of welcoming and hospitality on the school landscape, the living out of which she cultivated in all elements of the holistic framework: physically, mentally, emotionally, and spiritually.

Esther's Narrative: Reflecting in Debbie's Backyard

I join Debbie in her beautiful backyard for some cold lemon water and conversation. As I sit down, my eyes wander to a meandering river of stones that curves around the grass and the fire pit, bringing together the space in a cohesive and welcoming way. There is something visually interesting about the way these stones sit together, side by side, none of them standing out individually, working together to create an artistic element in the backyard. I mention this to Debbie and we engage in a lively discussion about the similarities between this unassuming river and the work that Linda accomplished at Edgeview School.

We recognize that Janet, as landscape architect, has intentionally created this visual element in Debbie's backyard, placing stones side by side on the earth in ways that work in relationship with the landscape. We also recognize that Linda was just as intentional. She stated, "We sit shoulder to shoulder…to have a strong circle everybody has to come to it and bring their strengths, because we can't, I guess in the spiritual sense, have a balanced earth or peace on earth unless everybody's part of that circle" (Recorded conversation, March 3, 2020). She approached the role of a leader as one who is not always the knower, but one who listens and learns, who is not apart from the circle but a part of the circle. Relationality is an important part of Indigenous worldview as we learned from Wilson's (2008) recounting of his friend's statement, "It's collective, it's a group, it's a community. And I think that's the basis for relationality. That is, it's built on the interconnections, the interrelationships and that binds the group" (p. 80). As Linda worked with the elements of design, resource management, and human ecological sensitivities in moral, ethical, and intellectual ways, the thread of relationality became the meandering river that worked to weave the architectural elements together on the Edgeview school landscape and in so doing re/centring the lives of students, parents, teachers, and leaders.

Rock river (Photograph by Debbie Pushor, 2021, used with permission)

References

Abbott, M. (2018). Placing design, and designing's place, in landscape architecture research. *Landscape Review, 18*(1), 89–107.

Canadian Society of Landscape Architects. (n.d.). *What is landscape architecture?* https://www.csla-aapc.ca/what-is-landscape-architecture

Clandinin, D. J., & Connelly, F. M. (1995). *Teachers' professional knowledge landscapes.* Teachers College Press.

Elwood Martin, R., Hanson, D., Heminway, C., Ramsden, V., Buxton, J., Granger-Brown, A., Condello, L. L., Macaulay, A., Janssen, P., & Hislop, T. G. (2012). Homelessness as viewed by incarcerated women: Participatory research. *International Journal of Prisoner Health, 8*(3/4), 108–116. https://doi.org.libproxy.uregina.ca/10.1108/17449201211284987

Ermine, W. (2017). The ethical space of engagement. *Indigenous Law Journal, 6*(1), 193–203.

Henderson, A. T., & Mapp, K. L. (2002). *A new wave of evidence: The impact of school, family, and community connections on student achievement.* Southwest Educational Development Laboratory (National Center for Family & Community Connections with Schools).

Little Bear, L. (2000). Jagged worldviews colliding. In M. Battiste (Ed.), *Reclaiming Indigenous voice and vision* (pp. 77–85). UBC Press.

Lyle, E. (2021). *Re/centring lives and lived experience in education* (call for proposals). Yorkville University.

Makokis, L., Kopp, K., Bodor, R., Veldhuisen, A., & Torres, A. (2020). Cree relationship mapping: nêhiyaw kesi wâhkotohk – how we are related. *First Peoples Child & Family Review, 15*(1), 44–61.

Mapp, K. (2013). *Partners in education: A dual capacity-building framework for family-school partnerships.* Southwest Educational Development Laboratory.

Nawre, A. (2016, May 26). Developing landscapes of resource management. *Landscape Architecture Magazine.* https://landscapearchitecturemagazine.org/2016/05/26/developing-landscapes-of/

Ozhanci, E., & Yilmaz, H. (2018). Sensitivity analysis in landscape ecological planning: The sample of Bayburt. *Journal of Agriculture Faculty of Bursa Uludag University, 32*(2), 77–98.

Pushor, D. (2001). *A storied photo album of parents' positioning and the landscape of schools* [Unpublished doctoral dissertation]. University of Alberta.

Pushor, D. (2015). Conceptualizing parent knowledge. In D. Pushor & the Parent Engagement Collaborative II (Eds.), *Living as mapmakers: Charting a course with children guided by parent knowledge* (pp. 7–19). Sense.

Weiss, H. B., Lopez, E. L., & Rosenberg, H. (2010). *Beyond random acts: Family, school, and community engagement as an integral part of education reform.* Research Project.

Wilson, S. (2008). *Research is ceremony: Indigenous research methods.* Fernwood.

Young, R. (2019). Introduction: Ecological wisdom as discourse. In B. Yang & R. F. Young (Eds.), *Ecological wisdom: Theory and practice* (pp. 1–13). Springer.

CHAPTER 14

Freirean Variations

Toward Humanistic Dialogue and Listening in Piano Lessons

Jee Yeon Ryu

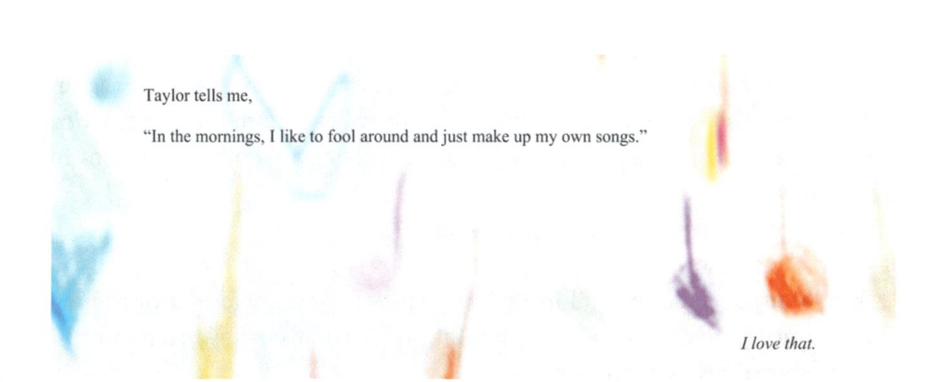

Freirean Inspired Theme

In this chapter, I share a collection of autoethnographic living stories[1] (Bochner & Ellis, 2016; Gouzouasis & Ryu, 2015; Ryu, 2018), digitally edited photographs, and reflective-reflexive, critical narratives (Lyle, 2009, 2013) as artful and empathetic (Eisner, 1997) forms of understanding to explore what it means to teach, learn, and be with young beginner piano students.

Theoretically framed by Paulo Freire's (1970/2005) humanistic concepts of dialogue as love, humility, faith, hope, and critical thinking, I use a first-person voice to tell stories of my lived experiences as a piano teacher (*auto*), and describe the interactions, events, and situations in our lessons that moved and resonated with me. I recall moments, memories, and conversations about the ways in which I am learning to listen to my students' unique, individual ways of learning to play the piano. By drawing attention to the emotions, objects, and experiences, I highlight my engagement and relationships with young children and their parents (*ethno*) that have deeply influenced my piano teaching practices. As an autoethnographic storyteller (*graphy*), I actively participate and collaborate in the (re)creation of our stories.

For me, our stories are *stories in motion* (LeBlanc et al., 2015). I explore, evoke, and share my learning journey, which is still in the process of *be*(com)*ing*.

© KONINKLIJKE BRILL NV, LEIDEN, 2022 | DOI:10.1163/9789004521186_014

They are metaphorical variations of my life stories (Leggo, 1995) about the value and importance of placing humanistic dialogue and listening at the heart of children's lived experiences of learning to play the piano.

Variation 1: Listening with Love

The first thing Andy[2] says to me as he walks into the studio is that he is stressed today. He has a science project due tomorrow and has yet to finish his homework.

"I have to end piano right at 4:30 pm," he says as he checks the clock on the wall. He also tells me that he might even have to skip the soccer practice because he needs to finish the school project. Then, suddenly, he decides to play *Chopsticks*.

"Let's play my favourite," he eagerly says.

"Yes, please. I love to hear your favourite, too," I encourage him.

But, to my surprise, when I invite him to play *Chopsticks* for our upcoming music concert, he declines without hesitation, "No thanks; they're *too* short."

"Too short?" I thought to myself.

Even when I ask him about his new favourite, *Hello Drums*, one of the longer compositions he is learning to play, he declines yet again: "Nah, maybe I'll play in the concert when I can play something *a little more complex*."

"A little more complex?"

Once more, he surprises me.

Although it has been a long time since Andy first learned *Chopsticks*, he still loves to play it all the time. During the last two years that I've known him, he has never declined the opportunity to play it in our lessons. He loves to play *Hello Drums*, too. He especially likes it when I accompany his playing with the little African hand drum.

"Can you be the drummer?" he invites me.

So, every week, we happily play his old and new favourites over and over again. Even as he hurriedly packs up his music bag ready to go at 4:30pm, he changes his mind about finishing our lesson right on time.

"I think I'll play it once more before I go," he says as he drops his music bag back onto the floor.

Andy loves to play *Chopsticks* that much.

∴

> Love is an act of courage…love is commitment to others. (Freire, 1970/2005, p. 89)

I meet many young children like Andy who worry that their songs might be too short and too easy to play in the concerts. Sometimes, they think that their playing is not good enough, and they constantly compare themselves with others. This seems exacerbated with children whose parents request a more teacher-directed, technique-oriented, and grade-driven approach to piano instruction; improvisations and other creative activities like drawing, storytelling, and composition that we like to integrate in our piano playing gradually fade away.

In the early stages of piano learning, teachers *and* parents play a critical role in nurturing a child's musical journey. To support my students' love for their favourite piano music, I invite parents to (re)consider the happy piano playing that comes from children to be a rich source of inspiration and foundation for new ways of imagining, understanding, and making joyful connections with music. In listening for all things that bring happiness, smiles, and laughter to young children, we can attend to the beauties in our everyday moments that we share with one another. We can lead creative, he*art*ful ways of cultivating children's musical ways of *be*(com)*ing*.

Duck of York

After playing Duke of York,
Sara suddenly reaches over for one of my pencils
and explains to me that she wishes to change the title of the song.

As she crosses out the word Duke,
she looks up with a smile and says,
"There! Now it's Duck of York!"

We laugh and giggle as we play the new song
with all the newly added sound effects of our little Duck.

Variation II: Listening with Humility

Sally loves to share her writing with me. She keeps a notebook full of stories and poems. Sometimes, she has drawings to accompany her writing. But, whenever I ask about her writing, she says, "I want to read you a poem, but I have to read it fast!"

Sally explains that we can't take too much time with her stories and poems. "It's our piano time," she tells me.

While quickly flipping through her pages to find something that she wants to share with me, she reminds me again, "I can only read one page because my mom will be mad. She doesn't want me to waste my piano lesson time."

And, as she packs up her notebook and music books at the end of our lesson, Sally with a concerned look asks me to promise, "Don't tell my mom about my poem, okay?"

∴

Dialogue cannot exist without humility. (Freire, 1970/2005, p. 90)

Just like Sally, many of my young students are very conscious about *wasting* our piano lesson time. Some children constantly check the clock and, although they wish to share more stories, drawings, and anything else that they like to explore in our lessons, many of them are very reluctant to do so.

Thinking about Sally and other students who worry about what we *should* or *ought* to do in our lessons moves me to keep searching for what it means to teach and learn piano. By focusing on children's creativity, curiosity, and wonder about music and life, we can (re)create piano curriculum and pedagogy that calls upon teachers, students, and parents to be attentive—to question, to ask, and to listen in new ways. In welcoming our students' willingness to share what is important and meaningful in their lives with us, we can develop a deeper connection to all the possibilities in children's ways of exploring music and piano playing.

With Sally, I am learning to teach music through poetry and stories. She inspires me to practice poetic ways of knowing (Leggo, 2005). As I listen to her poems, I imagine her four elemental fairies—*sky, earth, water,* and *fire*—happily dancing around the secret gardens. As we create music about her mysterious creatures living in a magical forest in a distant star, Sally's creative piano playing humbles me with its newness and beauty and inspires awareness for children's musical, magical ways of learning to play the piano.

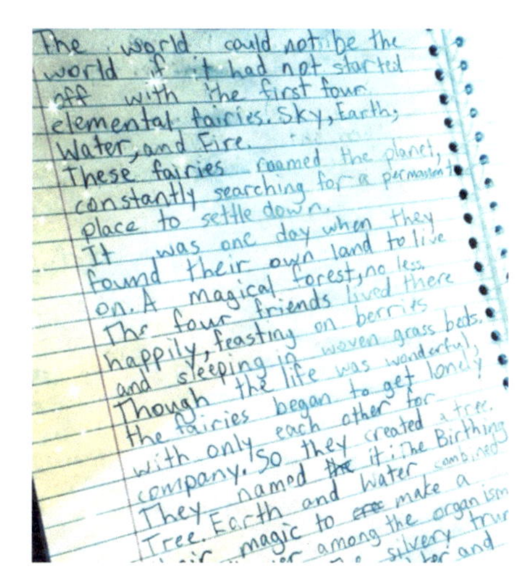
The world could not be the
world if it had not started
off with the first four
elemental fairies. Sky, Earth,
Water, and Fire.
These fairies roamed the planet,
constantly searching for a permanent
place to settle down.
It was one day when they
found their own land to live
on. A magical forest, no less.
The four friends lived there
happily, feasting on berries
and sleeping in woven grass beds.
Though the life was wonderful,
the fairies began to get lonely
with only each other for
company. So they created a tree.
They named ~~the~~ it: The Birthing
Tree. Earth and Water combined
magic to ~~cre~~ make a

Variation III: Listening with Faith

For Brianna, the music notes remind her of the different planets in our galaxy. Pointing to the Middle C, D, and E on her music page, she explains to me, "E is for earth and there is the Moon beside it! Middle C is like Saturn with a ring around it!"

When I ask Brianna why the note D is for the Moon, she pauses for a moment and replies, "Moon dance!"

So, I ask again, "Saturn has a ring around it but it doesn't start with the letter C. Is there another planet name that starts with a letter C?"

With no hesitation, she immediately cries out, "Oh, yes! Cumanon!"

"Cumanon? Whoa! What a beautiful name. Can you tell me more about your special planet?"

As I invite her to describe her planet for me, Brianna happily shares a wondrous, magical story about a planet named Cumanon, a very special far away planet where happy dreams, smiles, and hugs await us.

"Cumanon is made up of many rainbow colors. There are 200 rings around it and everybody's favourite dreams are on it. The name rhymes with Pokémon and, if you come close, the rings will spread out like the big arms and hug you!"

∴

> [Dialogue] requires an intense faith in humankind,
> faith in their power to make and remake,
> to create and re-create, faith in their vocation to be more fully human.
> (Freire, 1970/2005, p. 90)

In *Experience and Education*, Dewey (1938) defined education as a continuation of growth in an "ever-present process" (p. 50). I am deeply drawn to his ways of thinking about education and the ways in which he brings awareness to our *present experiences* (Ryu, 2017a) because I am learning that "music is, for young children, primarily the discovery of sound" (Moorhead & Pond, 1941, p. 17).

Children love to *play* with sound.

For them, music is an integral, natural, and inseparable part of their lives, and they need to explore it and play with it to pursue their own musical interests, curiosities, and purposes.

To my students, piano playing is an *ever-present* journey.

Each thought, story, and question is meaningful.

Their present ideas and life experiences are what *matters* in our lessons.

For these reasons, I embrace *pedagogic listening* (Aoki, 1993) whereby both teachers and students take time to truly listen to one another. We attend to our present and stay *attuned* (Aoki, 1986, 1991, 2004) to the flow of our piano lessons because there is no singular approach to piano teaching that will work for all children.

There are many ways to learn to play the piano.

Every moment in our lesson calls for individuality, creativity, imagination, and flexibility for all the different ways in which children can learn about music and piano playing.

And so, from my students, I am learning that piano teaching and learning are ongoing processes of shared meaning making. They inspire me to embrace our

lessons as opportunities for new discoveries—new musical ways of knowing. They help me to see what may seem *irrelevant* and *distractive* in one moment could incite new ideas, directions, and possibilities that I couldn't have imagined. They teach me to have faith in their creative and imaginative ways of thinking about music and piano playing.

Variation IV: Listening with Hope

Ever since Jasmine started her piano lessons, she has been rushing through the door to give me a big hug.

"J-e-e-yeon...Guess what?"

"Yes, Jasmine?"

"I have a new song for you~"

Full of smiles and energy, she always rushes down the hallway ready to play me her new piano songs.

But, because she has yet to learn to read and write traditional music notation, Jasmine and I improvise and draw pictures to represent our music. We make up our own symbols to notate our musical ideas.

"Look! Here is my picture for my song!" Jasmine says as she holds the picture right up to my face.

And there it was, all the little animals underneath a big colorful rainbow, and a huge bluish-purple coloured monkey smiling.

"Jasmine, who is this?" I ask with great curiosity.

"It's my music monkey!"

"Whoa...this is a very special monkey...it's a magical monkey!"

"Yah, do you like it?"

"I love it! What does your musical monkey sound like?"

"Like this!"

Jasmine immediately starts to improvise her colourful notes all over the piano keys like the magical blue monkey jumping up and down across the rainbow.

∵

> Hope is rooted in [our] incompletion,
> from which [we] move out in constant search—
> a search which can be carried out only in communion with others.
> (Freire, 1970/2005, p. 91)

Jasmine's unchecked courage in improvisation leads me to think about all the students who no longer improvise to create artworks about their music. I wish we could have lingered a little longer in their ways of exploring music and piano playing. How wonderful it would be to dance across the piano keys without worrying about the *wrong* notes, rhythm, and timing—an improvisational way of playing the piano freely with imagination, creativity, and wonder.

In listening to my students' own wonderful, creative ways of learning to play the piano, I remain hopeful as I continue to ask myself: *what if we develop piano curriculum and pedagogy based on children's lived experiences of music making and piano playing? What if teachers and parents openly support, value, and acknowledge many of the extra musical learning—knowledge and meanings gained through sharing stories, questions, conversations, and drawings—that takes place in piano lessons as precious and important in child's reality? What if we seek for new meanings and possibilities of piano teaching and learning? What if we mindfully listen to all things that capture children's curiosities and imagination as a natural process of learning to play the piano? What if we embrace piano pedagogy as an emergent living process of shared inquiry? What if teachers and parents trust and have faith in the humanistic ways of knowing through music to create more joyful, meaningful piano playing experiences in our lives?*

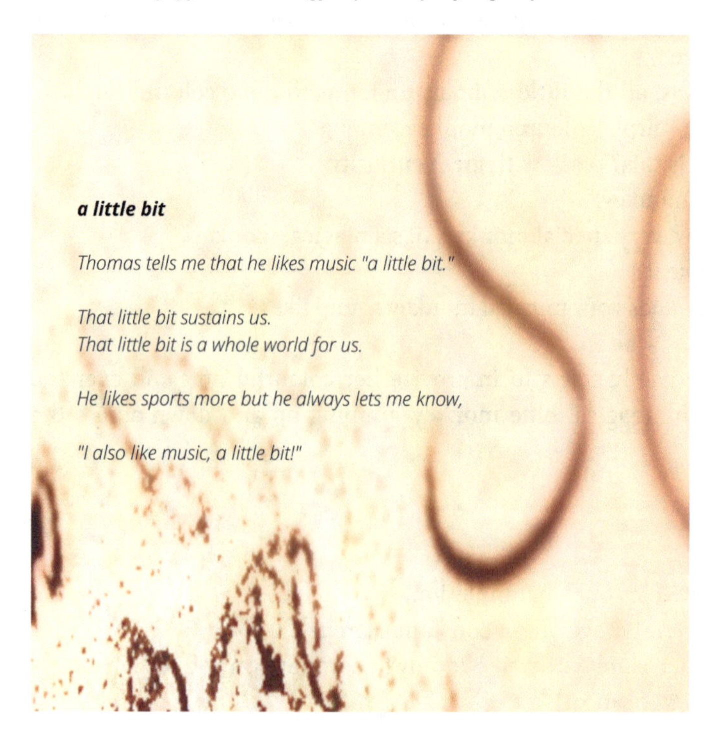

Variation v: Listening with Critical Thinking

Whenever Katie places her hands on the piano ready to play, I hold my breath. I know what's coming. I know I need to be ready.

Katie always happily plays all the notes *incorrectly*.

No rhythm.

No dynamics.

Wrong notes everywhere.

Whatever she is playing is not what is on the music score.

Nonetheless, I remind myself to breathe, patiently wait, and wholeheartedly listen until she finishes her playing.

No comments.

No interruptions.

Just listening.

Every time Katie finishes her piano playing, she asks me, "There! I did it! Was it *good*?"

I know she is not reading. She is not interested in learning to read. She doesn't like to play the music as written on the page.

Yet, Katie and I are expected to carry on our piano lessons. We are required to learn to read the *real* notes. We are asked to *fix* the mistakes and to count together. We are reminded that we *should* and *ought* to play the *right* notes and be steady.

"But why?" she asks.

"Yes, why?" I ask myself the same question all the time.

∴

> [Critical thinking] perceives reality as process, as transformation. (Freire, 1970/2005, p. 92)

Building a relation of care and trust for one another takes time (Noddings, 2012), and part of this emergent, reciprocal process needs to include all the things that our students may wish to share with us. Sometimes, my students *interrupt* their piano playing to tell me how much they like my sparkling earrings or a ring that I have on for the day. Other times, they show me their new wiggly teeth or a flower that they picked on their way to our piano lesson. The stories that they want to share, the little gifts that they find, and all the questions, ideas, and unique, individual ways of playing the piano call for our caring attention, understanding, and openness to possibility.

How teachers and parents think, feel, and respond to the expressed needs, interests, and ideas matter to young children. Our ways of being with young students have the capacity to motivate or discourage their curiosities, joy, and growth in learning. That is why it is critical that we have the sincere willingness to accept their ways of being even as we place great value in enabling young children to grow and develop at their own paces (Hua, 2012). When given the time and opportunity, children richly invest in their own *wonderful ideas* (Duckworth, 2006). When piano learning connects to children's interests, curiosities, and life experiences, they engage more meaningfully with music.

For these reasons, I take time to participate in reflective dialogical practice (Freire, 1970/2005) with my students to encourage them to trust themselves as authentic learners, thinkers, and creators (Rodgers & Raider-Roth, 2006). As Freire (1970/2005) explains: "without dialogue there is no communication, and without communication there can be no true education" (pp. 92–93). By engaging in a dialogical approach to piano teaching and learning, I can enable young students to have confidence and freedom to "critico-creatively" (Greene, 1984, p. 127) express and communicate their own ways of imagining music. In (re)conceptualizing piano pedagogy as an "act of creation and re-creation" (Freire, 1970/2005, p. 89), I can embrace music learning as an ongoing pedagogical process of (re)discovery.

As we listen with *love* for all our students' unique, individual ways of musical being, we celebrate children's stories, ideas, and interests about music, including everything else that brings them joy and happiness in life. When we listen with *humility*, we trust the process of transformation and growth in our students' present interests, questions, stories, and needs. In listening with *faith*, we place value in their own "power to make and remake, to create and re-create" (p. 90). As we listen with *hope*, we move closer to (re)creating what Aoki (1986/1991/2004) calls an "extraordinarily unique and precious place, a hopeful place, a trustful place, a caring place—essentially a human place" (p. 164). In *thinking critically* about piano teaching and learning, we begin "yearning towards possibility" (Greene, 1977, p. 134). We engage in "dialogue about what is it to be human, to grow, to *be*" (p. 123).

For me, the humanistic qualities of Freirean dialogue and listening infused with love, humility, hope, faith, and critical thinking inspire me to commune mindfully *with* and care *for* my students as we continually embark on our search for meanings. They enable me to *hear* all aspects of being in *pedagogical presence* (Rodgers & Raider-Roth, 2006). In listening for what matters most to my students, I welcome and commit to piano teaching and learning as an ever-present living practice—a joyful, beautiful part of our shared life journeys.

Codetta: 38+ Ways of Listening to Children's Piano Playing

What *is* piano playing?
For Kieran, piano is about music math with sounding numbers.
For Zoe, piano playing is about letting it go.
For Ashley, piano is time for play.
For Hael, music brings close friends together.
For Lysander, music keeps going and going.
For Jahan, learning to play the piano is so easy.
For Cameron, music is quiet stillness.
For Joy, piano is always inviting.
For Chelsea, piano learning is about happy don't-know(s) and not-sure(s).
For Tony, making music should always be like the Monster Boogie.
For Lily, music happens when her little brother begins his bouncy dance.
For Emilia, piano is about singing and dancing with her tiny little ballerina fingers.
For Kenny, piano playing is something that he can do all on his own.
For Julie, piano is fun only when accompanied by a guitar.
For Sarah, music is everything she loves.

For Minu, playing the piano is about making beautiful noise.
For Jenny, piano is flowing with happiness.
For Anthony, piano learning is about doing your best and never ever giving up.
For Jamie, piano play needs to be filled with endless Yays.
For Alexandra, music reminds her of all the Winx fairies with magical powers.
For Roman, piano play includes Mario, Luigi, and all other little mushroom Toads.
For Markus, music is everywhere.
For Valeria, piano playing is full of laughter and flying fingers.
For Sammy, music is filled with blue monkeys.
For Josie, piano playing is shining shyness.
For Chloe, music is filled with I-love-yous, kisses and hugs.

'I love music' heart-note composed by my young piano student

For Charlotte, playing the piano is happy, fun playtime with her little sister.
For Raina, music is poetry made up of colourful musical haiku.
For Katy, the process of learning to play the piano is full of untold, never-ending stories.
For Kathleen, music is full of sounding mystery.
For Lilian, piano playing is about sharing our songs with the little *Fuzzy*.
For Brenda, piano lesson is a great way to begin her weekend.
For Ben, piano brings endless smiles.
For Jessica, playing the piano is something that she likes to do every day.
For Joe, making up new songs brings new dreams.
For Emily, piano time is quiet nocturne over and over again.
For Kay, music is always bubbling fun.
And, for…
Piano playing *is*…

Notes

1 A selection of autoethnographic stories in this paper belong to a collection of stories included in the author's doctoral dissertation (see Ryu, 2017b).
2 All the student names are pseudonyms.

References

Aoki, T. T. (2004). Legitimating lived curriculum: Toward a curricular landscape of multiplicity. In W. F. Pinar & R. L. Irwin (Eds.), *Curriculum in a new key: The collected works of Ted T. Aoki* (pp. 199–215). Lawrence Erlbaum. (Original work published 1993)

Aoki, T. T. (2004). Teaching as indwelling between two curriculum worlds. In W. F. Pinar & R. L. Irwin (Eds.), *Curriculum in a new key: The collected works of Ted T. Aoki* (pp. 159–165). Lawrence Erlbaum. (Original work published 1986/1991)

Bochner, A. P., & Ellis C. (2016). *Evocative autoethnography: Writing lives and telling stories*. Routledge.

Dewey, J. (1938). *Experience and education*. Kappa Delta Pi.

Duckworth, E. (2006). *"The having of wonderful ideas" and other essays on teaching and learning*. Teachers College Press.

Eisner, E. W. (1997). The new frontier in qualitative research methodology. *Qualitative Inquiry, 3*(3), 259–273.

Freire, P. (1970/2005). *Pedagogy of the oppressed: 30th anniversary edition*. Continnum.

Gouzouasis, P., & Ryu, J. (2015). A pedagogical tale from the piano studio: Autoethnography in early childhood music education research. *Music Education Research, 17*(4), 397–420.

Greene, M. (1977). Toward wide-awakeness: An argument for the arts and humanities in education. *The Humanities and the Curriculum, 79*(1), 119–125.

Greene, M. (1984). The art of being present: Educating for aesthetic encounters. *Journal of Education, 166*(2), 123–135.

Hua, Z. (2012). Turning to the pedagogy of "listening": *Complicity: An International Journal of Complexity and Education, 9*(1), 57–74.

LeBlanc, N., Davidson, S. F., Ryu, J., & Irwin, R. L. (2015). Becoming through a/r/tography, autobiography and stories in motion. *International Journal of Education Through Art, 11*(3), 355–374.

Leggo, C. (1995). Storing the word/storying world. *English Quarterly, 28*(1), 5–11.

Leggo, C. (2005). The heart of pedagogy: On poetic knowing and living. *Teachers and Teaching, 11*(5), 439–455.

Lyle, E. (2009). A process of becoming: In favour of a reflexive narrative approach. *The Qualitative Report, 14*(2), 293–298.

Lyle, E. (2013). From method to methodology: Narrative as a way of knowing for adult learners. *The Canadian Journal for the Study of Adult Education, 25*(2), 17–34.

Moorhead, G., & Pond, D. (1941). *Music of young children, I: Chant.* Pillsbury Foundation for the Advancement of Music Education.

Noddings, N. (2012). The caring relation in teaching. *Oxford Review of Education, 38*(6), 771–781.

Rodgers, C. R., & Raider-Roth, M. B. (2006). Presence in teaching: *Teachers and Teaching: Theory and Practice, 12*(3), 265–287.

Ryu, J. (2017a). Deweyan fragments: Erasure poetry, music, and a story. In P. Sameshima, K. James, C. Leggo, & A. Fidyk (Eds.), *Poetic inquiry III: Enchantment of place* (pp. 297–304). Vernon Press.

Ryu, J. (2017b). *Exploring music and piano playing with young children: A piano teacher's pedagogical stories* [Unpublished doctoral dissertation]. University of British Columbia.

Ryu, J. (2018). I wish, I wonder, and everything I like: Living stories of piano teaching and learning with young children. *LEARNing Landscapes, 11*(2), 319–330.

CHAPTER 15

Re/centring *Montage* in Artistic | Educational Practices

Natalie LeBlanc

FIGURE 15.1 Still from *Bajorat: A Visual Narrative* by Amber MacGregor (Photograph by Amber MacGregor, used with permission)

The French word *montage* refers to the technical process of film editing (the cut from one shot to another). It is commonly known as a cinematic technique for compressing space, time, and information. However, as Willerslev and Suhr (2013) argue, montage also plays a crucial role in artistic, cultural, and academic practices, offering "alternative ways of venturing into the realm of the invisible" (p. 3).

In this chapter, I argue that montage is a material mode of engagement in which artistic practices and techniques, such as selection and juxtaposition, encourage a thinking *in* materials that has important implications for artistic and educational practices. I share a series of digital films made by artist-teachers in a course designed to teach technical and creative applications for digital presentations, the final course in a three-year program that places equal emphasis on studio and teaching practices in which artist-teachers work to investigate their artistic and pedagogical practices in and through visual arts. I theorize ways in which montage re/centres lived experience in artistic educational practices and addresses the capacity of lived experience to advance

© KONINKLIJKE BRILL NV, LEIDEN, 2022 | DOI:10.1163/9789004521186_015

relationality, both human and more than human. Through a new materialist lens, montage reveals processes of *diffraction* (Barad, 2007, 2010, 2014, 2017) becoming attentive to how differences are made and what effects they produce (LeBlanc et al., 2019). Through this work, I explore ways that montage provokes artist-teachers to think deeply with/in their practices making *diffractive-cuts* in which agencies emerged through entanglements and relationships between subjects and objects, bodies and media, and the visible and invisible.

Visual | Narratives

Montage always and necessarily involves the re/configuration of images, clips, and footage that diffractively/differentially re/constitute each other producing new entanglements. As an alternative to reflection, a mode of self-positioning that mirrors sameness through the totalization of narratives, montage offers a way of attuning to the movements, the ambiguities, and the differences that arise in bodies and things as they mutually intra-act. In the summer of 2020, teaching and learning quickly pivoted to an online format and, as such, students were (socially) distanced from the computer lab and had to use whatever technology they had available to them.

Through an exploration of non-linear modes of visual storytelling, artist-teachers presented their studio work using various artistic and cinematic effects. In the two following sub-sections, I examine a series of short films capturing the dynamic forces of materials and I discuss the vibrancy of these assemblages. Each montage is highly layered in which sound, light, colour, shape, line, and objects gather together, at once amplifying the rich textures of practice, and as a collection of experiences, events, and memories, fade in their temporal materiality.

Deleuze (1986, 1989) argues that the complexity of the cinematic experience resides in the *excess* of the storyline, which creates new potentials through the intensity of the image that produce new images of thought. For Deleuze, the plot is relatively rudimentary, whereas the complexities of life are in the image, "which achieves a diversity of realizations impelled through divisions within images, the play between images, their assemblages, sets, framing, angles, close-ups [and] shadings" (Kepferer, 2013, p. 23). Through unique sensorial configurations, montage produces affective intensities (Figure 15.2). Flows, movements, and forces will be explored by attending to the *practices/doings/actions* enacted through *diffractive/cuts* that montage makes possible and by extending what anthropologist Bruce Kapferer (2013) argues cinema does best, "concerning the way human beings construct their realities through a capacity

FIGURE 15.2 Still from *Bajorat: A Visual Narrative* by Amber MacGregor (Photograph by Amber MacGregor, used with permission)

to go outside the human and also to penetrate deeply within" (p. 24). This last act will be performed by *cutting/together/apart*.

Diffractive | Cuts

In the Master's program, artist-teachers spend three summers developing a reflective studio practice through the production of a focused body of artwork and contextualizing their work within contemporary artistic and art education practices. Through the pursuit of an individual project, several practices for conducting inquiry are encouraged: selecting a topic; developing a question; situating the inquiry within a theoretical framework; and relating the inquiry to art education practices. This final course provided an extensive exploration of the tools and processes used in presenting their inquiries, and it required artist-teachers to organize studio materials, processes, ideas, and resources into dynamic presentation structures through a combination of still/motion, visuals, text, and audio.

Cuts are normally used to convey actions and create reactions through an effect of continuity. A temporal ellipsis, for example, refers to ways in which cuts are made and used in order to omit parts of/or events. Through montage, and temporal ellipses in particular, there can be a speeding up of time in addition to breaks in time through techniques such as reverse-shots, flashbacks, and dream sequences. In such sequences, the addition of transitions such as fades, are used to signify a change in time. Through contrast and juxtaposition,

FIGURE 15.3 Stills from *The Promise of Intra-Actions* by Nadine Bouliane (Photograph by Nadine Bouliane, used with permission)

montage also has the ability of showing multiple shots simultaneously, inviting viewers to make connections and comparisons. In such instances, our vision becomes entangled within different, multiple, converging, and diverging perspectives.

Nadine's montage is a mixture of video clips with/in still images (freeze frames), causing the viewer to "jump between divergent perspectives" (Willerslev & Suhr, 2013, p. 6). She combines images and bits of nature collected from places that inspire her studio art practices with drawings and paintings made of traditional materials, photographs, and short video clips (Figures 15.3 & 15.4). Gestural lines, made of paint and graphite, sit on rectangular fields of colour held in place with what appear to be small pieces of masking tape. Many of the frames within these compositions are reminiscent of analogue polaroid pictures or pages ripped from a sketchbook.

In time, the images within these frames begin to move and what we first assume are still images become animated. In many instances, they begin to play a short video clip, pulling us through a small portal into another dimension—the sound of frozen ground crunching loudly under a pair of winter boots, or the shimmering and dancing of light moving across water. Nadine's entire montage repeats similar yet different assemblages such as these throughout its entirety. Through a variety of images and compositions, each with its own unique sequences and juxtapositions, including different combinations of still and moving images.

In a second example, Evelyn uses animated transitions, freeze frames, and the juxtaposition of still images and video to combine a series of her digital

FIGURE 15.4 Still from *The Promise of Intra-Actions* by Nadine Bouliane (Photograph by Nadine Bouliane, used with permission)

artwork, featuring small repeating diagonal lines on top of images of landscape and nature. In several scenes, we see a grid in which the small digital markings in a variety of colours begin to form before our eyes through repetition and pattern (Figure 15.5). Her montage presents multiple collections of *colour palettes* as well as the processes of making them and looking for them in her everyday surroundings.

A range of colour palettes and the scenes that inspire them are shown one after another in sequence. There is a speeding up of time during some of these compilations and a slower pace for emphasizing certain colour combinations and juxtapositions. At times, it appears as though these scenes are stills; however, micro-movements like a breeze-blown flower reveal that they are long, continuous shots that work to stretch time out to create a tension in the viewing experience. Our sight begins to move along with the camera's movements as it jumps between the foreground and the background, between the colourful diagonal lines that seemingly float on an invisible skin of film while the landscape recedes into the distance.

FIGURE 15.5 Montage of stills from *Designing your Art Palette* by Evelyn Crossley (Photograph by Evelyn Crossley, used with permission)

In a third example, Gina uses a series of macro shots, animation, and parallel editing. Different shots combined together in one frame alternate with one single cropped and close-up image extracted from her painting process creating a world of swirling colour. The circle, as a motif, appears and repeats throughout. First, as a canvas that supports the action of painting and, then, like lens capturing the fluidity of the bleeding colours and the performative acts of brushing and pouring paint onto canvas (see Figure 15.6). Through movement and animation, the circle jumps and swirls in and between the series of frames and shots. At times, it is unclear if we are examining a specimen through a

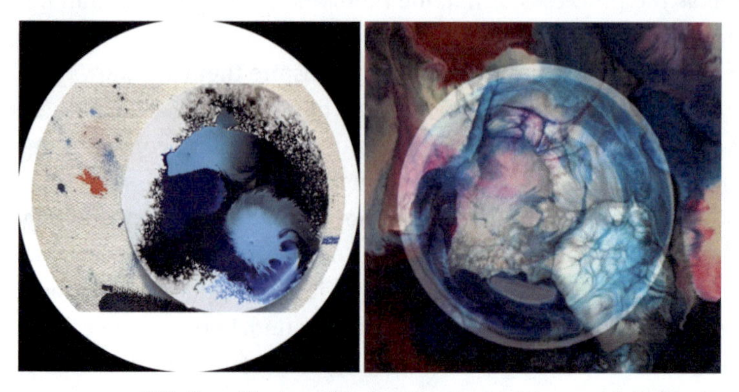

FIGURE 15.6 Stills from *The Art of Play* by Gina Sicotte (Photograph by Gina Sicotte, used with permission)

microscope or a distant planet through the lens of a telescope. Through various and exaggerated modes of magnification and cropping, we are brought into close proximity with her material explorations, moving in-between micro and macro perspectives, immersing the viewer into a completely different reality.

Cutting | Together | Apart

Whether in analogue or digital form, the artist's task is to make aesthetic choices regarding the *why* and *how* of making cuts that have a direct impact on the film's narrative. This section attends to montage and the *practices/doings/actions* of making cuts as an experience-driven approach. Barad (2014) argues that "intra-actions enact agential cuts, which do not produce absolute separations, but rather cut together-apart" (p. 168). The concept of cutting together/apart is a process that both "joins and disjoins" (Barad, 2010, p. 244), producing dis/continuity. Barad (2014) points out that this is the hauntological nature of quantum entanglements, she writes,

> There is no smooth temporal (or spatial) topology connecting beginning and end. Each scene diffracts various temporalities, iteratively differentiating and entangling, within and across, the field of spacetimemattering. Scenes never rest but are reconfigured within and are dispersed across and threaded through one another. (pp. 244–245)

It is here where I would like to address the ghost in the room, a fourth example of an artist-teacher's montage created by Amber, entitled, "*Bajorat*" (Figures 15.1, 15.2, & 15.7), a small meditation on a cyanotype[1] inspired by the poem

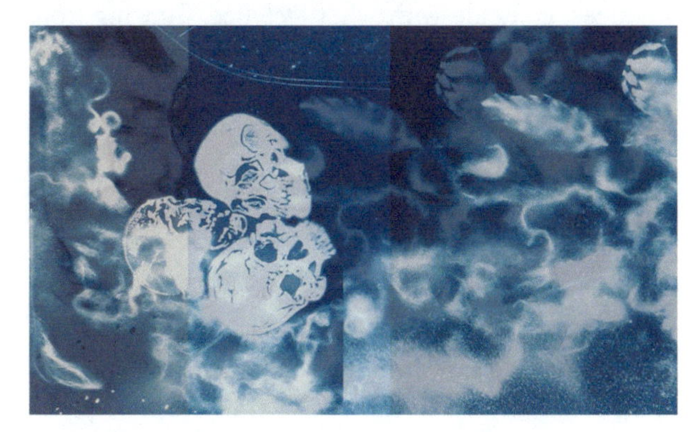

FIGURE 15.7 Still from *Bajorat: A Visual Narrative* by Amber MacGregor (Photograph by Amber MacGregor, used with permission)

Dolphin Catcher's Mummy Man by writer Astrid Van der Pol. In 2016, a sailboat was found listing in the South Pacific Ocean and onboard were the remains of Manfred Fritz Bajorat, a German sailor, who had been mummified by hot, dry weather and salt. At the time, it was unknown how long his corpse had been floating undiscovered or when he had died. Amber writes:

> I wanted to observe that time frame between Bajorat's death and the discovery of his mummified body. I used the technique of temporal expansion through slow transition dissolves and sound, to create a sense that the images exist outside of a common time-frame. I wanted to heighten the uncertain quiet, amidst the ocean waves before that rush of noise and activity that exposed the image of his greyed and desiccated corpse for all the world to see. (Artist Statement, 2020)

In this outer/other world, Amber's montage asks, *what if Bajorat's secrets remained undiscovered by the human world?* It shares an aesthetic quality with the film *La Jetée* created in 1962 by Chris Marker, unfolding like a photomontage, a composite image made of multiple, overlapping images. Unlike the standard 24 frames per second that conventional filmmakers utilize to create a feeling of continuity in the viewing experience, Amber's technique deliberately makes movements between images *feel* slower. There is an uncanniness in the viewing experience, a haunted and ghostly feeling produced in the atmosphere for which Bajorat's body makes an appearance on screen as a peculiar and supernatural event—a force and a form—a living/dead.

Amber's montage helps shed light on what montage *does*, particularly the *cutting/together/apart* that has become our focus. Fragments that have been combined in such a way as to draw attention to the movements between shots and to the affect this produces, coincide with what Deleuze, drawing from Soviet filmmaker Eisenstein, argues create a *collision*. For Deamer (2016), this style of editing is meant "to draw attention to itself" (p. 169) to produce a cut[2]—to "a more radical Elsewhere outside homogeneous space and time" (Deleuze, 1986, p. 17). The virtual[3] does not pertain to the on-screen images but to the *interstices*, the *gaps*, and the *out-side*—"that which is not given" (Deamer, 2016, p. 171).

Practice-led researcher Barbara Bolt (2013) argues that materialist films, with non-narrative as their object, open alternate encounters that are *truer to life*. She writes, "materialist films create situations where memory is re-experienced in the present rather than the recalled" (p. 10). Through "techniques of fragmentation, defamiliarization and abstraction" (Knowles, 2020, p. 27), they function beyond signification and representation (O'Sullivan, 2006) by revealing how the timing/layering of shots and imagery "creates a complexity and intensity that is affectively powerful and works performatively" (Bolt, 2013, p. 10). Bolt (2013), drawing from Deleuze's theory of time informed by Henri Bergson's notion of *duration*, rejects the notion that time is an external force built on linear sequencing of events. Rather, through duration, time is multiple, affective, and embodied, capable of bringing the past and the future together into the *living present* (see also Boulton, 2019). Through the cutting and re-arranging of shots, Amber's cyanotype became something else. As Colebrook (2006) argues:

> By presenting the image of the very production of a set of images cinema gives a direct confrontation with time. Time is no longer that which measures movement within the world, but is the creation of images that alter just what counts as the world. Cinema presents an image of the opening of relations of another world from within an actual world. This is time: the production of worlds, not the passage from one moment to another 'in' time, but the opening of time, the creation of the new. (p. 91)

Re-turning to the three previous artist-teachers' films, we may begin to recognize how they, too, are productions of a world-becoming with haptic and tactile qualities, bringing "the virtuality of life to presence" (Colebrook, 2006, pp. 84–85). Nadine's montage (Figure 15.8) renders aesthetic moments for her

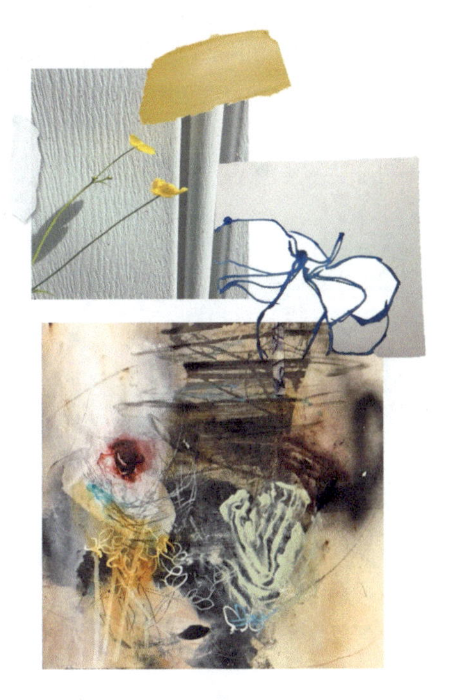

FIGURE 15.8
Still from *The Promise of Intra-Actions* by Nadine Bouliane (Photograph by Nadine Bouliane, used with permission)

viewers to feel the wild places that ispire her artwork through movement, gesture, translucency, and opaqueness. She recounts, "I included short video clips that could create sensory pauses, mirroring the kinds of aesthetic gathering I find myself responding to in my work" (Artist Statement, 2020).

Evelyn's digital *petits points* or digital *cross-stitches* (Figure 15.9), are woven through temporal holes and visual gaps echoing her daily art practices that function on the repetition of gesture and the performative power of being immersed in the present, helping her to sustain both her artistic and educational practices. She writes, "I wanted to maintain a dreamlike quality...the pieces slowly make their way to fill a void...the flood of artwork breathing life" (Artist Statement, 2020).

Gina's montage (Figure 15.10), guided by processes of experimentation and invention, produces playful events through the intimacy and proximity of materials—and by attending to the movement and transitions between fragments, layers, and flows that relinquish outcomes in favour of curiosity, wonder, and an attunement to, and discovery of, pattern. Gina explains, "My film [depicts] the journey from exploring media to discovering moments of playful creation where the beauty of the unknown resides. Honouring the subtle moments of noticing potential, noticing patterns, noticing opportunities" (Artist Statement, 2020).

Within the context of new materialism, *cutting/together/apart* resonates with the agency of materials and how relations between humans and non-humans challenge human exceptionalism (Barad, 2007). For Barad (2014), there is a spectral quality to the process of cutting/together/apart—a "quantum weirdness"

FIGURE 15.9 Still from *Designing your Art Palette* by Evelyn Crossley (Photograph by Evelyn Crossley, used with permission)

FIGURE 15.10 Still from *The Art of Play* by Gina Sicotte (Photograph by Gina Sicotte, used with permission)

that transforms into "quantum queerness"—that she argues increases uncanny phenomena. Bolt (2011) argues that montage and photomontage are an *assemblage* "that produces new resemblances with non-resembling means" (p. 271). By mixing fragments in new ways, Bolt argues that montage is "simultaneously both homely (Heimlich) and unhomely (Unheimlich)" (pp. 271–272)—the uncanny—which Freud (1955) infamously describes as being *strangely familiar* rather than mysterious.

For Massumi (2011), "there is the slightly uncanny sense of feeling sight in the invisible" (p. 44). This pertains to the thinking-feeling of an event and the experiential, lived reality of the virtual—"a sense of aliveness that accompanies every perception. We don't just look, we sense ourselves alive" (Massumi, 2011, p. 43). Montage, as affect and embodiment, is a re-occurring thread in all of the montages presented in this chapter, *relaying* between the digital and the analogue as self-varying abstractions. Massumi (2011) writes, that abstract art "makes felt a dynamic, a vitality affect, that has no object. It's not animation *of* anything. It's pure animatedness, a vitality affect that comes from no thing and nowhere in particular" (p. 69).

When Deleuze (1978) argues that "the abstract *is* lived experience…you can live nothing but the abstract and nobody has lived anything else but the abstract" (Massumi, 2011, p. 43), he means that life is lived in rhythms of intensity and affect (Adkins, 2016) and that this lived experience also pertains to non-human life—and matter itself. In this *strangely familiar* world, "sensations, percepts and affects are *beings* whose validity lies in themselves and exceeds any lived" (Deleuze & Guattari, 1994, p. 27).

Adema (2014), drawing on Barad, argues that cuts do not function through representations or "allegories *of* the world but [are] direct interventions *in* the world" (p. 245). For Adema (2014), "cutting becomes a technique not of rendering or representing the world, but of managing, ordering, and creating it, of giving it meaning" (p. 246). This resonates with how Marcus (2013) argues that montage is a visual way of thinking, a "deep tactile, and immersive form of play in which "concepts, ideas, allusions, and gestures emerge as intellectual 'things'" (p. 304). As an apparatus, montage became a way for artist-teachers to collate, to curate, and to present their artistic inquiries through aesthetic processes that provoke further experiences in the unfolding of events and the ways in which they entangle through *practices/doings/actions* of selecting, gathering, inventing, compositing, and re/mixing. Each *cut* diffracts in images and durations of artist-teachers' practices as they differently and performatively intra-act within a network of agencies, both human and non-human, producing on-going relational movements of living.

One of the most striking elements pertains to the sensitivities enacted with/in how the artwork is visually presented. Colour and movement disperse in radiant motions across the surface of the screen provoking "an experience of seeing" (Massumi, 2011, p. 74). As an event of *pure perception*—"a feeling of seeing sight caught in its intensive act" (Massumi, 2011, p. 70)—what becomes apparent are the agentic, non-human forces and their vital materialism. Artwork becomes dis/mantled, dis/membered and, at times, in/discernible. Paintings, drawings, photographs, cyanotypes, collage, and video transform into lines, shapes, marks, tones, and reflections of light that shimmer each producing their own distinct and unique rhythms that result in a multiplicity of connections and movements, generating new fields of possibility.

Conclusion

In this chapter, I discussed the potential of montage for provoking new and creative thought through a series of films made by artist-teachers in their final course in a Masters of Education program. Drawing on Barad's (2007, 2010, 2014) concept of *cutting/together/apart*, I argued that montage presents a sense of dis/continuity in which agencies emerge through forces and entanglements between subjects and objects, bodies and media, and the visible and invisible. Unlike traditional filmmaking techniques that make cuts *seamless*, montage re/centres lived experience through affect/ions, percept/ions, and sensations that not only speak to the complexity of lived experience, but make experience lived in the present through duration.

Acknowledgements

I thank Nadine Bouliane, Evelyn Crossley, Amber MacGregor, and Gina Sicotte for their creative and artistic insight that contributed substantively to the writing of this manuscript. My gratitude extends to Valerie Triggs and Ellyn Lyle for their generous feedback, helping me to strengthen this chapter.

Notes

1 Cyanotypes are photographic-like impressions that use a mixture of iron compounds that when exposed to UV light and washed in water, oxidize creating Prussian Blue images.
2 The time-image For Deleuze (1989) and more specifically *Lectosigns*, pertains to "the virtual arising from the disruptions of the image and narration—a new image of thought, the unthought" (Deamer, 2016, p. 163).
3 For Massumi (2002), "Images of the virtual make the virtual appear not in their content or form, but in the fleeting, in their sequencing or sampling. The appearance of the virtual is in the twists and folds of formed content, in the movement from one sample to another. It is in the ins and outs of imaging. This applies whether the image is verbal, as in an example or parable, or whether it is visual or aural. No one kind of image, let alone any one image can render the virtual" (p. 133).

References

Adema, J. (2014). *Cutting scholarship together/apart. Rethinking the political-economy of scholarly book publishing*. Routledge.
Adkins, B. (2016). Who thinks abstractly? Deleuze on abstraction. *The Journal of Speculative Philosophy, 30*(3), 352–360.
Barad, K. (2007). *Meeting the universe halfway: Quantum physics and the entanglement of matter and meaning*. Duke University Press.
Barad, K. (2010). Quantum entanglements and hauntological relations of inheritance: Dis/continuities, spacetime enfoldings, and justice-to-come. *Derrida Today, 3*(2), 240–268.
Barad, K. (2014). Diffracting diffraction: Cutting together-apart. *Parallax, 20*(3), 168–187.
Barad, K. (2017). No small matter: Mushroom clouds, ecologies of nothingness, and strange topologies of spacetimemattering. In A. Tsing, H. Swanson, E. Gan, & N.

Bubandt (Eds.), *Arts of living on a damaged planet* (pp. 103–120). University of Minnesota Press.

Bolt, B. (2011). Unimaginable happenings: Material movements in the plane of composition. In S. Zepke & S. O'Sullivan (Eds.), *Deleuze and contemporary art* (pp. 266–285). Edinburgh University Press.

Bolt, B. (2013). Toward a 'new materialism' through the arts. In E. Barrett & B. Bolt (Eds.), *Carnal knowledge: Towards a new materialism through the arts* (pp. 1–13). I.B. Tauris.

Boulton, A. (2019). Artistic inquiry in art teacher education: Provoking intuition through a montage of memory in and of place. *The Canadian Review of Art Education, 46*(2), 3–16.

Colebrook, C. (2006). *Deleuze: A guide for the perplexed.* Continuum.

Deamer, D. (2016). *Deleuze's cinema books: Three introductions to the taxonomy of images.* Edinburgh University Press.

Deleuze, G. (1986). *Cinema 1: Movement-image* (H. Tomlinson & B. Habberjam, Trans.). University of Minnesota Press.

Deleuze, G. (1989). *Cinema 2: Time-image* (H. Tomlinson & R. Galeta, Trans.). University of Minnesota Press.

Deleuze, G. (1991). *Bergsonism* (H. Tomlinson & B. Habberjam, Trans.). Zone Books

Deleuze, G. (1994). *Difference & repetition* (P. Patton, Trans.). Columbia University Press.

Deleuze, G., & Guattari, F. (1994). *What Is philosophy?* Columbia University Press.

Freud, S. (1919/1955). The 'uncanny.' In *The standard edition of the complete psychological works of Sigmund Freud, volume XVII (1917–1919)* (pp. 218–252). Hogarth.

Kepferer, B. (2013). Montage and time: Deleuze, cinema, and a Buddhist sorcery rite. In C. Suhr & R. Willerslev (Eds.), *Transcultural montage* (pp. 20–39). Berghahn.

Knowles, K. (2020). *Experimental film and photochemical practices.* Palgrave MacMillan.

LeBlanc, N., Triggs, V., & Irwin, R. L. (2019). Sub/versing mentoring expectations: Duration, discernment, diffraction. *The Journal of Social Theory in Art Education, 39*(1), 82–96.

Marcus, G. E. (2013). Afterword: The traffic in montage, then and now. In C. Suhr & R. Willerslev (Eds.), *Transcultural montage* (pp. 302–307). Berghahn.

Massumi, B. (2002). *Parables for the virtual: Movement, affect, sensation.* Duke University Press.

Massumi, B. (2011). *Semblance and event: Activist philosophy and the occurrent arts.* MIT Press.

O' Sullivan, S. (2006). *Art encounters Deleuze and Guattari: Thought beyond representation.* Palgrave Macmillan.

Willerslev, R., & Suhr, C. (2013). Montage as an amplifier of invisibility. In C. Suhr & R. Willerslev (Eds.), *Transcultural montage* (pp. 1–16). Berghahn.

CHAPTER 16

Awakening Conscious Bodies in Relational Learning/Living Places

Danielle Denichaud, Andrea Nann, Michelle Silagy and Philip Davis

> Conscious Bodies aims to nourish how we support each other…so that each member of our shared circle can find something of value for themselves—a gift of care to celebrate the uniqueness of our individual embodied stories, and an experience of kind connection to ripple out into our broader communities and Lands we call home.
>
> DREAMWALKER (2020, p. 2)

∴

Invitation to the Reader

This chapter broaches embodied communication in shared physical places and across digital landscapes. We offer this introduction to Conscious Bodies Methodology and the Cycles of Activation pedagogy as an opportunity to awaken felt awareness of "the body as a receptive space," providing reflection and experience of the ways we are learning to welcome inner worlds into shared learning places (Snowber, 2009, p. 31). The appropriate pathway to share our discoveries of this work as a somatic journey to meet "ourselves as *mental, physical, spiritual and emotional* beings in relationship with…all of Creation" would be to invite readers to co-create a circle together (Dreamwalker, 2020, p. 6). In lieu of this opportunity, we offer this theoretical and pedagogical introduction to the embodied, sensorial, imaginative, and kind inquiry that potentiates the ongoing evolution of Conscious Bodies Methodology.

In terms of flow, this chapter will present the Dreamwalker Dance Company research team and the inquiry we conducted during two Conscious Bodies community engagement projects, which includes transitioning from in-person to an online facilitation format in response to the global pandemic. Following this framing, the reader will encounter Conscious Bodies Methodology, its genealogy, conceptual pillars, and key pedagogical awarenesses, along

© KONINKLIJKE BRILL NV, LEIDEN, 2022 | DOI:10.1163/9789004521186_016

with the central pedagogical structure the cycle of activations. This section is followed by pedagogical entry points for educators who wish to engage with this embodied pedagogy, either as individuals or within their education spaces and amongst community. Interactive links provide the reader with a range of guided supports as well as examples of the community artistic creations that resulted from the highlighted research contexts. A conclusion provides the reader with questions and considerations to support their own reflective awareness about their experience with the chapter material.

Research Team & Foci

Between summer 2019 and summer 2021, Andrea Nann (Dreamwalker Dance Company Founder, Artistic Director, and Project Instigator), Michelle Silagy (Inclusion Facilitator), Danielle Denichaud (Wellness Facilitator/Researcher), and Philip Davis (Indigenous Liaison) engaged in collaborative inquiry to perceive and identify criteria for the co-creation of empathetic learning places.

Research Contexts

Conscious Bodies of Methodology (CBM) and the Cycles of Activations (COA) pedagogy take distinct form through various community engagement actions, whose variables include number of sessions, population size, population demographics, and artistic/community engagement outcome.

Conscious Bodies Methodology

CBM is an embodied community practice created by Dreamwalker Dance Company Artistic Director Andrea Nann. CBM was born in 1995 from Nann's experiences working with Grade 6 students on the topic of Cambodian refugee camps in Thailand after the Khmer Rouge genocide. Since its first expression, CBM has evolved through sessions with hundreds of individuals from diverse communities, seasons of life, and cultures, bringing artists and non-artists together for collaborative multi-modal artistic projects. Multi-generational learning fulfils a core intention of the practice, inviting new and perennial practitioners to co-create in shared spaces.

Cycle of Activations

The Cycle of Activations (COA) is the pedagogical journey of CBM; specific, embodied intentions orient participants through various sensorial discoveries of self, space, each other, and environs. Through a practice of aesthetic embodied inquiry (Snowber, 2009, 2019), participants are guided to marvel at the ordinary materiality of their physical bodies and living places using an immersive gaze of "radical amazement" (Anderson & Suominen Guyas, 2012, p. 234). Resonant with Snowber (2019), we celebrate that "the body has a huge capacity to open up places of knowledge and wisdom where the feet, hands, hips and heart literally uncover multiple realities and perceptions weaving inquiry, research and pedagogy together" (p. 236). Valuing the subjective experience of both facilitators and participants, COA evokes individuals' memories, imaginings, and dreams, "stewarding our collective togethering into kind connection" (Dreamwalker, 2020, p. 15).

Co-Creating Relational and Empathetic Dialogue Processes

The malleable pedagogical space or "container" intentionally created by the COA is functional to welcoming individuals' inner worlds into a *dialogue process* with group members (Holmes, 2015). According to Holmes, "the Dialogue Process can change the total felt quality of its own process as an experience; its own ritual structures serve as constraints…[which] are created and maintained by group members" (p. 292). Centering "the productive, creative quality of [group] communication" (DeTurk, 2001, p. 376), CBM embraces a sociological definition of relational empathy, as "the imaginative, intellectual and emotional participation in another person's experience" (p. 418). Years of experiences with CBM/COA have taught us that embodied relationality or "kinesthetic empathy" requires not only an awakening of one's own sensorial, imaginative, and emotional receptors, but also a softening of one's membrane to the living, breathing, co-creative space among bodies (Rae, 2018, p. 95).

The two contexts presented here are exemplars of our work; they are not an exhaustive representation of Conscious Bodies community engagement projects.[1]

Body Space Creation Place (2017–present)

Body Space Creation Place (BSCP) offers one-off individual movement sessions, open to all bodies, genders, and cultures, stewarded by Andrea Nann and dance artist facilitators. True to CBM's core intention, each year, select new artists are welcomed into BSCP facilitator training to create a faceted generational lens on the evolution of the work. At the time of the research (2019–2021), the facilitation team consisted of nine members, representing a diversity of interests, dance/movement practices, and communities. The research was conducted during the beginning and peak of the global pandemic, stimulating a shift from in-person offerings to online formats. The embodied and non-directive nature of this work raised the stakes for ensuring the maintenance of methodology and pedagogy integrity across digital landscapes. Pedagogical considerations and insights gleaned from ongoing reflective sharing circles between the research team and facilitators will be shared in future sections.

The Welcome Project: Sharing Stories (2019–2021)

The Welcome Project: Sharing Stories (TWP:SS) is an evolution of The Welcome Project (TWP) (2018–2019), which brought together hundreds of newcomers and dance artists to experience a series of *Conscious Bodies* workshops with the intention to embody the positive public action, *The Welcome Gesture*. TWP:SS was created in response to the isolated realities caused by the global pandemic. Acknowledging the need for togethering and authentic connection, Nann designed intimate *petal* experiences where one facilitator, one ambassador, and two participants explore the cycles of activation towards the creation of 2-minute stories reflecting the theme of home. Partnering with local communities, artists, non-artists, and individuals who self-identified as marginalized (BIPOC, 2SLGBTQI+, youth, dis/abled, seniors, newcomers) the project has completed two chapters in Guelph and Niagara. An intimate look at the transition from an in-person to the online format, including insights into the experiences of creating text, sound, movement, and heart story creations is told from the perspective of organizers, facilitators, ambassadors, and participants in the documentary *The Welcome Gesture Project*.[2]

CBM/COA Philosophical Pillars

Distilling the information shared by the core team during The Welcome Project: Sharing Stories pre-petal training sessions, we offer essential awarenesses and pedagogical considerations that orient how we co-create empathetic learning places.

The Human Is a Caring Being

Our work is grounded in the assumption that humans long for connection and have a capacity to relate to others with kindness. Our body is in a continual dynamic of renewal, so we continually come back to noticing our breath in order to soften our minds, to listen and feel into the newness of each moment. Returning to our breath with curious attention awakens us to the present of our perceptive, receptive, feeling body, inviting our emergence into spaces of possibility.

Impregnating our noticing with *positive emotional investment* and *radical amazement* awakens and cultivates our innate empathy (Anderson & Suominen Guyas, 2012). Whole being sensing in the context of playful relationship with the body and physical space helps bridge to places of real experiences of ourselves as kind creative beings. We awaken the sensorial imagination to frame the miraculous reality of our interconnectedness with life, which "brings love, passion, wonder and magic" (p. 234) because we're entering with wonderment, instead of knowing what is.

The Body Is Conscious

In CBM, we constantly practice noticing the body, beginning with witnessing the body and following the body as guide to our felt presence with self, each other, Land, and Cosmos. This work brings therapeutic effect to individuals' overall wellbeing because all feelings and sensations that arise are appreciated and respected in our shared spaces, welcoming somatic expression according to individual desire, pacing, and comfort to participate. The various somatic pathways of embodied noticing in COA are trauma-informed through their support of a frequent return to "a bodily sense of safety in the present moment…to help everyone…connect with our bodily capacities for feeling centred, grounded, balanced, and awake" (Rae, 2018, pp. 126–127).

As we move together, we trust that by embracing all aspects of our being, by returning to a fluid breath and listening to our heart beats, we can create space for the wholeness of each individual to emerge with/from conscious embodied felt awareness. In this way, words, memories, dreams, sensations, and feelings that long to be expressed are welcome to naturally arise as a part of the group journey.

Honouring Our Circle/The Space Is Alive

We desire to co-create environments where kindness, care, creativity, and reciprocity are possible. Philip Davis reminds us that The Medicine Wheel Teachings have brought our circles to life while obliging an empathetic due diligence to treat our safe spaces as sacred entities. Tending the aliveness of our shared spaces welcomes our bodies into compassionate presence and shows us how to care for each other as mental, physical, emotional, and spiritual beings. Ensuring that each member of the circle is looked after—is invited to look after each other and our circle—is how we seed equity into our shared learning spaces. Resonant with Opaskwayak Cree scholar Shawn Wilson (2008), who wrote in his book *Research is Ceremony,* "rather than viewing ourselves as being *in* relationship with other people or things, we *are* the relationships that we hold and are part of" (p. 80).

Best Practices for Online Facilitation[3]

Pedagogical insights from reflective circles between Dreamwalker researchers and Body Space Creation Place facilitators are selectively shared in this section, demonstrating that co-creativity can be stewarded across physical distances and amongst diverse expressions of presence.

Stewarding Pathways for Relationality

Quality of connection, belonging, and inclusion are at the forefront of CBM/COA facilitation. Great intentionality is given to the creation of direct and non-direct entry points for individuals to participate with movement invitations and the collective group experience. Navigating the natural awkwardness and anxieties that are expected from new workshop participants proved challenging giving the limitations of digital relationality. The use of movement "dialoguing" in the form of group flocking exercises, "pinning" a partner for brief duets, and the use of verbal *noticing* were elements of COA that became grounding components to support participant engagement.

The practice of *noticing* is used to verbalize observations of unique and synchronous movement choices emerging during movement processes (i.e., "I see some interesting shapes and use of rhythm right now"). While group synchrony happens organically in physical spaces, the absence of peripheral vision in digital landscapes creates accessibility challenges for natural movement scaffolding. This required more attention on verbal *noticing* to encourage and support renewed creativity from workshop participants.

Welcoming Shades of Participation

Shades of participation is a foundational concept of CBM and key element of inclusivity for welcoming all bodies. While dark screens and silent presence can initially be challenging, facilitators reflected on the hypocrisy inherent to inviting individuals to create their own experience and then insisting that they visually and aurally invite strangers into their personal space. Countering the assumption that participation with distance is of lesser quality, our research revealed that online spaces were experienced by some as serendipitous places to connect more intimately with one's own inner world, as well as provided empowering opportunities for individuals to follow their personal level of comfort towards co-creative presence with others.

Through their embrace of participants' shades of participation, facilitators made greater use of the multi-literacies integrated into the COA pedagogy. For example, music and silence are often used to support movement experiences; participants are invited to lay down in their space, walk away from the camera, journal or rip paper, make sounds while muted, write words in the chat, or hold words written on paper up to the screen. Respecting a participant's right to choose their shade of participation also supported the facilitators' experience of equity in workshop co-creation, releasing some of their responsibility to manage participant experiences.

Imagination as a Communication/Connection Tool

Coherent with CBM/COA principles, imaginative language is used by facilitators to create pathways for aesthetic wonderment and sensorial listening during embodied explorations. Intentionally using "imagination as a humanizing capacity" (Lake, 2013, p. 2), perennial facilitator Sid consciously maintains a visceral connection with participants through the digital screen *portal*.

> I scroll through people's names, and I create a tether to them…I take time to imagine the whole map of where everybody is, and that I can magically transport myself at any point. I'll go into the power of my imagination to do that—I'm genuinely quite worried about how everyone else is doing and I really want to make sure everyone else is okay. (July 12, 2020, Reflective Circle)

This is an example of the "empathetic imagination" (Lake, 2013, p. 82) that informs *Conscious Bodies* facilitation. Loyal to the intentional heart of this work, facilitators and participants are honoured as unique worlds of knowledge, so imagination is continually evoked to inspire "the conditions out of which personal meaning is continually created *from within*" (p. 102).

Celebrating the Diverse Worlds of Each Other

Transitions into, among, and from guided physical explorations and group discussions invite individuals' inner worlds to the forefront of awareness. The use of silence, joyful exploration, and care-filled listening weave inclusion into our co-created learning places. Michelle Silagy creates frequent space for individuals to meet the currents of their own learning path:

> I'm wondering if you'd like to take a few moments to jot or note down anything that you absorbed…about what you heard or felt, what you thought about or even daydreamed. How are you going to commune with what was said? How do you process in the presence of each other?

Slowing down time to create opportunities for meeting subjective places of understanding relaxes attention on the outcome, and circle members are supported to respect their natural learning rhythms.

Facilitation Frameworks for Educators

To support the reader's integration of CBM and COA amongst their communities, we offer a guiding framework of embodied sensibilities towards the co-creation of inclusive, caring, and empathetic learning places. Instead of prioritizing all elements, we encourage a balanced consideration of four facets of embodiment. We invite you to intuitively choose a facet and notice your responsiveness to the different elements while paying attention to any experiences of curiosity and resistance in your body.

Identifying Embodiment

- Preparing the space (welcome music, warm up movements, check in/greeting)
- Physical positioning (with relation to each other, in the digital frame)
- Use of silence/stillness/transitions

Activating Embodiment

- Intention activation/reactivation (balance verbal/kinesthetic)
- Multi-sensorial explorations of self/other(s)/space
- Connection with environs/Earth/Land, Four Directions and Realms

Noticing Embodiment

- Discovering a shared group language: encourage vocal/physical expressions
- Witnessing, following, and generating movement
- Where are sparks happening between self, circle, other, place, group?

Deepening Embodiment

- Allow integration time (feel into the rhythm of group learning)
- Nurture sensitivity and responsiveness to the group mind and group heart
- How is community being created? (sharing power/authority)

Interactive Pedagogical Entry Points

Conscious Bodies Methodology is an embodied community practice, experienced and co-created on the lands of Turtle Island. Integrating the

> Medicine Wheel and Traditional teachings from the First Peoples invites us to deepen our awareness of holistic interconnections among the diverse experiences of self, others, and our environs. (Dreamwalker, 2020, p. 2)

Philip Davis, who is Haudenosaunee of Six Nations of the Grand River, has woven his knowledge into the Conscious Bodies pedagogical framework, imbuing the organizational structure with perennial wisdom of his ancestors and First Peoples of the Lands where our work is conducted. At the beginning of all project training sessions, facilitators and participants are invited to engage with a Thanksgiving Address, Land Acknowledgement, and The Medicine Wheel Teachings; we invite you to explore these before you engage with the guided embodied practices that follow.

- *Thanksgiving Address – The Words Before All Else*[4]
- *Land Acknowledgement*[5]
- *The Medicine Wheel, Four Directions & Four Realms*[6]

Examples of Guided Embodied Experiences

Body Space Creation Place Home/Tune In! Sessions

These two sessions vary from 18–21 minutes in length and can be experienced alone in one's own space or as a group (in-person or digital). The visual and audio experience supports the inclusion of diverse bodies, mobility, and abilities. This is an excellent introductory pathway to CBM and the COA.

> Dreamwalker Dance Company invites you to join us in expanding and opening our bodies and minds through a series of free wellness movement experiences facilitated by skilled artists. ...You will be guided into flowing gentle stretches, simple vocal play, image rich visualizations and movements. No experience is required, just bring a curiosity for exploring, sensing, feeling and moving in space. (Dreamwalker, n.d.)[7]

'Quick Start' Daily Practice

Andrea Nann guides a 17-minute Conscious Bodies practice integrating the Four Realms and Four Directions of The Medicine Wheel Haudenosaunee Teachings. Similar to all COA, embodied, sensorial, and imaginative invitations are made through this audio-only practice that is appropriate for individuals and groups.[8]

Examples of Community Co-Creations

The following resources provide educators and learners with video experiences of how Conscious Bodies has been used towards the artistic creation of multi-modal public offerings, in shared physical and digital landscapes, on small and large scales.

The Welcome Project
Introduction: https://www.youtube.com/watch?v=1mXYg-I5e6g&t=24s
Newcomer Day: https://www.youtube.com/watch?v=ziaUYgZMAck
Godstone Park: https://www.youtube.com/watch?v=HrmQD2VAdRw

The Welcome Project Sharing Stories
Story Seed Offerings:

Chapter One Guelph:
https://www.youtube.com/playlist?list=PL135LDz13FV4I8RAO-e7GfXKeuHB8D-wS

Chapter Two Niagara:
https://www.youtube.com/watch?v=dkzXxBqC28o&list=PL135LDz13FV5RwZteDIG938EA4Vg03VQ3

Self-Guided Practice

Reflective awareness is an integrated practice of CBM and the COA. The practice of journaling, making marks on paper, or recording one's voice supports the practice of "paying attention to shifts and evolution throughout the CBM/COA processes. In addition to heightening sensitivity to how embodiment is enlivened in participation, you are asked to accompany your own journey with [active] reflection…to enhance our personal and collective experience" (Dreamwalker, 2020, p. 12).

The following framework visually guides you through an extremely condensed experience of how The Medicine Wheel Teachings, Four Directions, and Realms are woven with CBM and prompts for reflective awareness. The different directions invite you to physically orient yourself geographically, the bolded words separated by semi-colons can be thought of as "*destinations, aims, objectives, landmarks, signposts & invitations*. Allow yourself to intuitively experience these destinations, let your mind, heart, and body settle into a direction and flow along your subjective present experience" (Dreamwalker, 2020, p. 7).

Italicized text are excerpts from a guided COA. You are invited to embody these activations, following your own rhythm and expressing movement in ways that feel safe and comfortable for your body. The prompts provide entry points for reflective awareness, and you are encouraged to speak the questions out loud and answer them in ways that feel natural and authentic. Perhaps you will make marks on paper, write words, draw images, hold stillness, speak, hum, sing, or move your intuitive responses. Before you begin, clear your space so that you will not trip over anything and put on comfortable clothing that will allow free movement. You may wish to dim the lights, open or close a window, move in silence, or put on a favourite playlist that will help you sink into kind presence with yourself. Take your time to read each word slowly. Let yourself linger as though you were encountering them for the first time; enter in wonderment and discover how they live within your conscious body.

CENTRE

growing awareness; kindness;
trust; safety; resilience; joy; flow; inspiration

Allow your eyes to gaze into your space. Invite your breath to participate.
Notice where you might have some thresholds in your body today,
maybe even in your mind, maybe it's in your emotional self.
Notice and allow yourself to ease into stretching and yawning a bit.

Reflective Prompt: Bring awareness to your current expression of Self
- Do you feel curiosity, openness and/or resistance to this chapter?
- Do you have any questions or objections you wish to be answered?
- Name one word that describes your present state/dynamic of being.

EAST

curiosity; awakening; attuning;
sensing; discovering; exploring; gathering; welcoming

Let's invite our bodies to face the direction where the sun rises
blink your eyes open to this vision of East.
Allow your hands to come towards your body and land somewhere.
Allow your eyes to softly close,
softening the backs of your knees and underneath the soles of your feet

Reflective Prompt: Bring your awareness to your physical body:
- Where in your body do you feel your breath?
- Can you feel/sense your heartbeat and its rhythms?
- Which parts of your body are most full/empty of vibration/sensation?

SOUTH

clarity of mind; dreaming; imagining; seeing and been seen; touching and being touched; experimenting; creating; innovating;

Turning your awareness to the South
rubbing your hands together, say aloud to yourself in your space,
'anything is possible.'
Wash that intention over your whole body, your whole being.
Notice how your breath might change, how your heartbeat might quicken
then, offer your hot palms outwards.

Reflective Prompt: Bring your awareness to your heart space:
- How are you presently feeling (relaxed, engaged, irritated, distracted, nervous, sad)?
- What is the intensity of your emotions?
- How does your heart feel (soft, guarded, aching, open)?

WEST

openness; listening; giving; receiving; empathizing; relating; accepting; remembering

Settle here in the West the way that we might settle in to experience a sunset.
How does your body want to respond to that? Does it want to stretch or yawn?
Does it want to slow down and maybe open in the legs and the feet?
Invite your body to do what it needs to do...bring wellness to you.

Reflective Prompt: Bring awareness to your mind:
- What is the speed of your thoughts (spacious, slow, overlapping)?
- What is the quality of your thoughts (positive, negative, functional)?
- What are the time and location of your thoughts (present, past, future)?

NORTH

reciprocity; interconnecting; reflecting; sharing; knowing; togethering; collaborating; belonging

Look around and see again the environment where you find yourself
with curiosity, allow yourself to find North.
Let's open here, whatever that means to you.
Inviting this sensation of the holistic aspect of our being

Our body is a Wellspring for what we need
listen to the body, what does it need to thrive?

Reflective Prompt: Bring your awareness to your spirit:
- Do you feel connected to a place/person/being(s)?
- Do you feel isolated from a place/person/being(s)?
- Do you feel supported by a place/person/being(s)?

CENTRE

growing awareness; kindness;
trust; safety; resilience; joy; flow; inspiration

Starting to relax, come to a place,
where like leaves falling softly,
you will just allow your body, your being to settle
whatever last moments of gesturing you want to do
if that feels good, tap your heels or touch your hands to the floor
whatever your body desires, to bring a sense of completion to the cycle.

Reflective Prompt: Bring your awareness to your current expression of Self:
- What is an essence of your experience with this chapter?
- What is a metaphor/image that represents your experience?
- Do you have any lingering questions about what you encountered?

This work becomes pedagogically alive and methodologically coherent through embodied experience with seasoned Conscious Bodies facilitators. We encourage you to explore and return to the guided and interactive resources made available and, should curiosity awaken your desire to experience a COA in your community, please reach out; we would be honoured to move, learn, connect, care, and co-create with you. Thank you. Merci. Nià:wen.

Notes

1 Please see The Welcome Project, The Whole Shebang, & The Ontario Shebang at https://www.thewelcomeproject.ca/; https://www.dreamwalkerdance.com/projects-1; http://theontarioshebang.com/
2 See https://www.youtube.com/watch?v=3dZuc50oR9g
3 Permission has been granted through informed consent to use the proper names and direct quotations of facilitators.
4 https://vimeo.com/493744111/e9c928179e

5 https://vimeo.com/493762864/261e779209
6 https://vimeo.com/493765421/1909088df5
7 https://www.dreamwalkerdance.com/body-space-creation-place
8 https://www.youtube.com/watch?v=fvDR6iScXhY

References

Anderson, T., & Suominen Guyas, A. (2012). Earth education, interbeing, and deep ecology. *Studies in Art Education, 53*(3), 223–245. doi:10.1080/00393541.2012.11518865

DeTurk, S. (2001). Intercultural empathy: Myth, competency or possibility for alliance building? *Communication Education, 50*(4), 374–384. doi:10.1080/03634520109379262

Dreamwalker Dance. (n.d.). *Stay home/tune in! Daily movement practice.* Dreamwalker Dance. https://www.dreamwalkerdance.com/body-space-creation-place

Dreamwalker Dance. (2020). *Conscious bodies companion handbook* [facilitation manual]. Dreamwalker Dance.

Holmes, S. (2015). Intercultural communicative performance and the body. *Contemporary Pragmatism, 12*, 275–301. doi:10.1163/18758185-01202006

Johnson, R. (2018). *Embodied social justice.* Routledge.

Lake, R. (2013). *A curriculum of imagination in an era of standardization.* Information Age.

Snowber. C. (2009). An aesthetics of everyday life. In C. Snowber, & S. Richmond (Eds.), *Landscapes of aesthetic education* (pp. 65–77). Cambridge Scholars.

Snowber, C. (2019). Embodied inquiry in holistic education. In M. Binder, S. Crowell, J. P. Miller, K. Nigh, & B. Novak. (Eds.), *International handbook of holistic education* (pp. 232–239). Routledge.

Wilson, S. (2008). *Research is ceremony.* Fernwood.

CHAPTER 17

Extending Scientific Literacy

A Scientist's Lived Experiences and Relational Connections through Hula

Poh Tan

> 'A'ohe pau ka 'ike i ka halau ho'okahi
> (All knowledge is not taught in the same school)
>
> MARY KAWENA PUKUI

∵

My journey in understanding who I am as a scientist and science educator is a messy one. It is not linear and does not have a destination. It requires being uncomfortable, open, and vulnerable to ideas and questions that provoke or evoke. As a scientist, I was trained to remain objective about my research and research subjects. I was trained to analyze evidence collected in systematic ways to help build on theory and scientific discovery. I acknowledge that I am speaking in general of all scientific disciplines while referring specifically to the *hard sciences* that are practiced within controlled laboratory microenvironments.

When I began this research journey, I limited scientific literacy to include only scientific knowledge and its critical application from and to testable, controlled laboratory environments. I made *assumptions* as a scientist about teaching science. There were times when I felt significant *tension* between how I taught science and how I saw science being taught by others. I know from experience that "discomfort [can be] pedagogically transformative" (Driussi, 2019, p. IV). As I immersed myself in reading about multiple approaches to acquiring knowledge, I learned about intersections between knowledge gained from science and from wider lived experiences. I started to ask *questions* about other ways of acquiring knowledge about science that comes from collective experiences, holistic observations, and relational connections. In doing so, my understanding of what constitutes a scientifically literate person began to shift. Along this journey, I encountered moments of assumption, tension, questioning, and transformation. I explore these four moments within an Indigenous Hawaiian seascape epistemology (Ingersoll, 2016), and I draw on

© KONINKLIJKE BRILL NV, LEIDEN, 2022 | DOI:10.1163/9789004521186_017

hula to help unpack my identity as a scientist who is continuously negotiating my understanding of what constitutes a scientifically literate person.

Briefly, a scientifically-inclined person is categorized into two terms: science literate and scientifically literate. The two categories have their own set of criteria and are labelled as Visions I and II, respectively (Roberts & Bybee, 2014). Vision I's principles are about curriculum, knowledge built from pre-existing techniques, and methods that are well tested with explanations for the events and objects of the natural world. Vision I came about during the Sputnik era. Vision II's principles were developed later and encourage an understanding of science through a more critical lens, considering human endeavour and life situations as part of the solution to creating a scientifically literate person (Roberts, 2007; Roberts & Bybee, 2014).

Both Visions I and II are well understood amongst science education scholars but, as we move into a new era in science education, perhaps it is time to talk about science literacy from multiple perspectives—a worldview that embeds Indigenous ways of knowing and non-Western approaches with Western paradigms (Murray, 2016). This new perspective on science literacy can be seen in Vision III that "allows us to imagine a different relationship with the world" (Kimmerer, 2013, p. x). Vision III identifies a scientifically literate person as one who places equal importance on different understandings of science (e.g. Indigenous knowledge, philosophy and art). Vision III is based on theoretical concepts on relationality with/in "others" by acknowledging that scientific understanding and thinking is a fluid process and recognizing that this process is continual and perpetual.

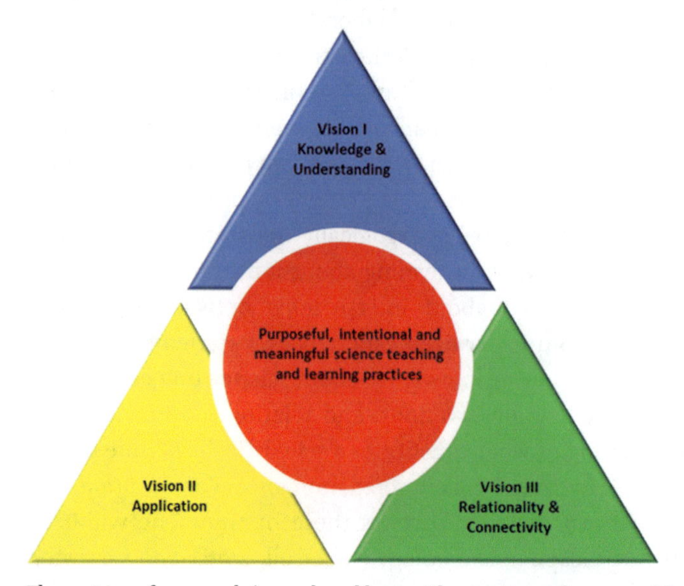

Three visions framework (reproduced here with permission from SFU Educational Review)

My interpretation of Vision III's transformational possibilities are deeply rooted in Indigenous Hawaiian understanding and specifically with Hawaiian seascape epistemology and hula. Hula dancing became a critical component in extending my understanding of Vision I and II and gave me deeper understanding about my identity as a scientist and as a scientifically-literate person. The three visions helped me question my teaching practice, and I began to build towards more intentional, purposeful, and relational learning experiences for my students (Tan, 2020). This aligned well with Indigenous Hawaiian epistemology, which asserts a *one-ness* or blurring of boundaries. Finding resonance with Manulani Aluli Meyer's work, I understand Hawaiian epistemology as rooted in experience, relationality, and reciprocity. Meyer (2008) explains in depth how each of us experiences and relates to the world differently and how these multiple interpretations matter. Meyer, a descendent of the first peoples of Hawai'i, is a Kānaka Maoli scholar, professor, and researcher within the field of Hawaiian epistemology. As ocean people from a warm climate, she says that "Hawaiian epistemology differs from those who occupy the shores" (Meyer, 2008, p. 218). Hawaiian epistemology is based on seven categories that bring us back to knowledge and knowing: spirituality and knowing; physical space and knowing; cultural nature of the senses; relationship and knowledge; utility and knowledge; words and knowledge; and body/mind question (Meyer, 2001, 2014). For the scope of this chapter, I focus on relationship and knowledge as it pertains to teaching scientific concepts from a place of relationality.

The concept of relationship and knowledge is not exclusive to Kānaka Maoli. Indigenous knowledge of one population may be useful to another group; in other words, it is *generalizable* (Simonds & Christopher, 2013). Deloria Jr., a Lakota scholar, discussed place-relationships where the universe is alive and personal and, thus, the universe demands that each and every entity seek and sustain personal relationships (as cited in Snively & Williams, 2016). Relationship or interdependence is a key opportunity for Hawaiians to "practice reciprocity, exhibit balance, develop harmony with land, and generosity with others" (Meyer, 2001, p. 134). This notion of acknowledging and respecting all types of life forms speaks to forming kinships, which is especially important when teaching science where the subject of study is often objectified perpetuating a relational distance from the learner (Kealiikanakaoleohaililani et al., 2018).

Kānaka Maoli's paradigm of knowledge is relational and uses body, mind, and spirit "to asks us to extend through our objective knowing, into spaces of reflection…and deeper realities where science can follow into but not lead or illuminate" (Meyer, 2008, p. 265). The aim of this approach is to "incorporate to the fullest degree all aspects of interactions of human in and of nature from interaction of the body, mind, soul, and spirit with all aspects of nature" (Cajete, 2000, p. 64).

> To see a child speaking with a tree does not carry the message of mental instability. On the contrary, this is a child engaged in coming to know the connections of the universe and to feel empathy with another living entity. (Snively & Williams, 2016, p. 39)

As a scientist-dancer, I live in the liminal space between science and art. Living in this liminality surfaced questions about how I was teaching science and about my identity as a scientist and science educator. Living, practicing, teaching, and learning within this space of tension hybridized my identity as a hula dancer, scientist, and science educator.

Moving beyond biological and scientific definitions of interconnectedness involves "multiple sensory experiences and understandings of how [students] make sense of the interconnections [i.e., relationality to] of the planet" (Snively & Williams, 2016, p. 39). This is vital to creating space where students experience a connection to nature via the senses of the body. For example, in Kānaka Maoli epistemology, the sense of touch has references that extend beyond the biological and scientific definition of touch: to touch with the hand; the touch of the blowing salty sea wind or the falling of rain drops; the touch of light; and touching the mind (Meyer, 2001). The senses play a vital role in relational knowledge. Working through the lens of Kānaka Maoli epistemology, an "Indigenous [Kānaka Maoli] science with Western science can establish a relationship, an obligation of sorts to give, to receive, and to reciprocate" (Snively & Williams, 2016, p. 3). Teaching science with a Kānaka Maoli lens may start to eliminate a dualistic and objectified worldview, thus moving towards a deeper understanding of "science citizenship and global interdependence" (Bybee, 2018, p. 61).

My journey unfolds from a place of *assumptions* informed by how I was taught science and how I teach science to my students. I have always designed and focused my lessons on three principles when teaching science: knowledge accuracy, in-depth understanding, and objective questioning. I used these principles to guide the design and intentions of my teaching focus. I remained very much within Vision I (Bybee, 2018) of scientific literacy, and I felt I had a responsibility as a scientist to ensure accurate information was transmitted. I was driven by the three principles because, as a stem cell scientist, I bear the burden to ensure I deliver accurate, precise, and objective information to the public to prevent misconception, misinformation, and misinterpretation about my work. It was important to me that I maintain an objective perspective as a scientist to ensure the research I contributed to the field was valid, credible, measurable, accurate, and objective.

I began to feel tension about my *intentions* when teaching science, and I started to question my teaching techniques. As time passed, I noticed that

I frequently described my desire to teach science *differently* by using phrases such as: hands-on activities; the five senses; feeling; experimentation; and *getting your hands dirty*. I was introduced to Karen Barad's (2007) work on relationality, and I began to wonder if *fluffy science* may have helped guide my scientific identity my whole life after all. I began to question my *gut-feel* in the laboratory, and wondered if it was strange that I cried the first time when I danced hula. I began to examine how the Hawaiian culture shaped, informed, and connected my mind, body, and spirit about science, as a scientist, and as a science educator.

I was first introduced to the history, culture, and stories of Hawai'i in 2004 when I attended my first hula class at my Kumu, Josie de Baat halau hula, called Halau Kia O Ka Hula (Guardians of the Hula). Josie is not native Hawaiian but has been a Hawaiian at heart since she was 16 years old.

My *kumu hula* (Photograph by Paulus Mau, used with permission)

Hula is a moving encyclopedia "inscribed into the sinews and postures of dancers' bodies [and] carries forward the social and natural history, philosophy, literature, and the *scientific knowledge* [emphasis added] of the Hawaiian people" (Rowe, 2008, p. 31). Kumu Josie often reminds us:

> We do not perform the hula for ourselves, but for each other and with each other, and the most important thing of dancing the hula, is to know, learn, and embrace Hawaiian culture, history, and mo'olelo (stories, legends) with your whole heart, and most important, with *Aloha*. And when you dance hula, you have to feel it…simply feel it and don't think so much about it. (de Baat, personal communication, March 29, 2019)

Before I begin a discussion of hula, it is important to understand the meaning of Aloha. If you have visited Hawai'i or have been part of Hawaiian theme gatherings, the word Aloha is often used to greet each other, to say goodbye, or merely as a *fun-thing* to say. However, Aloha is "grounded in tenets of Hawaiian education" (Kahakalau, 2020, p. 1), and it is "affiliation-oriented with all involved, constituting an extended, intergenerational family of learners where everyone is valued and loved" (p. 3). In addition, pedagogy of Aloha "utilizes Hawaiian knowledge as the curricular foundation for all content areas, integrating Hawaiian language, culture, knowledge, and history to make the curriculum relevant and personal to the students" (p. 4). Grounded in the value of Aloha, exhibiting Aloha becomes an "inherent responsibility to each other where all are interconnected" (p. 1). Thus, a Science of Aloha supports and enhances a collective Aloha that makes us better stewards of the Earth (Kealiikanakaoleohaililani et al., 2018), and "shifts our current scientific culture into one that embodies the Aloha spirit and strengthens the foundation of the science that we do" (Kamai, 2018, para. 6). Aloha is the heart and Hula is the heartbeat of the Hawaiian people.

Connecting the haumana (student) to mele (song) and oli (chant) (Photograph by Paulus Mau, used with permission)

Before a single hula step is learned, the history, story, legend, and meaning of each mele (song) and oli (chant) is learned. My Kumu reminds us that understanding and appreciating the history and purpose of an oli helps us connect and *feel* the song. For the first few years, I was trying to memorize the steps by counting the beats in my head and listening for the specific words to remind me where my hands need to be and remembering to display cued expressions on my face. Accuracy and *getting the steps right* was important and akin to how I was teaching science at the time. My scientific identity of a commitment to methodical steps (mis)guided me. However, even when I placed my feet and hands exactly on beat, a deeper connection to the mele (song) was still missing, and my Kumu always noticed. Kumu Josie frequently reminds us:

> Ladies, you have to take in the story and chant. You cannot just memorize it, and if you memorize it, you look like you have a fake smile on your face, and your hands are just placed here and there. You don't look like you care. Just don't think. Just dance, and remember you have to feel it; you must feel it—otherwise, why dance? (De Baat, personal communication, 2019)

I have heard these words ever since I started dancing in 2004. She reminds us to *feel the music* with every mele, oli, and kahiko (ancient hula), and I always thought I had understood what she meant. I assumed she meant preciseness, accuracy, and *on-beat* steps. It was June 2019, on Thursday night's hula practice, when I saw her eyes focused on me, and a flood of images from my time teaching hit me like lightning striking a tree. This is a moment when my identity as a rigorous scientist began to embrace an embodied science. Specifically, it affirmed that not all knowledge and understanding is measurable, and not all knowledge and understanding NEEDS to be measurable, to be valid, accurate, and precise. As a cell biologist who studies the microscopic world, it is easy to forget or dismiss the importance of a larger context for which we are studying. Hula created a space for me to be open to other ways of gaining scientific knowledge—to allow relational aspects of emotion and spirituality with/in my scientific practice.

As a scientist and science educator with preconceived notions about teaching and learning science, I danced and floated between trepid waters of assumption and tension, and encountering islands of questions and multiple knowing expanded and challenged my notion about science and science education. Through Hula and Aloha, I relinquished a sense of control of tensions and assumptions, and I immersed myself within the movements and spiritual connections with my Kumu and halau.

Combining Aloha and Hula, my connection to science and my practice of teaching science has become deeper and more relational, moving beyond

Vision I and Vision II of scientific literacy. Although words can help articulate my new relational connection with science, embodying science through hula creates a deeper and more meaningful connection and respect regarding *how* I study science. It is a permanent mark that hula has made in my scientific identity where my logical and rational mind moves fluidly in rhythm with hula. This rhythmic dance opens multiple ways of knowing, being, and becoming.

First hula performance in an academic setting (Photograph by Jacky Barreiro, used with permission)

References

Barad, K. M. (2007). *Meeting the universe halfway: Quantum physics and the entanglement of matter and meaning.* Duke University Press.

Bybee, R. W. (2018). *STEM education more than ever.* National Science Teachers Association Press.

Cajete, G. (2000). *Native science: Natural laws of interdependence.* Clear Light.

Driussi, L. (2019). *Wayfaring: A phenomenology of international teacher education* [Doctoral dissertation, Simon Fraser University]. Summit SFU. http://summit.sfu.ca/item/19322

Ingersoll, K. A. (2016). *Waves of knowing: A seascape epistemology.* Duke University Press.

Kahakalau, K. (2020). Pedagogy of Aloha. In M. Peters (Ed.), *Encyclopedia of teacher education.* Springer.

Kamai, B. (2018, May 17). Bringing Aloha into science. *March for Science.* https://medium.com/marchforscience-blog/bringing-aloha-into-science-9290f0c40011

Kealiikanakaoleohaililani, K. K., Asing, C., Asing, K., Block, T., Browning, M., Camara, K., Camara, L., Dudley, M., Frazier, M., Gomes, N., Gordon, A., Gordon, M., Irvine, A., Kaawa, N., Kirkpatrick, S., Leucht, E., Perry, C., Replogle, J., Salbosa, L. L., Sato, A., Schubert, L., Sterling, A., Uowolo, A., Uowolo, J., Walker, B., Whitehead, A, Yogi, D., & Heu, L. (2018). Ritual + sustainability science? A portal into the science of Aloha. *Sustainability, 10*(10), 1–17.

Kimmerer, R. W. (2013). *Braiding sweetgrass. Indigenous wisdom, scientific knowledge, and the teachings of plants.* Milkweed Editions.

Meyer, A. M. (2001). Our own liberation: Reflections on Hawaiian epistemology. *The Contemporary Pacific, 13*(1), 124–148.

Meyer, A. M. (2008). Indigenous and authentic: Hawaiian epistemology and the triangulation of meaning. In N. K. Denzin, Y. S. Lincoln, & L. T. Smith (Eds.), *Handbook of critical and Indigenous methodologies* (pp. 217–232). SAGE.

Meyer, M. A. (2014). Hoea Ea: Land education and food sovereignty in Hawai'i. *Environmental Education Research, 20*(1), 98–101. https://doi.org/10.1080/13504622.2013.852656

Murray, J. (2016, May 29). *Science education in Canada to 2030.* Canadian Society for the Study of Education, Brandon, Manitoba. https://ocs.sfu.ca/csse/index.php/csse/CSSE2016/paper/viewFile/2928/38

Roberts, D. (2007). Scientific literacy/science literacy. In S. K. Abell, & N. G. Lederman (Eds.), *Handbook of research on science education* (pp. 729–781). Routledge.

Roberts, D., & Bybee, R. (2014). Scientific literacy, science literacy and science education. In N. G. Lederman (Ed.), *Handbook of research on science education* (pp. 545–558). Routledge.

Rowe, S. M. (2008). We dance for knowledge. *Dance Research Journal, 40*(1), 31–43.

Simonds, V. W., & Christopher, S. (2013). Adapting western research methods to Indigenous ways of knowing. *American Journal of Public Health, 103*(12), 2185–2192. https://doi.org/10.2105/AJPH.2012.301157

Simon Fraser University. Three Visions Framework. https://apastyle.apa.org/style-grammar-guidelines/tables-figures/sample-figures

Snively, G., & Wanosts'a7, L. W. (2016). *Knowing home: Braiding Indigenous science with western science.* University of Victoria. https://pressbooks.bccampus.ca/knowinghome/

Tan, P. (2016). Science education: Defining the scientifically literate person. *SFU Educational Review, 9*. https://doi.org/10.21810/sfuer.v9i.307

Tan, P. (2020). Towards a new teaching approach for scientific literacy. *SFU Educational Review, 13*(1), 91–95. https://doi.org/10.21810/sfuer.v13i1.1262

CHAPTER 18

Situated English Language Learning

Lessons Learned from a Jamaican Inner-city Classroom

Shawnee Hardware and Clement Lambert

The voices and in-school experiences of Jamaican inner-city high school students have been largely underrepresented in research studies on student engagement (Nero & Stevens, 2018; Roofe, 2018). Moreover, the lived and out of school experiences of most Jamaican inner-city students are left out of the Jamaican English Language Arts (ELA) classrooms. *Inner-city*, within this context, is defined as urban communities characterized by poverty, overcrowding, poor social amenities, and habitual violence (Kinkead-Clark, 2016). The students in these urban centres sometimes have low educational attainment and school engagement. The low educational attainment contributes to and reinforces the cycle of the poor socio-economic conditions in which they live.

Typical research on Jamaican student engagement tends to privilege middle- and upper-class funds of knowledge and canon literacy (Dodman, 2021). In this chapter, we highlight how including Jamaican high school inner-city students' lived experiences has the potential to transform ELA learning by affirming the students' identities and improving their academic engagement. Although we critique the predominance of canon literacy and rote learning in Jamaican ELA teaching and learning processes, we do not critique Western-based theories. In fact, we used two such theories, *multiliteracies pedagogy* (Burke & Hardware, 2015) and *sociocultural theory* (Swain et al., 2015), to situate the students' ELA learning in the study discussed in this chapter.

Research Context

Jamaica is a post-colonial Caribbean island with a population of almost three million people. The nation has grappled with a history of slavery, colonization, and more recent efforts to function as a country independent of its former colonizers. Vestiges of Jamaican history include complex social structures and unique language and learning contexts. These legacies of its colonial past are visible in the education systems where there is a divide between schools for the upper and middle classes and those for the working classes. Schools

© KONINKLIJKE BRILL NV, LEIDEN, 2022 | DOI:10.1163/9789004521186_018

for the former are well funded while those for the latter are underfunded—especially the ones located in rural and inner-city communities. The inner-city site selected in this study amplifies the classroom challenges faced in post-colonial education in Jamaica. Convenient sampling was used to select this site as Shawnee, the primary researcher in this inquiry, taught there briefly as a language educator eight years prior to conducting this fieldwork.

One of the key subjects that the students in this study struggle with is ELA. Due to limited research conducted in inner-city high schools, there is no current information on the number of students who are underperforming in ELA. The most recent figure reported in the Jamaican news media in 2015 was that about 80% of inner-city students are assigned failing grades in their end of high school (Grade 11) English examinations (Thompson, 2015). This is exacerbated by the fact that not all Grade 11 inner-city students sit the high school ELA exam, and a significant percentage of students either drop out of school or do not attend school at all (Caribbean Policy Research Institute, 2018). There are no comparative statistics that highlight the differences between inner-city high school students' school leaving ELA rates and the national ELA average.

The politics of language in Jamaican society strongly influences Jamaican ELA policy (Devonish & Jones, 2017). Jamaican inner-city students' ability to speak standard Jamaican English (SJE) is vital for them to achieve positive academic outcomes just as it is required for their career development. In Jamaica, English is considered the language of power, *civility,* and education. Due to its colonial history, Jamaica is a diglossic society in which members of the middle and upper classes typically speak English in *polite society* while often code switching between Patois and English when they are angry or wanting to appear more nationalistic (Simmons-McDonald & Robertson, 2006). This creates a dichotomy in language use in which English is classified as the only Jamaican official language while Patois, the mother tongue of over 80% of Jamaican citizenry, is relegated to an illegitimate language for the private domain (Brown-Blake, 2017; Devonish & Carpenter, 2007).

Although the Jamaican Ministry of Education has made efforts to reform the education system to include more learner-centered pedagogies, these adjustments have not extended to including Patois as language of education. In many cases, Jamaican classrooms continue to be influenced by colonial approaches to education, specifically teacher-centered approaches that privilege rote learning as standard (Hibbert, 2020).

Jamaican teachers, especially at the post-primary levels, continue to use mostly *chalk and talk* methods that require students to consume knowledge rather than engaging them in a process of knowledge production (Iyare et al., 2018).

Jamaican inner-city students in a strong teacher centered classroom (Photograph by Shawnee Hardware, used with permission)

Positionality

Acknowledging that who we are affects what and how we know, we disclose that we have both completed our first degrees in Jamaica and earned our terminal degrees in Canada. We have also taught in Jamaica in various capacities, and we are currently teaching in Canada and the United States of America. Therefore, we have an insider–outsider perspective on the Jamaican education system and the historical legacies that continue to impact its aspiration to be equitable.

Grounding Perspectives

Shawnee opted to use multiliteracies pedagogy (MLS) as the grounding perspective for her PhD work, from which this data is derived. Despite being a Western framework, she saw its potential for improving the Jamaican ELA pedagogical processes because of its focus on situated learning and transformational practice (Burke & Hardware, 2015). MLS also places an onus on schools to recognize the cultural and linguistic diversity that students bring to school and draw on them as learning resources (Burke et al., 2013; New London Group, 1996). In recent years, MLS has been used in many non-Western countries such as South Africa (Andrews et al., 2020) and Papua New Guinea (Kitson et al., 2007), given its critique of canon literacy practices and its advocacy for the inclusion of under-represented students' lived experiences in classrooms.

Shawnee also used sociocultural theory (SCT) as her theoretical framework. There is a link between multiliteracies pedagogy and SCT. Like MLS scholars,

SCT scholars advocate for the inclusion of underserved students' culture in their school learning. Following sociocultural theorizing, these students' lived experiences are labelled as their funds of knowledge (Moll, 2019). Answering MLS's call to include student knowledge in the classroom (Taylor et al., 2008), and aligned with sociocultural theorizing (Macy, 2016), Shawnee designed all her collaborative, group-based lessons to ensure that students were encouraged to make meaning in their ELA classroom through the inclusion of their cultural knowledge and lived experiences.

Methodology

Shawnee engaged in qualitative case study research because of its ability to support researchers in observing, noting, and incorporating participant narratives, which offer rich insights into their emic perspectives during the research (Stake, 2000; Yin, 2013). She obtained ethical clearance from her university and permission from the Jamaican Ministry of Education to conduct this study. She also received consent from the students' parents for their participation so that recordings could be made and pictures taken of the students to include in future publications. Obtaining approval and consent were vital since the research was conducted with a vulnerable population—children from a low-income background.

The time spent at the research site allowed Shawnee to build relationships with student participants and learn more about the research context. Her research was conducted in a sequential manner: a classroom observation occurred in Mrs. Brown's[1] classroom (the original classroom teacher) during which time Shawnee took field notes and video-recorded the teacher's lessons; teaching an intervention of 23 communicative, collaborative, group-based task-based lessons, covering three topics and seven sub-topics occurred over a 2-month period of time. Mrs. Brown returned as the classroom teacher for one week, and after the one week of Mrs. Brown's instruction, Shawnee conducted another set of observations to see how the students assessed their agency and engagement—four student focus groups and one teacher interview were included in this phase. Shawnee conducted document analysis of the students' individual work, which included after-lesson reflections. The 2-month interventions were key to this inquiry as they involved creating and teaching task-based lessons that required students to produce texts such as posters, drama pieces, and songs that accessed their funds of knowledge and artistic talents. Akin to the multiliteracies framework (Burke & Hardware, 2015), the students became producers of knowledge and created texts that helped them to understand their lived realities.

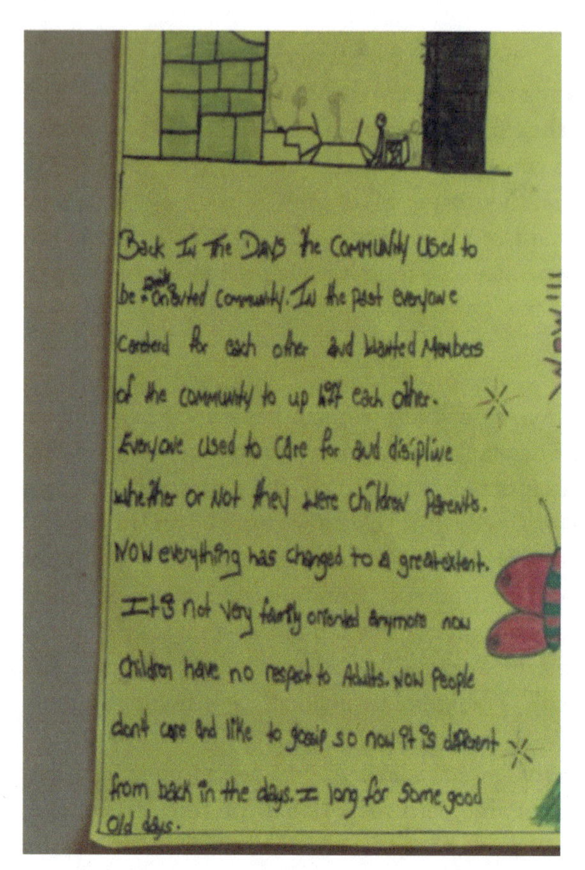

Student-designed poster that compared their community in the past and present (Photograph by Shawnee Hardware, used with permission)

The poster above was the culmination of five interdisciplinary lessons, the first three of which were completed before the poster writing sessions. The last two lessons were used to complete the poster: class discussion about the students' perspectives about their community; practice with writing interview questions with the target language *used* to; and a panel discussion with members of the students' community including one of their grandmothers to investigate how their community was in the past.

Findings and Discussion

Analysis of the focus group interviews, the pictures taken, and the submitted work in the study revealed three themes: collaborative and multimodal activities as catalysts for academic engagement; collaborative and multimodal activities as catalysts for emotional engagement; and the conundrums of developing appropriate classroom management techniques to match student-centred learning in a space where students are accustomed to stringent forms of behavioural management strategies.

Theme 1: Collaborative and Multimodal Activities as Catalysts for Academic Engagement

It is evident from the poster that the students got adequate practice with two ELA learning objectives: the grammar form *used to* and making comparisons. Outside of learning about this grammar form and writing technique, the students also learned vital information about their community, which connects with the Grade 7 social studies curriculum. Therefore, completing this collaborative and multimodal task led to their broader academic engagement. Evidence from the focus group suggests that students recognized the value of completing this collaborative task in promoting their engagement as they acknowledged "Ms. moare wen wi in grup…, Ms wi anderstan Ms."[2] This finding supports sociocultural theorizing that social interaction contributes to students' cognitive development (McLeod, 2020). Group work is also important to identify here as some of the students noted that "[dem] nuh use to group work."[3] Working in groups seemed to allow students the opportunity to occupy various learning positions.

Students practicing for their storytelling in Shawnee's class (Photograph by Shawnee Hardware, used with permission)

According to Kirshner (2008), while working in groups, students can perform multiple roles: (a) the knowledgeable and capable participant (participatory appropriation) who scaffolds their group members' understanding; (b) a learner who fluctuates between a knowledgeable participant and dependent learner in team (guided participant); and (c) a dependent learner with very little working knowledge of how to complete tasks (apprenticeship). These roles are not stationary, and one person can shift positions from participatory appropriation to apprenticeship. For example, in completing the poster, some participants were skilled at drawing but struggled with writing; hence, they would fluctuate between participatory appropriation and apprenticeship in the activities.

Theme 2: Collaborative and Multimodal Activities as Catalysts for Emotional Engagement

The students also shared that they enjoyed designing multimodal activities and showcasing other forms of literacies. One student noted that "Ms. lik wen wi do di stories an' we cum up an' ack it out an al dem tings deh, Ms we lik dem likkle tings deh."[4] This indicates that at least some students felt that activities used in this research made them "feel nice" and caused them to enjoy the class. This emotional engagement is vital to both their cognitive and academic engagement (Fredricks et al., 2004).

In accessing the students' socio-cultural knowledge and by placing them in groups, the study followed the well-established evidence in SCT research (Bass-Dolivan, 2011), which recognizes that students become engaged once teachers embed their lessons in their students' home culture, lived experiences, and socio-cultural knowledge. In this study, engagement involves meaning making, interest, and participation in activities. In short, the lessons that were based in MLS and SCT led to students' engagement through situated practice, student agency, student meaning-making, and the cultivation of a warm classroom environment (Ganapathy, 2014; Healy, 2016; Mann, 2001).

Theme 3: Classroom Management Conundrums as Unintentional Consequence

Although the students shared that they experienced emotional and academic engagement in this study, we identified one main limitation. Shawnee strived to establish positive relationships with the students as a means of improving their academic and behavioural engagement. The students seemed unaccustomed to the free range of movement and increased opportunities to talk; hence, they had difficulty regulating their behaviours in the first month of her study. Noticing this, she co-constructed rules and consequences in the classroom and had discussions when the students did not adhere to these classroom rules. It appears that students who are accustomed to more authoritative forms of discipline saw this disciplinary style as being *too soft* (Hardware, 2020).

There is a need for more research from both SCT and MLS to discuss how to address disciplinary problems in classrooms where lessons are informed by these frameworks. We recommended that MLS and SCT scholars become *warm demanders* to address this challenge (Delpit, 2012). Warm demanders establish strong relationships with their students and enact good "classroom management based on explicitness and insistence which is communicated in both subtle and straightforward ways" (Bondy et al., 2013, p. 5). Being a warm demander has the capacity to create a third space between the traditional teacher-centred approach and an unstructured, undisciplined space.

Conclusions

In this chapter, we discussed the adaptations we have made to the Jamaican Grade 7 curriculum to accommodate the students' lived perspectives and students' responses to these adaptations. These amendments to the curriculum were important since the Jamaican education system builds on historically didactic, teacher-centric perspectives that paint working class students' lived experiences as a deficit for their learning. Understandably, creating multimodal activities that affirm the students' funds of knowledge requires more time initially to plan (Roswell & Burke, 2009), which might give teachers concern about extra preparation time since many are experiencing high workload demands (Walker, 2020). However, once the students are engaged in knowledge production, they will become facilitators of learning and less dependent on the teachers.

Using multimodal activities built on the students' lived experiences and improved their investment in learning (cognitive engagement) and their sense of belonging (emotional engagement). Both tenets are important for their overall academic engagement and learning. While this study is focused on adaptation made to curriculum to improve the students' learning and engagement, these modifications would not have been successful if Shawnee did not build strong relationships with the students. A key aspect of teacher-student relationship is teacher disposition. Future research can explore how Jamaican teachers' dispositions impact students' academic engagement and learning to ultimately influence policies and practical considerations regarding the education of Jamaican youth.

Notes

1 All names are pseudonyms.
2 When we are placed in groups…, we understand more.
3 They are not accustomed to group work.
4 Miss. Like when we do the stories and we act them out and all those things. Miss, we like those little things.

References

Andrews, G., Prozesky, M., & Fouche, I. (2020). Environment as decolonial nexus: Designing for decolonial teaching in literacies courses at a South African university. *Scrutiny2*, *25*(1), 64–85.

Bass-Dolivan, D. W. (2011). *Students' engagement with second language learning: A socio-cultural approach* [Unpublished doctoral dissertation, University of Wollongong]. University of Wollongong, Australia.

Bondy, E., Ross, D. D., Hambacher, E., & Acosta, M. (2013). Becoming warm demanders: Perspectives and practices of first year teachers. *Urban Education, 48*(3), 420–450.

Brown-Blake, C. (2017). Supporting justice reform in Jamaica through language policy change. *Caribbean Studies, 45*(1/2), 183–215.

Burke, A., & Hardware, S. (2015). Honoring ESL students' lived experiences in school learning with multiliteracies pedagogy. *Language, Culture and Curriculum, 28*(2), 143–157. doi:10/1080/07908318.2015.1027214

Burke, A., Hughes, J., Hardware, S., & Thompson, S. (2013). Using multiliteracies to rethink literacy pedagogy in elementary classroom. *Education Matters, 1*(2), 1–23.

Caribbean Policy Research Institute. (2018). *Situation analysis of Jamaican children-2018.* https://www.unicef.org/jamaica/media/546/file/SituationAnalysisofJamaicanChildren–2018.pdf

Delpit, L. (2012). *Multiplication is for white people: Raising expectations for other people's children.* New York Press.

Devonish, H., & Carpenter, K. (2007). Bilingual education in Creole situations: The Jamaican case. *Society for Caribbean Linguistics*. Occasional paper No. 35, p. 48.

Devonish, H., & Jones, B. (2017). *Jamaica: A state of language, music and crisis of nation.* https://journals.openedition.org/volume/5321

Dodman, J. (2021). The best glass? Equitable access to quality education in inner-city Kingston, Jamaica. *Environment and Urbanization, 33*(1), 83–98.

Fredricks, J. A., Blumfield, P. E., & Paris, A. H. (2004). School engagement: Potential of the concept, state of the evidence. *Review of Educational Research, 74*(1), 59–109.

Ganapathy, M. (2014). Using multiliteracies to engage learners to produce learning. *International Journal of e-Education, e-Business, e-Management and e-Learning, 4*(6). http://www.ijeeee.org/Papers/355-A001.pdf

Hardware, S. (2020). What's so critical about critical reflection? The role of critical reflection for improving doctoral research practice. *Caribbean Journal of Education, 42*(1&2), 87–109.

Healy, A. (2016). Transforming pedagogy with multiliteracies in the English classroom. *Literacy Learning: The Middle Years, 24*(1), 7–17.

Iyare, N., James, J., & Amonde, T. (2018). Effectivities of integrating interactive technology in reading comprehension: A case study of Jamaica's grade school. *JITE-Research, 17*(1), 227–246.

Kitson, L., Fletcher, M., & Kearney, J. (2007). Continuity and change in literacy practices: A move towards multiliteracies. *Journal of Classroom Interaction, 41*(2), 29–41.

Kinkead-Clark, Z. (2016). Bridging the gap between home and school-perception of classroom teachers and principals: Case studies of two Jamaican inner-city schools. *Education and Urban Society, 48*(8), 762–777.

Kirshner, B. (2008). Guided participant in three youth activism organizations: Facilitation, apprenticism, and joint work. *Journal of the Learning Sciences, 17*(1), 60–101.

Macy, L. (2016). Bridging pedagogies: Drama, multiliteracies, and the zone of proximal development. *The Educational Forum, 80*(3), 310–323.

Mann, S. (2001). Alternative perspectives on the student experience: Alienation and engagement. *Studies in Higher Education, 26*, 7–19.

McLeod, S. (2020). *Lev Vygotsky's sociocultural theory.* https://www.simplypsychology.org/vygotsky.html

Moll, L. (2019). Elaborating funds of knowledge: Community-oriented practices in international contexts. *Literacy Research: Theory, Method, and Practice, 68*(1), 130–138.

Nero, S., & Stevens, L. (2018). Analyzing students' writing in a Jamaican Creole-speaking context: An ecological and systemic function approach. *Linguistic and Education, 43*, 13–24.

New London Group. (1996). A pedagogy of multiliteracies: Designing social futures. *Harvard Educational Review, 66*(1), 60–93.

Roofe, C. (2018). Schooling, teachers in Jamaica and social responsibility: Rethinking teacher preparation. *Social Responsibility Journal, 14*(4), 916–827.

Rowsell, J., & Burke, A. (2009). Reading by design: Two case studies of digital reading practices. *Journal of Adolescent & Adult Literacy, 53*(2), 106–118.

Simmons-McDonald, H., & Robertson, I. (2006). *Exploring the boundaries of Caribbean Creole languages*. UWI Press.

Stake, R. E. (2000). Case studies. In N. K. Denzin, & Y. S. Lincoln (Eds.), *Handbook of qualitative research* (2nd ed., pp. 134–164). Sage.

Swain, M., Kinnear, P., & Steinman, L. (2015). *Sociocultural theory in second language education. An introduction through narratives* (2nd ed.). Multilingual Matters.

Taylor, L. K., Bernhard, J. K., Garg, S., & Cummins, J. (2008). Affirming plural belonging: Building on students' family-based cultural capital through multiliteracies pedagogy. *Journal of Early Childhood Literacy*, *8*(3), 269–294.

Thompson, K. (2015, August 13). 2015 CSEC results show increase in Mathematics passes-while English language declines. *The Jamaican Observer*. https://www.jamaicaobserver.com/news/2015-CSEC-results-show-increase-in-mathematics-passes--while-English-language-declines

Vygostsky, L. S. (1978). *Mind in society: The development of higher psychological processes*. Harvard University Press.

Walker, A. (2020). God is my doctor: Mindfulness meditation/prayer as a spiritual well-being coping strategy for Jamaican school principals to manage their work-related stress and anxiety. *Journal of Educational Administration*, *58*(4), 467–480.

Yin, R. K. (2013). *Case study research: Design and methods* (5th ed.). Sage.

CHAPTER 19

Ethnodramatic Inqueery

Re/centring Queer Lives and Queer Experiences

Patrick Tomczyk

Queering

As a queer scholar and educator, I often use the word *queer* as a re-appropriated identifier—reclaimed from its disgraceful history and pejorative uses—to think and act with/in the world outside of epistemology and ontology. Contemporary queer research is anti-normative. It seeks to subvert, disrupt, and critique *stabilities* in everyday life (Browne & Nash, 2010). By using queer to situate my work in a non-hetero/cisnormative perspective, I can challenge our current ways of thinking, being, and knowing. Foremost, I use this term as an inclusive term (a noun or an adjective) for lesbian, gay, bisexual, trans, two spirited, and all other non-conforming gender and sexual identities and expressions. I also use queer as a verb to define what I am doing, to queer / query. I wish to be specific here that queering and querying are not limited to asking questions. As Sullivan (2003) stated, "to queer [is] to make strange, to frustrate, to counteract, to delegitimize, to camp up—hetero[/cis]normative knowledges, and institutions, and the subjectivities and socialites that are (in)formed by them and that (in)form them" (p. VI). Queering moves away from the hetero/cisnormative binary and into a space of possibility, an adjacent space that permits us to challenge normative categories, by "decenter[ing], destabili[zing] and deconstruct[ing]" normative practices (Pinar, 1998, p. 44).

Thinking queerly opens up ideas to imagine other possibilities. Rincón-Gallardo (2019) wrote that "ideas are powerful forces. They shape not only how we think about the world but, perhaps most importantly, how we act on it… Our ways of thinking about the world delimit what we believe is possible and desirable" (p. 1). As a queer educator, I have a role to play in disrupting and destabilizing the ongoing hetero/cisnormative discourses in schools, as they perpetuate a hegemonic power and authority that is designed to oppress. The future of educational change is to hone in on "deep learning," which is defined as the manner and outcome of making meaning of questions that matter (Rincón-Gallardo, 2019, p. 7). It was these questions that I sought to answer in my research—questions and answers that give learning an intrinsic value

© KONINKLIJKE BRILL NV, LEIDEN, 2022 | DOI:10.1163/9789004521186_019

by becoming a liberating act and an intentional practice with larger societal implications, and specifically one that re/centres sexual and gender minority (SGM) youth and their experiences in schools.

The function of education is to build a community of practice working towards freedom and emancipation, which can be achieved by means of *praxis*, by reflecting and acting upon the social world in order to transform it (Freire, 1970/1990). The transformation alluded to is a change in the paradigm that recognizes how hetero/cisnormativity acts as an agent of oppression, and, in turn, leads to homo/bi/transphobia (HBT) in our schools. Centring SGM youth and their lived experiences builds agency and advocacy by highlighting how hetero/cisnormative oppression directly impacts them. Emancipation occurs through the development of critical literacy and, thus, students become conscious of the different forces at play that affect their lives. Freire (1970/1990) referred to this process as a raising of critical consciousness or conscientization. In order to raise a *queer conscientization*, I propose that ethnodramatic inqueery can serve this purpose by centring queer lives and queer experiences in schools.

Educational systems are a major social and political instrument that can stifle open dialogue and reinforce a "culture of silence" (Freire, 1970/1990, p. 30). A culture of silence can result in the continued oppression of sexual and gender minorities and further reinforce the hetero/cisnormativity upheld by those with privilege and power, and those who have been oppressed and silenced. I have witnessed this silencing in schools, as educators and students turn a blind eye to homonegative remarks such as *fag* or *that's gay*. I have also seen heterosexual educators freely speak of their husbands or wives with their students while SGM teachers prefer not to speak about their partners out of strong discomfort in disclosing their sexualities. This silencing can also have a consequential negative impact on youth expressing their sexualities and genders in non-normative ways. Ethnodramatic inqueery centers SGM youth and their experiences, thereby activating their stories and generating voice for those who may experience silencing practices of the mainstream hetero/cisnormative culture.

The larger social world is continually changing and, as a result, it poses a dynamic challenge that constantly requires caring for and responding to. Using critical pedagogy and queer theory, I have begun to discover and expose the incoherency that exists within the normalizing discourse of hetero/cisnormativity. Freire (1970/1990, 2005) further expressed that our *ontological vocation* is to act upon and change the social world, and he called upon teachers to become cultural workers for social change. Despite this call to action, Grace and Wells (2015) indicated that few educators have heeded this call to support

SGM students. I am determined to respond to this call in cultivating a praxis that is situated in a search for social justice, fairness, and equity with particular focus on SGM students.

Critical Pedagogy and Queer Theory

Critical pedagogy and queer theory share an emphasis on challenging the hegemony of the dominant culture and, within the context of my research, a hetero/cisnormative culture. These theories converge in a place that disrupts the status quo with the aim of questioning, disrupting, and interrogating (Hackford-Peer, 2019; Mayo & Rodriguez, 2019; Meyer, 2019). Through these actions, I can re/centre participants and the issues that matter to them.

Emancipatory practices are fundamentally countercultural. They address the hierarchical relationships of control and authority inculcated in systems and structures in culture and society, which have implications for the educational, social, and political arenas (Rincón-Gallardo, 2019). Edelman (1994) indicated that queer is "a zone of possibilities" (p. 114); within this space, I have enacted my work of questioning, disrupting, and interrogating. Giroux (2011) and Kincheloe (2011) wrote that critical pedagogy is about issues of social justice and, thus, works towards critical manifestations. It is within Edelman's zone of possibilities that I took up my work of queering humanness in these challenging times by addressing the crossroads of injustice and oppression within the social world. It is at the centre of these crossroads that I was able to locate the participants and their narratives. Through dialogue, an essential element of critical pedagogy, SGM youth can envision possibilities; "dialogue is the process through which participants are able to name and rename their world" (Hackford-Peer, 2019, p. 87). It is through this dialogue that SGM youth can posit new ways of thinking and being where they can hope and aim for change and cultural transformation to improve their lives (Giroux 2011; Kincheloe, 2011). Such emancipation is not an instantaneous effect, nor does it solve all problems; rather, it is a process that creates potential for SGM youth to envision a better world as it "attempts to disrupt the usual power dynamics…so that previously marginalized or silenced voices can be centered, empowered, and heard" (Hackford-Peer, 2019, p. 88).

I learned, through preliminary interactions with SGM youth in and outside of school contexts, that even though their diversity in sexualities, gender expressions, and sexual orientations are generally invisible, they are one of the highest targeted groups to suffer from bullying and harassment (Kosciw et al., 2020; Taylor et al., 2011; The Trevor Project, 2021; Wells, 2012). Meyer (2019) said that it is seemingly "difficult to effectively intervene to stop bullying when the qualities that bullies embody are the ones most valued by many and demonstrate a form of power generally esteemed in a male-centered, or patriarchal, society" (p. 45).

Culture must be understood *in relation* to a hetero/cisnormative culture, school culture, institutional culture, power, and capacity for change. It is essential to operationalize this term, because *default culture* can have a neutralizing effect on any attempts at transformation. Rather, it is characteristically a conservative force that is powerful at preventing change (Evans, 2000). This impacted my research, as I proposed a rationale for queer theory as an agent of counterculture, and I drew on Gramsci's (1971) concepts of *hegemony* and *counterhegemony* to intentionally position the act of queering to open up the larger cultural context of social relations of power, authority, and control. I did this by centring SGM youth participants and their stories at the heart of the ethnodramatic inqueery. If I am to queer the dominant forces of culture, such as hetero/cisnormative forms of hegemony, heteropatriarchy and hetero/cisnormative oppression, then I need to bring to focus the products of dominant and default culture. Giroux (1988) posited that critical educators should become *transformative intellectuals*. I heed this call through my approach to using theatre to investigate liberated queered research.

Ethnodramatic Inqueery

I situate my practice in a queer space that weaves creativity and pedagogy into an impetus that seeks opportunities for more inclusion in schools through *ethnodramatic inqueery*. This work empowers students to find their own voice so that they can become agents of change and advocate for a more caring and equitable world that accepts, celebrates, and accommodates SGM students.

Ethnodrama, as a research methodology, is the scripting and theatrical staging of qualitative research (Saldaña, 2005, 2011). Unlike a scholarly article that is read in a performative manner, ethnodrama actively reconstructs fieldwork data into a monologue or dialogue to resemble a theatrical performance mounted for an audience. Saldaña (2005) described ethnodrama quite simply as "dramatizing the data" (p. 2) and *ethnotheatre* as performing the ethhnodrama on stage (Saldaña, 2011). I use the term *ethnodramatic inqueery* to encompass the whole process from conceptualization to performance.

Ethnodramatic inqueery is countercultural by definition; it examines those values that control social actions by "looking at life's rules" through re-creation (Bolton, 1998). Exploring these life rules generates opportunities for change beyond the context of the stage. Ethnodramatic inqueery allows for an understanding of the performed content in ways that are contextual, constructive, and collaborative, because the themes are enacted and social. Ethnodramatic inqueery permits a rethinking of attitudes surrounding marginalized populations by allowing opportunities for change to occur. As a form of ethnographic research, ethnodramatic inqueery focuses on the lived experiences of a given group or community and, with community members' consent, uses their authentic narratives in an embodied expression to enlighten other community members by means of theatrical performance. Ethnodramatic inqueery uses action methods to facilitate creativity, imagination, learning, insight, and growth.

An ethnodramatic inqueery in service to understanding the experiences of SGM students holds the potential to empower the participants and audiences to initiate change in their schools and community cultures. If queering the hegemony of hetero/cisnormativity can raise an awareness of people's fears, then this "discomfort is greeted as a good sign of our attachments and aversions, and welcomed as an opportunity to investigate its source and nature and practice acceptance and release" (Eppert, 2008, p. 98). Saldaña (1995) explained that the goal of ethnodrama is to use the methods and techniques of theatre and performance to portray a live representation of a particular facet of the human condition authentically, vividly and convincingly. The goal is to inform the audience by raising the awareness of pressing social issues.

As originally practiced by Mienczakowski (1995a), the ethnodramatic method involves the "construction of ethnographic interviews into dramatized form" (p. 364). One of the main purposes of this type of interview is to build relationships, which is particularly relevant in instances where the participants are involved throughout the research, as in my study. This type of interview can be viewed as a friendly conversation. While asking semi-structured questions such as "Can you describe a situation when you witnessed homophobic bullying in school?", it was important to listen attentively, take a passive voice, and express interest in what the participant was saying. While I selected lists of themes and questions that I introduced throughout the interviews, a semi-structured interview allowed me to insert question probes as necessary, dependent on participant responses and as different themes emerged. This type of interview also permitted the participants to respond in a manner that suited them. A principal foundation of this ethnographic approach is participant validation. This validation ensures that the authenticity of a participant's narrative is not lost, and they remain at the centre of the work.

Once I transcribed the interviews, I used *dramaturgical coding* (Miles et al., 2014; Saldaña, 2013) to analyze the narratives from the interviews. The function of dramaturgical codes, as described by Miles et al. (2014), is to apply theatrical conventions, such as, scenes, character, and setting, to qualitative data. Dramaturgical coding aligns well with centring participants and their lived experiences as it explores intrapersonal and interpersonal experiences and actions, power relationships, motivations, intentions, and agency (Miles et al., 2014).

In ethnodrama, the partnership between the researcher and participants continues through script writing into the performance; nothing goes into the script or the performance without first being validated by the participants. The writing of the script is an iterative process, where either monologues or dialogues are developed to construct a larger narrative. The participants are actively engaged in this process, contributing their ideas and their voices in the writing of the script. Dialogue throughout the ethnodramatic process is a significant marker, as it is woven throughout the entire process. Essentially, the participants become the co-authors of the script and this, in turn, creates the truthfulness of the performance. This co-research process ensures the authenticity of the lived experiences of the participants and facilitates an ownership of their stories, thus creating a convincing representation for script and performance and re/centring the work on those who matter.

Ethnodramas are performed for an audience within the community of stakeholders from which the data was generated. In order for an ethnodrama to offer a significant contribution to the community, it must hold relevance for an audience. Ethnodramas can help enact a politics of resistance and possibility by engaging the voices of those living on the margins of society by co-creating a space with audiences and performers to actually engage in meaningful dialogue and discourse. While the need to reach wider audiences beyond stakeholders is very important, it is within the community, itself, that dialogue and action can begin.

Research-informed theatre presents a powerful mirror to reflect the deficiencies of a particular system (Conrad, 2004; Goldstein, 2013; Selman & Heather, 2015). Ethnodramatic inqueery can offer more than just a powerful mirror. It can also offer a powerful window. As a powerful mirror, ethnodrama has the capacity for participants and members of a particular community to reflect critically on their lives and identify systems of oppression. As a powerful window, ethnodramatic inqueery helps people in the hetero/cis mainstream to witness queer identities, lived realities, and struggles of which they might not be aware. This is why I propose ethnodramatic inqueery as a vehicle for queer conscientization, not only for participants but also for the audiences. It is through this reflection and witnessing that SGM students may engage in discourse to seek emancipation. To borrow from the language of theatre, this work directly places the participants and their lived experience *centre stage.*

The umbrella under which ethnodrama resides is qualitative, art(s)-based inquiry. McNiff (2013) stated that art-based research is a principal way of "understanding and examining experience by both researchers and participants who are involved in the studies. He further argued that art-based research has the potential to generate data that is more authentic and richer in that it "often feels more accurate, original, and intelligent than more conventional descriptions" (p. 30). Barone and Eisner (2012) explained that arts-based research affords us the opportunities to make deeper and more complex understandings of some particular aspects of people's lives and, in turn, the broader social world. They wrote that arts make "empathic participation possible because they create forms that are evocative and compelling" (p. 3).

Mienczakowski (2001) noted that ethnodrama's "overt intention is not to just transgressively blur boundaries but to be a form of public voice ethnography…that has emancipatory and educational potential" (p. 469). Through ethnodrama, the researcher and participants seek to communicate the importance of issues that may have been silenced otherwise. In this sense, the art is not only aesthetic; it also possesses *emancipatory potential* for motivating change within participants and audiences (Mienczakowski 1995a, 1995b). Furthermore, as Eisner (2002) suggested in relation to all arts, "work in the arts is not only a way of creating performances and products; it is a way of creating our lives by expanding our consciousness, shaping our dispositions, satisfying our quest for meaning, [and] establishing contact with others" (p. 3). As such, this work has potential to create more welcoming, caring, diverse, and inclusive classrooms.

Impact of Ethnodramatic Inqueery

Ethnodramatic inqueery performs a significant role as it encourages students and teachers to delve into and question normative structures and institutions that re/produce positions of power and contribute to a hierarchical society across a magnitude of crossroads that lead to HBT. What is further significant is that, in raising queer consciousness about the very issues that oppress SGM youth in high schools, I have come to understand how our lives are impacted by the dominant sexual and gender cultural norms. This is because "hitching our hopes to policies to fix intractable problems, when policies themselves are designed to protect a normative status quo, is not enough" (Mayo & Rodriquez, 2019, p. 3). The significance of this work is in its queer critique of heteronormativity and cisnormativity to interrupt HBT bullying and harassment even as it queerly highlights how school culture, policies, and teaching, learning, and curriculum reinforce normalized beliefs and attitudes around power, privilege, and oppression in schools.

References

Barone, T., & Eisner, T. (2012). *Arts based research*. Sage.

Bolton, G. (1998). We do drama: The cultural dimension of classroom drama. In C. O'Sullivan & G. Williams (Eds.), *Building bridges: Laying the foundations for a child-centered curriculum in drama and education* (pp. 20–25). The National Association of the Teaching of Drama.

Browne, K., & Nash, C. (Eds.). (2010). *Queer methods and methodologies: Intersecting queer theories and social science research*. Ashgate.

Conrad, D. (2004). Exploring risky youth experiences: Popular theatre as a participatory, performative research method. *International Journal of Qualitative Methods, 3*(1), Article 2. http://www.ualberta.ca/~iiqm/backissues/3_1/pdf/conrad.pdf

Edelman, L. (1994). *Homographesis: Essays in gay literary and cultural theory*. Routledge.

Eisner, E. (2002). *The arts and the creation of mind*. Yale University Press.

Eppert, C. (2008). Fear, (educational) fictions of character, and Buddhist insights for a witnessing curriculum. In C. Eppert & H. Wang (Eds.), *Cross-cultural studies in curriculum: Eastern thought, educational insights* (1st ed., pp. 55–108). Lawrence Erlbaum, Taylor and Francis.

Evans, N. (2000). Creating a positive learning environment for gay, lesbian, and bisexual students. *New Directions for Teaching and Learning, 82*, 81–87. https://doi.org/10.1002/tl.8208

Freire, P. (1990). *Pedagogy of the oppressed* (M. B. Ramos, Trans.). Continuum. (Original work published 1970)

Freire, P. (2005). *Teachers as cultural workers: Letters to those who dare teach* (D. Macedo, D. Kolke, & A. Oliviera, Trans.). Westview Press.

Giroux, H. (1988). *Teachers as intellectuals: Toward a critical pedagogy of learning*. Bergin Garvey.

Giroux, H. (2011). *On critical pedagogy*. Continuum.

Goldstein, T. (2013). *Zero tolerance and other plays*. Sense.

Gramsci, A. (1971). *Selections from the prison notebooks*. International Publishers.

Grace, A. P., & Wells, K. (2015). *Growing into resilience: Sexual and gender minority youth in Canada*. University of Toronto Press.

Hackford-Peer, K. (2019). "That wasn't very free thinker": Queer critical pedagogy in the early grades. In C. Mayo & N. M. Rodriquez (Eds.), *Queer pedagogies: Theory, praxis, politics* (pp. 75–92). Springer. https://doi.org/10.1007/978-3-030-27066-7_6

Kincheloe, J. (2011). *Key works in critical pedagogy*. Sense.

Kosciw, J. G., Clark, C. M., Truong, N. L., & Zongrone, A. D. (2020). *The 2019 National School Climate Survey: The experiences of lesbian, gay, bisexual, transgender, and queer youth in our nation's schools*. GLSEN. https://www.glsen.org/sites/default/files/2021-04/NSCS19-FullReport-032421-Web_0.pdf

Mayo, C., & Rodriquez N. M. (Eds.). (2019). *Queer pedagogies: Theory, praxis, politics.* Springer. https://doi.org/10.1007/978-3-030-27066-7_1

McNiff, S. (2013). *Art as research: Opportunities and challenges*. Intellect.

Meyer, E. J. (2019) Ending bullying and harassment: The case for a queer pedagogy. In C. Mayo & N. M. Rodriquez (Eds.), *Queer pedagogies: Theory, praxis, politics* (pp. 41–58). Springer. https://doi.org/10.1007/978-3-030-27066-7_4

Mienczakowski, J. (1995a). *The application of critical ethno-drama to health settings* [Unpublished doctoral dissertation]. Griffith University.

Mienczakowski, J. (1995b). The theatre of ethnography: The reconstruction of ethnography with emancipatory potential. *Qualitative Inquiry, 1*(3), 360–375. https://doi.org/10.1177/107780049500100306

Mienczakowski, J. (2001). Ethnodrama: Performed research – limitations and potential. In P. Atkinson, A. Coffey, S. Delamont, J. Lofland, & L. Lofland (Eds.), *Handbook of ethnography* (pp. 468–476). Sage.

Miles, M., Huberman, M., & Saldaña, J. (2014). *Qualitative data analysis: A methods sourcebook* (3rd ed.). Sage.

Pinar, W. (Ed.). (1998). *Queer theory in education.* Lawrence Erlbaum Associates.

Rincón-Gallardo, S. (2019). *Liberating learning: Educational change as social movement.* Routledge.

Saldaña, J. (Ed.). (2005). *Ethnodrama: An anthology of reality theatre*. Altamira Press.

Saldaña, J. (2011). *Ethnotheatre: Research from page to stage*. Left Coast Press.

Saldaña, J. (2013). *The coding manual for qualitative researchers* (2nd ed.). Sage.

Selman, J., & Heather, J. (2015). *Theatre, teens, sex ed: Are we there yet?* The University of Alberta Press.

Sullivan, N. (2003). *A critical introduction to queer theory.* New York University Press.

Taylor, C., Peter, T., McMinn, T. L., Schachter, K., Beldom, S., Ferry, A., Gross, Z., & Paquin, S. (2011). *Every class in every school: The first national climate survey on homophobia, biphobia, and transphobia in Canadian schools. Final report.* Egale Canada Human Rights Trust. https://egale.ca/wpcontent/uploads/2011/05/EgaleFinalReport-web.pdf

The Trevor Project. (2021). *National survey on LGBTQ youth mental health 2021.* The Trevor Project. https://www.thetrevorproject.org/wp-content/uploads/2021/05/The-Trevor-Project-National-Survey-Results-2021.pdf

Wells, K. (2012). Generation queer: Sexual and gender minority youth and Canadian schools. *Education Canada, 48*(1), 18–23.

CHAPTER 20

Pedagogy, People, and Place

A Rural Experience

Barbara Gilbert Mulcahy

> The school environment of desks, blackboards, a small school yard were supposed to suffice. There was no demand that the teacher should become intimately acquainted with the conditions of the local community, physical, historical, economic, occupational, etc., in order to utilize them as resources. A system of education based upon the necessary connection of education with experience must, on the contrary, if faithful to its principle, take these things into account.
>
> DEWEY (1938, p. 40)

∵

Context for Inquiry

Curriculum rarely reflects the lived experiences of those for whom it is designed. Pinar (1991) suggests, "From its conceptions as a specialized field this century, curriculum has tended toward the abstract, for instance the formulation of principles of curriculum development applicable anytime and anywhere" (p. 165). Such standardization neither reflects the diversity within urban schools nor the local experience of students in rural schools. However, a meaningful curriculum is one in which all students see themselves reflected, thus affirming their identities (Comber & Nixon, 2013; Corbett, 2010a, 2010b; Delpit, 2006; Lyle, 2017; Montero et al., 2013). However, rather than recognizing diversity and difference, educational institutions have tended to be assimilative.

Historically, and contemporarily, the official school curriculum generally ignores the lived experience of rural students (Bartholomeus, 2006; Corbett, 2010b; Edmondson, 2003). This is reflected in a comment from a former teacher in the community that was the focus of my research. He noted:

© KONINKLIJKE BRILL NV, LEIDEN, 2022 | DOI:10.1163/9789004521186_020

> It was a generic program meant to serve everybody. If I can recall correctly, I think, it was like generic texts. You got in Cod Bight what you got in New Cove, what they got in Sandy Cove. So, it didn't focus on regional issues if I can recall. It was a program brought down, prescribed by, the Department [of Education]. We used that, and that was your sources.[1]

Rural identities, languages, and cultures have been marginalized or ignored. Research has demonstrated that the dominant discourses of politics, media, and education have perpetuated the belief that success equates with leaving rural areas (Corbett, 2010b; Donehower et al., 2012; Edmondson, 2003; Rebanks, 2015; Schafft & Jackson, 2010; Theobald & Wood, 2010). Moreover, schools "have also been sites of ideological positions that are, historically, hostile to the land, environment, and ecology and reproduce values of industrialization and globalization" (U. Kelly, personal communication, February 2, 2018). This ideological shift influenced by the marketplace results in the belief that successful employment is found outside rural communities, and there is little value for local experience.

While the primary purpose of schooling has been mobility-focused, Corbett (2010b) maintains that what schools should do is build awareness of the possibilities of either leaving or staying, both positive options. As Sterling suggests, "The key shift required is from a limited emphasis on 'education for jobs' towards the broader goal of building an ecologically sustainable economy and society" (as cited in University of Bath, 2005, para. 7). Education that focuses on preparation for work in a global economy with a focus on moving out does little to encourage a connection to, or a sense of importance of, small local communities. Such an approach does little to encourage reflective and critical thinking about how to live well in a place—to respect diverse and local knowledges and to sustain community. Furthermore, in a global marketplace with a primary focus on profit, there is less concern for the environment, especially local habitats. It is detrimental to community survival.

Curriculum should be rooted in a specific context, time, and culture with a focus on what is to be achieved with students in that setting (Kelly, 2009). Such a curriculum would build a connection and sense of belonging that would result in an ethic of care for the local. However, this cannot be achieved with a standardized curriculum that ignores local context. Place attachment would result in a deeper concern and care for the place (Kelly, 2008). While an ethic that is required for local sustainability, it is also one that might be transferred as students bring new understandings to global settings. Kelly (2009) believes it is an education that would examine loss as a means of hope, that is, a way to reconsider that which is taken-for-granted, to produce new ways of thinking, and build different kinds of connections. It is an approach that would have students take a critical look at what is happening in their local communities and encourage reflection and action based on this knowledge. Furthermore, Kelly (2009) contends:

> Sustainability is not only for a population seen to stay and nor should it be reduced to a common yet narrow view of upkeep of a social and ecological status quo—susSTAYnability. Rather, sustainability should be a centerpiece of an education that attends to a profound form of inhabitation, involving ethics, politics and affect—a complex and compelling call to care in which transience is a feature of life, a way of thinking, a mode of identification, a form of belonging, and a mark of loss as possibility and hope—of reparation, for people and their places. (p. 3)

According to Corbett (2010a), "If education takes places and spaces seriously, then it becomes difficult to justify a monolithic approach to teaching and learning. The rise of place-based education attests to this fact" (p. 83).

Building on previous research that explored the lived experience of individuals in one coastal community in Newfoundland and Labrador and their response to the ecological cod crisis (Gilbert Mulcahy, 2018), I extend that inquiry here to examine educational implications. Education that recognizes the importance of the lived experience of people and the places they inhabit might lead to a "sustainable and powerful curriculum practice" (Luke & Carrington, 2004, p. 5).

Place-based Education

This work is informed by critical pedagogy of place, a framework first advanced by Gruenewald (2003). Kerkham and Comber (2013) suggest "a critical pedagogy of place…can provide a strong basis for a proper education for rural-regional sustainability" (p. 213). They do so by offering educators and communities a way to help students to become local problem solvers—an act that is necessary as the world adjusts to the consequences of climate change, economic globalization, and resource depletion (Smith & Soebel, 2010). Creating this type of action-oriented consciousness is critical to humanity and the planet:

> Place-based pedagogies are needed so that the education of citizens might have some direct bearing on the well-being of the social and ecological places people actually inhabit. Critical pedagogies are needed to

challenge the assumptions, practices, and outcomes taken for granted in dominant culture and in conventional education. (Gruenewald, 2003, p. 3)

Exploring Lived Experience with/in Place

This critical qualitative study used an ethnographic methodology to explore the lived experience of one coastal community in response to an ecological crisis and the resulting cod moratorium of 1992 and to examine the role of education in contributing to loss, sustainability, diversity, and difference. I used critical ethnography to recognize and centre the experiences of this rural community. Those involved in the study included people who lived in the community prior to, during, and after the cod moratorium who offered observations on historical and longitudinal changes. I interviewed 21 individuals—six females and 15 males, ranging in age from 34 to 76. I designed an interview protocol to give the interview structure and for note taking purposes (Creswell, 2015). The research questions guided the interview protocol. Data was also collected through observation, field notes, and document analysis.

Local Context

In 1992, the near eradication of a species (Northern cod), resulted in the closure of the 500-year-old cod fishery in Newfoundland and Labrador and a loss of 30,000 jobs—the single largest job loss in Canadian history (Rose, 2007). Rural[2] areas bore the brunt of the closure, with a population loss of 18% between 1991and 2007 (Higgins, 2008). Residents relocated or commuted between their homes and new places of employment (Howard, 2007; Rose 2007). By 1994, it was hoped that the cod stocks would rebound and that the fishery would resume, but it did not happen (Rose, 2007). What was expected to be a 2-year closure is now in its 30th year.

Community Experience

Individuals related their experience of education in their community and suggested that the school curriculum included very little of their lived experience. A generic program, meant to serve all, often serves no one well. The term *generic* is often defined as *non-specific*. This language disguises the fact that the selection of both textbooks and curriculum materials are always specific, never neutral, and thus ignores the ideological nature of such choices. Such choices reflect the knowledge that is valued generally. Cheryl Allen, an Inuit pre-service teacher, states:

> By using local knowledge as a primary source in all areas of the curriculum, [teachers] can make learning more centred to the students, which in turn creates a deeper and more meaningful learning experience. By availing of local knowledge in our communities, we can make meaningful and strong connections that will foster relationships within the schools and communities. (Moore et al., 2016, p. 101)

In this case, the curriculum did little to enhance knowledge and understanding of their rural community.

Corbett (2010b), in his work in rural Nova Scotia, suggests, "if we were to look at the school as a large text, it was fundamentally a story about somewhere else" (p. 117). Edmondson and D'Urso (2008) insist that this kind of standardization furthers the "trend of rendering rural students invisible in the current contexts of public education" (p. 3). And Gruenewald (2003) argues that a standardized curriculum does not foster an attitude of concern for the local; rather it provides a "placeless" (p. 8) curriculum that is not meaningful. Yet, rarely do students see themselves represented in the curriculum, so it is nearly impossible to educate youth on local ecological crisis.

Individuals suggest this provincial ecological crisis and its impact was rarely addressed in school except in a cursory way. One person, a former teacher who was working in the community when the cod fishery closed, stated, "There may have been issues outside in the community, but it was never a community focus driven through the school." Although a community institution, the school too often stands apart from the reality of what is happening in local lives. Worse, ubiquitous curriculum does not include the possibility that one could make a life and a living in rural places; instead, it tends to position education as a way out of the community. One participant commented:

> Education wasn't centred around getting an education and going fishing and staying in rural Newfoundland. Education, and school, my recollection of it, was to get an education and move on to urban centres. And move into universities and get much more higher qualifications. And move on into more sustainable, land-based work.

Another participant remarked:

> Well, yes. And nine chances out of ten, when anybody said, well you're going, and you're going to go to university, or you're going to go college, or you're going to go and do these things, you're typically not going to stay in this smaller outport community.

Participants in general indicated that those who did not complete their schooling had to remain in the community—a choice viewed as less desirable. Corbett (2007) argues the same— that schools educate people to leave—but he believes that people must have a choice as to "how and where to construct an identity and to discover where one belongs" (p. 273). Such an education would provide not only knowledge but an ability to reflect and gain an understanding of how to move forward.

Community-Informed Discussion

The closure of the Northern Cod fishery was one of the most significant events in the history of Newfoundland and Labrador, but few students (rural or urban) are aware of the impact (Neis, 2012, as cited in Mair, 2012). This begs the question whether it is partly the result of an education system that offers a mandated standardized curriculum that ignores issues of local place. According to Gruenewald (2003):

> Abstract curriculum that has been designed and written elsewhere is inadequate to the task of 'learning to live well' within the limits and possibilities of specific places, and of understanding the cultural and political processes that shape what happens there. (p. 9)

An education that is community-focussed or place-based might consider critical issues such as how to *reimagine* life in the community. In this case, it would focus on ways of building a more sustainable fishery and protecting the resources to ensure that people have a way of making a living. It would also work to counter the prevailing attitude that to choose to live in a small rural place is a poor choice for a young person.

Finding a way to make a living in a way that is focused on the local would challenge the dominant discourse in education while contesting the unchecked movement toward globalization and industrialization. Such an education would be about community building as well as being more resilient and civic-minded. It could emphasize the importance and value of local culture as well as cultural preservation.

Kelly (2012) insists that "education in the context of loss must be committed to a learning that encounters the place of loss as a place from which to reimagine and to rebuild community" (p. 13). It is education that provides not only knowledge but an understanding of how to move forward in a positive and meaningful way. Likewise, Corbett (2010a) argues, good pedagogy would offer an education for not only those who leave but those who might choose to remain in a community that is threatened by "the encroachments of fast capitalism and the globalized (and increasingly depopulated) countryside" (p. 85).

Final Words

It is a deeply-rooted belief that outport Newfoundland and Labrador had, or has, very little to offer, so it is not surprising that many people have internalized this view. When dominant institutions promote such beliefs, it is difficult to counter, but a counter narrative is imperative to prevent such discourses from being accepted and normalized. The purpose of education in this small community was not about responsible citizenship and learning to live with/in a place as Gruenewald (2003) suggests is critical. Education that is true to its cause must consider the experiences and circumstances of those for whom it is designed (Dewey, 1938). In this case, we ought to be considering a place and people that have been impacted in significant ways by an ecological crisis that resulted in a loss of a way of being.

Notes

1 All place names are pseudonyms.
2 In Newfoundland and Labrador, *rural* is a relatively new term to describe what was originally called "outport life." The use of the term "rural" to describe the outport lifestyle was introduced as a government descriptor in 1949.

References

Bartholomeus, P. (2006). Some rural examples of place-based education. *International Education Journal, 7*(4), 480–489. https://files.eric.ed.gov/fulltext/EJ854303.pdf

Comber, B., & Nixon, H. (2013). Urban renewal, migration and memories: The affordances of place-based pedagogies for developing immigrant students' literate repertoires. *REMIE – Multidisciplinary Journal of Educational Research, 3*(1), 42–68.

Corbett, M. (2007). *Learning to leave: The irony of schooling in a coastal community.* Fernwood.

Corbett, M. (2010a). Backing the right horse: Teacher education, sociocultural analysis and literacy in rural education. *Teaching and Teacher Education, 26*, 82–86.

Corbett, M. (2010b). Wharf talk, home talk, and school talk: The politics of language in a coastal community. In K. Schafft & A. Jackson (Eds.), *Rural education for the twenty-first century* (pp. 115–131). Penn State University Press.

Creswell, J. (2015). *Educational research: Planning, conducting and evaluating quantitative and qualitative research* (5th ed.). Pearson.

Delpit, L. (2006). The politics of teaching literate discourse. In L. Delpit (Ed.), *Other people's children: Cultural conflict in the classroom* (pp. 152–166). The New Press.

Dewey, J. (1938). *Experience and education.* Simon and Schuster.

Donehower, K., Hogg, C., & Schell, E. (2012). *Reclaiming the rural: Essays on literacy, rhetoric and pedagogy.* Southern Illinois University.

Edmondson, J. (2003). *Prairie town: Redefining life in the age of globalization.* Rowman & Littlefield.

Edmondson, J., & D'Urso, A. (2008, January). Book review [Review of the book Rural literacies by K. Donehower, C. Hogg, & E. Schell]. *Journal of Research in Rural Education, 23*(1), 1–3. https://jrre.psu.edu/sites/default/files/2019-08/23-1.pdf

Gilbert Mulcahy, B. (2018). *Biological, linguistic and cultural change and education in one coastal community in Newfoundland and Labrador* [Unpublished doctoral dissertation]. Memorial University.

Gruenewald, D. (2003, May). The best of both worlds: A critical pedagogy of place. *Educational Researcher, 32*(4), 3–12. http://www.jstor.org/stable/3700002

Higgins, J. (2008). *Rural depopulation.* Memorial University. https://www.heritage.nf.ca/articles/society/depopulation.php

Howard, P. (2007). The pedagogy of place: Reinterpreting ecological education through the language arts. *Diaspora, Indigenous and Minority Education: Studies of Migration, Integration, Equity and Survival, 1*(20), 109–126. http://dx.doi.org/10.1080/15595690701293728

Kelly, U. (2008). Where biography meets ecology: Melancholy and transformative education. In M. Gardner & U. Kelly (Eds.), *Narrating transformative learning in education* (pp. 31–49). Palgrave Macmillan.

Kelly, U. (2009). Learning to lose: Rurality, transience, and belonging (A companion to Michael Corbett). *Journal of Research in Rural Education, 24*(11), 1–4.

Kelly, U. (2012, September 10). *Migration, modernity and education: A Newfoundland and Labrador case study* [Conference Session]. British Association for Comparative and International Education University of Cambridge, Cambridge, England.

Kerkham, L., & Comber, B. (2013). Literacy, placed-based pedagogies, and social justice. In B. Green & M. Corbett (Eds.), *Rethinking rural literacies: Transnational Perspectives* (pp. 197–218). Palgrave and Macmillan.

Luke A., & Carrington, V. (2004). Globalisation, literacy, curriculum practice. In T. Grainger (Ed.), *The RoutledgeFalmer reader in language and literacy* (pp. 52–65). RoutledgeFalmer.

Lyle, E. (2017). Autoethnographic approaches to an identity conscious curriculum. In E. Lyle (Ed.), *At the intersection of selves and subject: Exploring the curricular landscape of identity* (pp. 1–8). Sense.

Mair, R. (2012, July 7). Few lessons taken from moratorium: Researcher. *The Telegram,* p. A1.

Montero, M. K., Bice-Zaugg, C., Marsh, A. C. J., & Cummins, J. (2013). Activist literacies: Validating Aboriginality through visual and literary identity texts. *Journal of Language and Literacy Education, 9*(1), 73–94.

Moore, S., Allen, C., Andersen, M., Boase, D., Campbell, J. R., Doherty, T., Edmunds, A., Edmunds, F., Flowers, J., Lyall, J., Mitsuk C., Nochasak, R., Pamak, V., Russell, F., & Voisey J. (2016). Inuit-centred learning in the Inuit Bachelor of Education program. *Études Inuit Studies, 40*(2), 93–107.

Pinar, W. (1991). Curriculum as social psychoanalysis: On the significance of place. In J. Kincheloe & W. Pinar (Eds.), *Curriculum as social psychoanalysis* (pp. 165–186). State University of New York Press.

Rebanks, J. (2015). *The shepherd's life: Modern dispatches from an ancient landscape.* Doubleday Canada.

Rose, G. (2007). *Cod: The ecological history of the North Atlantic fisheries.* Breakwater Books.

Schafft, K., & Jackson, A. (2010). Introduction. In K. Schafft & A. Jackson (Eds.), *Rural education for the twenty-first century* (pp. 1–13). The Pennsylvania State University Press.

Smith, G., & Soebel, D. (2010). *Place- and community-based education in schools.* Routledge.

Theobald, P., & Wood, K. (2010). Learning to be rural: Identity lessons from schooling, history and the U.S. corporate media. In K. Schafft & A. Jackson (Eds.), *Rural education for the twenty-first century* (pp. 17–33). Penn State University Press.

University of Bath. (2005, February 18). *Education needs a "fundamental re-think" to assist sustainable development, says researcher* [Press release]. Retrieved July 18, 2021, from http://www.bath.ac.uk/news/archive/2005/2/18/sustainability.html

Printed in the United States
by Baker & Taylor Publisher Services